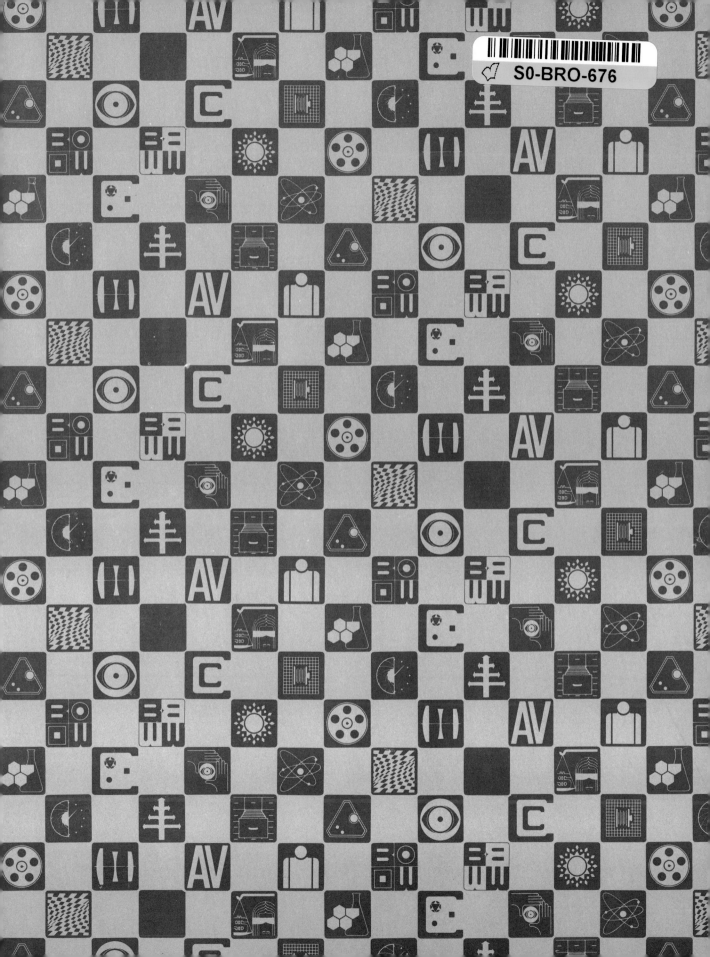

Encyclopedia
of Practical
Photography

Volume 7
Flo-Gum

Edited by and published for
EASTMAN KODAK COMPANY

AMPHOTO
American Photographic Book Publishing Company
Garden City, New York

Note on Photography

The cover photos and the photos of letters that appear elsewhere in this encyclopedia were taken by Chris Maggio.

Library of Congress Cataloging in Publication Data

Amphoto, New York.
    Encyclopedia of practical photography.

    Includes bibliographical references and index.
    1. Photography—Dictionaries. I. Eastman
Kodak Company. II. Title.
TR9.A46   770'.3   77–22562

ISBN 0–8174–3050–4 Trade Edition—Whole Set
ISBN 0–8174–3200–0 Library Edition—Whole Set
ISBN 0–8174–3057–1 Trade Edition—Volume 7
ISBN 0–8174–3207–8 Library Edition—Volume 7

Manufactured in the United States of America

Editorial Board

The *Encyclopedia of Practical Photography* was compiled and edited jointly by Eastman Kodak Company and American Photographic Book Publishing Co., Inc. (Amphoto). The comprehensive archives, vast resources, and technical staffs of both companies, as well as the published works of Kodak, were used as the basis for most of the information contained in this encyclopedia.

Symbol Identification

 Audiovisual

 Color Processing and Printing

 Picture-Making Techniques

 Biography

 Equipment and Facilities

 Scientific Photography

 Black-and-White Materials

 Exposure

 Special Effects and Techniques

 Black-and-White Processing and Printing

 History

Special Interests

 Business and Legal Aspects

 Lighting

 Storage and Care

 Chemicals

 Motion Picture

 Theory of Photography

 Color Materials

 Optics

 Vision

Guide for the Reader

Use this encyclopedia as you would any good encyclopedia or dictionary. Look for the subject desired as it first occurs to you—most often you will locate it immediately. The shorter articles begin with a dictionary-style definition, and the longer articles begin with a short paragraph that summarizes the article that follows. Either of these should tell you if the information you need is in the article. The longer articles are then broken down by series of headings and sub-headings to aid further in locating specific information.

Cross References

If you do not find the specific information you are seeking in the article first consulted, use the cross references (within the article and at the end of it) to lead you to more information. The cross references can lead you from a general article to the more detailed articles into which the subject is divided. Cross references are printed in capital letters so that you can easily recognize them.
Example: *See also:* ZONE SYSTEM.

Index

If the initial article you turn to does not supply you with the information you seek, and the cross references do not lead you to it, use the index in the last volume. The index contains thousands of entries to help you identify and locate any subject you seek.

Symbols

To further aid you in locating information, the articles throughout have been organized into major photographic categories. Each category is represented by a symbol displayed on the opposite page. By using only the symbols, you can scan each volume and locate all the information under any of the general categories. Thus, if you wish to read all about lighting, simply locate the lighting symbols and read the articles under them.

Reading Lists

Most of the longer articles are followed by reading lists citing useful sources for further information. Should you require additional sources, check the cross-referenced articles for additional reading lists.

Metric Measurement

Both the U.S. Customary System of measurement and the International System (SI) are used throughout this encyclopedia. In most cases, the metric measurement is given first with the U.S. customary equivalent following in parenthesis. When equivalent measurements are given, they will be rounded off to the nearest whole unit or a tenth of a unit, unless precise measurement is important. When a measurement is considered a "standard," equivalents will not be given. For example: 35 mm film, 200 mm lens, 4″ × 5″ negative, and 8″ × 10″ prints will not be given with their customary or metric equivalents.

How Articles are Alphabetized

Article titles are alphabetized by letter sequence, with word breaks and hyphens not considered. Example:

> Archer, Frederick Scott
> Architectural Photography
> Archival Processing
> Arc Lamps

Abbreviations are alphabetized according to the letters of the abbreviations, not by the words the letters stand for. Example:

> Artificial Light
> ASA Speed

Contents
Volume 7

Flower Photography

Flower photography can be a year-round project. During the winter months, flowers from the florist offer many picture possibilities. And after the pictures have been taken, the bouquet or plant can brighten up a room. Then as outdoor buds turn to blossoms during spring months, take the camera to a favorite garden and concentrate on capturing the change of season.

Such garden pictures can serve as a handy reference through the years. Annual pictures of flowers from the same plant or pictures of this year's garden can be compared with those taken in previous years.

Flower Close-ups

Most flower photography falls into the area of close-up photography because flowers and blossoms are generally rather small. This makes it necessary to use equipment at closer-than-normal distances for good results. To fill the viewfinder with a flower, or to focus on a single part of a blossom, close-up lenses, extension tubes, or a bellows extension unit will be needed. (*See:* CLOSE-UP PHOTOGRAPHY.)

Flowers Outdoors

Flower photographs can be taken either outdoors in sunlight or in the controlled atmosphere of a studio. Indoors, move the lights to create dramatic effects; outdoors, move the camera and select the best viewpoint to achieve dramatic lighting. Sidelighting emphasizes the shape of the flower and

Photographs of favorite flower gardens can serve as a record of past years, and make excellent means of comparison between one year or season and the next. Photo by Jan Lukas for Editorial Photocolor Archives.

brings out the texture of the petals. Backlighting accentuates the translucent, delicate quality of flowers and helps produce striking pictures.

Both types of lighting produce shadows, but since shadows help show shape and dimension, try not to eliminate them. They may, however, be lightened to reveal more detail. It is a good idea to have a reflector that will bounce light into the shadow areas. An inexpensive one can be made from crumpled aluminum foil fastened to a piece of cardboard. If this is not available, use a newspaper or a white shirt to reflect the light.

Bright sunlight is not required to make excellent flower photos. In fact, overcast days generally provide shadowless light that makes it possible to achieve good color saturation and a soft, even quality in photos. However, if the texture and shadows produced by strong lighting are preferred, use a flash on overcast days.

Flowers and Flash. When used close to the subject, flash illuminates so brightly that a small lens

FLASH EXPOSURE FOR FLOWER CLOSE-UPS*†

Flashbulb and Reflector	Lens Opening‡	
	Subject Distance: 10–20 inches	Subject Distance: 30 inches
Flashcube or magicube	f/16	f/11
Hi-power flashcube	f/22	f/16
AG-1B, shallow cylindrical reflector	f/16	f/11
AG-1B, polished-bowl reflector	f/22	f/16
M2B, polished-bowl reflector	f/22	f/16
M3B, 5B, or 25B, polished-bowl reflector	f/22 (with two layers of handkerchief)	f/22

*Use a shutter speed of 1/25 or 1/30 sec., and put one layer of white handkerchief over the flash.
†This table applies directly to films with a speed of 64. If films with a speed of 25 are used, select a lens opening one stop larger than the table indicates.
‡For very light subjects, use one stop less exposure or add another layer of handkerchief over the flash reflector.

◄ *(Far left) Extreme close-ups are best made with flash, which allows for smaller apertures and consequently greater depth-of-field. (Left) When used off-camera, flash can create interesting lighting effects; it will also darken the background to make the flower stand out in greater contrast.*

STARTING ELECTRONIC FLASH EXPOSURES FOR FLOWER CLOSE-UPS

| Film Speed | Output of Unit BCPS | Lens Opening | |
		Subject Distance: 10–20 Inches	Subject Distance: 25–35 Inches
25–40	350– 700	f/11 (1 layer)	f/5.6 (1 layer)
	700–1000	f/16 (1 layer)	f/8 (1 layer)
	1000–2000	f/16 (1 layer)	f/11 (1 layer)
	2800–4000	f/22 (1 layer)	f/16 (1 layer)
	5600–8000	f/22 (2 layers)	f/22 (1 layer)
50–80	350– 700	f/16 (1 layer)	f/8 (1 layer)
	700–1000	f/22 (1 layer)	f/11 (1 layer)
	1000–2000	f/22 (1 layer)	f/16 (1 layer)
	2800–4000	f/22 (2 layers)	f/22 (1 layer)
	5600–8000	f/22 (3 layers)	f/22 (2 layers)
100–160	350– 700	f/22 (1 layer)	f/11 (1 layer)
	700–1000	f/22 (2 layers)	f/16 (1 layer)
	1000–2000	f/22 (2 layers)	f/22 (1 layer)
	2800–4000	f/22 (3 layers)	f/22 (2 layers)
	5600–8000	f/22 (4 layers)	f/22 (3 layers)

BCPS OUTPUT OF ELECTRONIC FLASH GUNS (FILM SPEED 64)

Guide Number	BCPS	Guide Number	BCPS	Guide Number	BCPS
32	350	65	1400	130	5600
40	500	80	2000	160	8000
45	700	95	2800	—	—
55	1000	110	4000	—	—

opening can be used to attain the depth of field that is generally desirable in close-ups. Off-camera flash can be used to create sidelighting or backlighting. Flash can also make the background appear quite dark so that the flower stands out in striking contrast.

If the flash unit cannot be backed away from a subject for proper exposure, place one layer of white handkerchief over the flash to diffuse the light and to reduce the intensity of the light on the flower. The use of a handkerchief also helps to light the subject evenly. (*See:* FLASH PHOTOGRAPHY.)

The accompanying flash-exposure tables can serve as a guide in determining exposure for close-ups with on-camera flash.

Use any shutter speed with leaf-type shutters, or the fastest shutter speed that will synchronize with focal-plane shutters (usually marked on the shutter

(Left) A dewy, morning-fresh look can be created any time of day with a spray-bottle filled with water. (Right) Photographing flowers indoors allows for greater control over the subject in terms of lighting, arrangement, and weather conditions. In addition, certain flowers, such as these orchids, do not grow naturally in all climates.

speed dial with an "X"). Over the flash use the number of layers of white handkerchief material shown in the starting-exposure table.

For very light subjects, use one stop less exposure or add another layer of handkerchief over the flash. Since there are many variations in conditions, such as the thickness of handkerchief material, consider these as starting recommendations for making tests.

If the BCPS value of the flash unit is not known, check the flash dial on the unit to find the guide number for a film speed of 64, and look up the BCPS in the bottom table on page 1115.

The Background. Every photographer knows that a distracting background can ruin a picture. However, this is usually not a problem with close-

ups since the background is usually so out of focus that it becomes a soft blur of color. As a result, the subject stands out in sharp contrast. On the other hand, bright reflections or spots of bright color can be distracting even though they are out of focus. Look at the background carefully before taking the picture, and select the angle that will give the most pleasing results.

If the camera angle that gives the best background does not show off the subject to its best advantage, modify the background. Ask someone to stand so that his or her shadow falls on the background. This will cause it to turn out underexposed and will eliminate any distracting elements. Be sure to take a meter reading before shading the background so that the reading will not be affected by the shadow.

The mood of a photograph can be altered simply by changing the color of the background. (Left) A green background gives the impression of foliage. (Below left) An orange background tinges the flowers slightly and gives the picture a warmer look.

Or, make a background by using a large sheet of art paper. By so doing, the background can be any color. Using paper backgrounds gives the photographer complete control over the color and mood of a shot; the mood of a picture changes completely when a dark green background is substituted for one of vibrant orange. Hold the background paper away from the flower to keep distracting shadows from falling on it. A piece of colored cloth can also be used as the background, but be sure to keep it far enough away from the subject so that wrinkles in the fabric will be out of focus. Green backgrounds give the impression of out-of-focus foliage, while those of light blue can simulate a clear sky.

Helping Nature

The image of dew on flowers can be captured without getting up at dawn. "Instant dew," created with one spray of a window-spray bottle (or a plastic squeeze bottle) filled with water, will make flowers look fresh and "alive."

Another way to make flowers look fresh is to carefully remove any wilted or damaged petals and leaves. Try to avoid touching the blossom when positioning the flower; the petals of some flowers turn brown when handled.

Breezes and Flowers. Flowers will sway and bob in even the lightest breezes. Since a moving subject requires a fast shutter speed, and a fast shutter speed means a larger lens opening, depth of field will be lost. Also, since depth of field is so shallow, it is necessary to focus carefully, which is hard because the subject keeps moving. To help eliminate this movement, improvise a wind screen. One made from clear plastic sheeting stapled to wooden dowels works well. This type of screen is self-supporting;

Flower Photography

With strong close-up lenses, at close distances, focusing is critical. As the photographer cannot expect to get the entire flower in focus at the same time, he or she should concentrate on the nearest or most interesting part and let the rest go into a blur. Photo by Raimondo Borea for Editorial Photocolor Archives.

just drive the dowels into the ground, and it will stand alone. Although cardboard or heavy paper can be used for construction, the clear plastic offers two advantages:

1. It does not cast shadows.
2. It can be placed behind the subject and not show in the picture because it is transparent and will be out of focus.

Select Part of a Blossom. With a strong close-up lens, or several close-up lenses used together, focus on the center of a flower and discover a world of unique beauty. Tulips offer many colorful possibilities. In extreme close-ups, the petals become colorful backgrounds for unusual compositions in which the pistil and stamens are the center of interest. Since focusing is extremely critical at this ultra-close distance, focus on the closest stamen and let the petals go into an out-of-focus blur of color.

The centers of some blossoms look like unusual flowers in themselves—quite different from the entire flowers. For example, a center of a magnolia blossom looks like an unusual spiny cactus. All sorts of interesting designs and abstract photographs

can be created by moving in close and photographing only part of a flower. If flash is used, be sure that the light from it reaches down into the center of the flower. A ring-light electronic flash is very useful for this type of picture.

Photographing Flowers Indoors

The main advantage of working indoors is in control over lighting. Also, flowers swaying in the wind are not a problem. Most of the techniques discussed in the section on outdoor picture-taking, such as spraying water on the flowers and using art-paper backgrounds, are just as useful indoors.

With indoor flash, use the same techniques and exposures discussed in the section on outdoor flower pictures. However, it may be easier to use several reflector photolamps to illuminate subjects. Not only are photolamps less expensive than flashbulbs, but they also give the photographer the advantage of seeing the lighting before taking the picture.

Three reflector photolamps will give good control. Use one for the main light, one for the fill light, and a third for the background light or for adding extra highlights. Begin by placing the main light to one side of the flower to create strong sidelighting.

(Left) The soft light of an overcast day eliminates harsh shadows and emphasizes delicate colors. Photo by William T. Shore. (Right) A single, brilliantly colored, sharply focused blossom stands out against a dark, out-of-focus background. Photo by Servizio Editoriale Fotografico. (Below) One painted daisy in a field of dissimilar flowers catches the eye in this interesting composition. Photo by William T. Shore. All photos for Editorial Photocolor Archives.

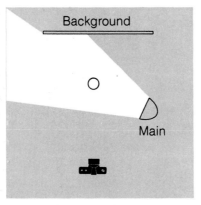

Photograph taken using main light only.
The diagram shows the lighting arrangement.

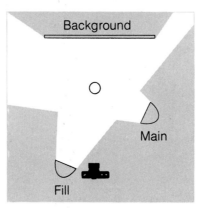

Photograph taken with main light and fill light. Fill light is positioned to the side and lights the subject from below.

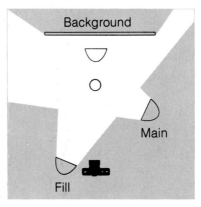

Photograph taken with main light and fill light, with a third light used as background light.

Then add a fill light at the camera position to lighten the shadow areas. Use the third light either to illuminate the background or to add highlights by aiming it from behind the flower. If very soft lighting is preferred, bounce the light by aiming a photolamp (or flash), at the ceiling. Experiment to see how many different effects can be created merely by changing the lighting arrangement.

• *See also:* CLOSE-UP PHOTOGRAPHY; FLASH PHOTOGRAPHY; LIGHTING; NATURE PHOTOGRAPHY.

Further Reading: Angel, Heather. *Nature Photography: Its Art and Techniques.* New York, NY: International Publications Service, 1973; ———. *Photographing Nature: Flowers.* Dobbs Ferry, NY: Morgan & Morgan, Inc., 1976; Guyler, Vivan V. *Design in Nature.* Worcester, MA: Davis Publications, Inc., 1970; Hannan, Hans W. *Flowers of the West Indies.* New York, NY: Hastings House Publishers, Inc., 1975.

A blurred background of neutral blue-gray flowers creates a perfect foil for this flame-colored dahlia. Photo by Editorial Photocolor Archives.

A brilliant burst of gold against a clear blue sky shows how aptly the sunflower is named. Photo by Editorial Photocolor Archives.

Fluorescence

When certain substances are subjected to energy beyond the shortest visible wavelengths—that is, ultraviolet and shorter wavelengths—they respond by radiating longer wavelengths. If the response occurs only while the stimulus energy is present, it is called *fluorescence;* if it continues after the stimulus is removed, it is called *phosphorescence.*

Fluorescence within the visible range can be photographed with conventional black-and-white and color films. The most common stimulus energy for such photography is ultraviolet radiation, which is readily available in easily controlled form in a variety of so-called "black light" lamps.

Visible fluorescence produces colorful pictorial effects, but more importantly it can reveal invisible information. For this reason it is widely used in investigatory and scientific photography. For example, underpainting in a work of art may be revealed if the lower-level paints fluoresce differently from those used for the visible surface painting. Or, the comparative amounts and distribution of a fluorescent substance in many different sample objects can be recorded.

Fluorescence is used in technical ways in photography. Some photographic papers contain white fluorescent dye in the baryta or resin layer just beneath the emulsion. When prints made on such papers are viewed in illumination that contains ultraviolet radiation, the material fluoresces white, giving added brilliance to the appearance of the print. Such materials are called "whiteners."

Radiography is the taking of pictures with x-rays. Films are made that are sensitive to x-rays, but they are relatively slow in reacting to straight x-ray radiation. Special screens made of materials that fluoresce when activated by x-rays are placed in contact with x-ray film, which is sensitive to light as well as to x-rays. When the x-ray is taken, the exposure is due to both x-rays and the fluorescent light, shortening the needed exposure. Since x-radiation can have severe side effects on tissue, this use of fluorescence lessens the exposure of people to x-rays, and increases the safety factor.

Electron beams are rays of energy with extremely short wavelengths. For this reason electron microscope pictures can be taken at much higher magnifications than with optical microscopes. Fluorescent ground-glass screens are used in electron microscopes in order to view the subject before the pictures are taken.

Computers can produce information much faster than mechanical printout devices can be made to operate. However, such printouts can be imaged in very small fractions of a second on a fluorescent screen. Equipment is made in which an automatic camera is focused on the fluorescent screen of a cathode-ray tube connected to a computer, photographing the computer printout. In this way, the rate at which the output of the computer can be recorded is speeded up significantly.

The techniques of fluorescence photography are explained in the articles in the following list of cross-references.

• *See also:* BLACK-LIGHT PHOTOGRAPHY; DOCUMENT EXAMINATION BY PHOTOGRAPHY; EVIDENCE PHOTOGRAPHY; RADIOGRAPHY; ULTRAVIOLET AND FLUORESCENCE PHOTOGRAPHY.

Fluorescent Light Photography

Scenes illuminated by fluorescent light usually appear pleasing and natural to the eye. Color photographs of these same scenes often have an overall color cast that makes them look different from the actual scenes. Fluorescent lamps emit a light that looks one way and photographs another. Since fluorescent light is weak in red and usually emits considerable blue and green, most color photographs taken without a filter in fluorescent light are also deficient in red and have an overall greenish appearance.

Yet there are benefits to be gained by using this type of illumination for picture-taking. Ordinarily, a room lighted with fluorescent lamps is brighter and more evenly illuminated than a room lighted with tungsten lamps. This makes it easier to get enough exposure for existing-light pictures, and shows good detail that might be obscured by the shadows caused by other types of lighting.

Fluorescent Lamps

There are several different types of fluorescent lamps, and each type produces somewhat different colors in a photograph. The differences are created by variations in the composition of the phosphor coating inside the tube. When these powdered phosphors are struck by ultraviolet radiation, they glow brilliantly and radiate visible light. The ultraviolet radiation that energizes the phosphors is produced by the mercury vapor in the tube.

The most common types of fluorescent lamps are standard cool white, deluxe cool white, standard warm white, deluxe warm white, and daylight.

The deluxe-type lamps emit more red light than the standard fluorescent lamps do. A deluxe warm white lamp closely approximates the visual appearance of a tungsten lamp. Cool white lamps emit relatively more blue light than warm white lamps do; and daylight-type lamps emit the most blue light.

Color Temperature Correction. Color films are usually designed for use with a specific type of light (daylight or tungsten). Ideally, the specified light source should be used, but when this is not practical, a conversion filter can be placed over the camera lens to adjust the color quality of the light to approximately that for which the film was designed.

The visual color quality of illuminants can be expressed in terms of "color temperature"—the color quality, designated in degrees Kelvin (K), of the light source. The higher the color temperature, the bluer the light; the lower the temperature, the redder the light.

Numbers such as 3200 K and 3400 K that are used in connection with light sources refer to color temperature. When it comes to color photography, however, the term should be used with caution. It designates only the appearance, or *visual* color, of the source and *not* the spectral energy distribution (relative amounts of energy at each wavelength). Color is the appearance of light as you, a human observer, see it, and visual color has no simple relationship to spectral energy distribution and the photographic effect that will result. To be effective for color photography, a filter should provide a certain change in color temperature and correction for the spectral energy distribution.

The output of a fluorescent lamp is best analyzed from a spectral-energy distribution (SED) curve. Such a curve depicts the relative energy of each wavelength put out by a light source. SED curves for typical deluxe warm white and daylight fluorescent lamps are shown in the accompanying diagrams.

The spectral-energy distribution curve for a typical deluxe warm white fluorescent lamp.

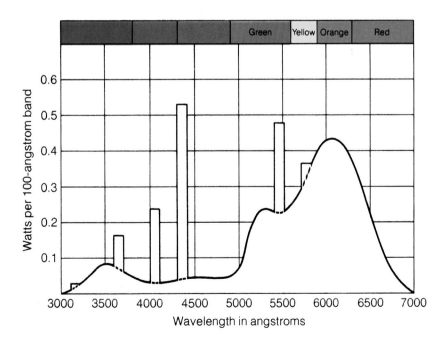

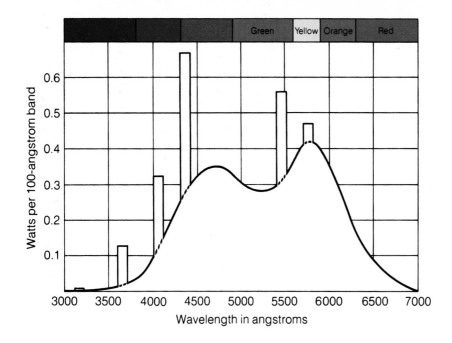

The spectral-energy distribution curve for a typical daylight fluorescent lamp.

The solid line is the spectral-energy distribution curve for a 500-watt, general-service tungsten lamp. The broken line is the spectral-energy distribution curve for a No. 2 photoflood lamp.

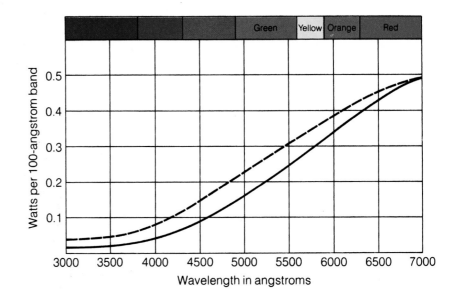

These graphs for the fluorescent lamps show a smooth but irregular-shaped curve with narrow vertical projections at several points along the curve. The smooth portion represents light from the glowing phosphors; the projections, light from the mercury vapor inside the lamp.

On the other hand, the energy output of a tungsten lamp is quite different, being a smooth curve without humps or spikes. The two tungsten lamps are quite similar.

Obtaining the Best Color Rendition

Color photographs made by fluorescent light involve some compromise, but there are two basic methods of obtaining satisfactory color pictures

Fluorescent Light Photography

when available fluorescent light is used as the predominant source of illumination:

1. Using color compensating filters in front of the camera lens.
2. Using supplementary lighting.

Color Compensating Filters. The density of each color compensating filter is indicated by the numbers in the filter designation, and the color is indicated by the final letter. In a typical filter designation, CC20Y, CC stands for Color Compensating, 20 for a density of 0.20, and Y for yellow.

You can use these filters singly or in combination to introduce almost any desired color correction. Such corrections are often required, as is the case with fluorescent illumination.

If you use several filters simultaneously in the camera-lens system, you may adversely affect definition and contrast by scattering the light. Try to use the minimum number of filters that will produce the desired correction. In most cases, the number should

A photograph taken by fluorescent light using tungsten film and no color compensating filter has a greenish appearance.

Use of a 20R filter in front of the camera lens gives the picture a warmer, reddish tone without apparent distortion of the natural colors.

not exceed three if definition is of major importance. Of course, definition is also affected by the condition of the filters. Keep them clean and free from scratches and other defects.

Tests and Tables. Although the light from fluorescent lamps appears to fall somewhere between tungsten and daylight, the usual color conversion filters do not give satisfactory results. The accompanying tables show that each type of fluorescent lamp requires a special combination of color compensating filters. If possible, you should make a series of photographic tests to ascertain the best filter or filter combinations for your film, the fluorescent lights that you will be working with, and your equipment.

Even with a table of suitable filter combinations, you are at a disadvantage because you seldom have the opportunity to find out what kind of lamps are installed in the area.

In public places where the fluorescent lighting is screened or hidden, it is often difficult to determine what kind of lamp is lighting the scene. Some-

Use of daylight film with fluorescent light and no filter results in a photograph with a bluish tinge.

A 30B filter reduces the amount of blue, resulting in a more natural-appearing picture.

Type of Fluorescent Lamp	Kodak Ektachrome EF Film 7241 (Daylight)		Kodak Ektachrome EF Film 7242 (Tungsten)*	
	Kodak Color Compensating Filters	Effective Exposure Index	*Kodak* Color Compensating Filters	Effective Exposure Index
Daylight	40M + 30Y	80	85B† + 30M + 10Y	64
White	20C + 30M	80	40R	64
Warm white	40B	64	30M + 20Y	64
Deluxe warm white	60C + 30M	50	10Y	100
Cool white	30M	100	50M + 60Y	50
Deluxe cool white	10Y	140–160	10M + 30Y	80

*Available in super 8 cartridges.
†Kodak daylight filter No. 85B.

FLUORESCENT LIGHT STARTING CORRECTION FILTER TABLE

Kodak Film Type	Deluxe Warm White	Warm White	White	Deluxe Cool White	Cool White	Daylight
	Filter	Filter	Filter	Filter	Filter	Filter
Daylight*	60C + 30M + 1⅔ stops	40C + 40M + 1½ stops	20C + 30M + 1 stop	30C + 20M + 1 stop	30M +⅔ stop	40M + 30Y + 1 stop
Type A (3400 K)	None —	30M + 10Y + 1 stop	40M + 30Y + 1 stop	10M + 20Y +⅔ stop	50M + 50Y + 1½ stops	85 + 30M + 10Y + 1⅓ stops
Type L† Tungsten (3200 K)	+10Y + ⅓ stop	30M + 20Y + 1 stop	40M + 40Y + 1 stop	10M + 30Y +⅔ stop	50M + 60Y + 1½ stops	85B+30M+10Y + 1⅓ stops

*Use these values for *Kodacolor* and Type S color negative films.
†Use these values for Type L color negative films.
NOTE: Increase the meter-calculated exposure by the amount indicated in the table. If the exposure times require, make the necessary additional corrections for reciprocity effect, both in exposure and filtration. With transparency films, run a filter test series up to ± CC20 from the given values (usually in the M ⟷ G and Y ⟷ B directions) under each lighting condition.

Filters specified above are *Kodak* color compensating filters and *Kodak Wratten* filters. Exposure increases for filters with the same designations from other manufacturers may differ.

These values are for undiffused lamps. Diffusers are apt to make the light more yellow. Remove a 10Y filter or add a 10B filter to those filters recommended above if diffused lamps light the subject area.

times the lamp types may be mixed. Manufacturers' sales figures indicate that the most common lamps are white, warm white, and cool white.

A less precise but simpler system for taking color pictures under fluorescent lamps is to always use a filter that provides a rough *average* correction for the three most popular lamps. For daylight color-slide films and some color-negative films, try a CC30M filter and an opening two-thirds of a stop wider. For tungsten films, use a CC50R filter and a lens opening one stop wider. *These recommenda-*

tions are only approximate, but will produce acceptable results in most cases.

One manufacturer offers single filters for overall average correction with daylight and tungsten color films. They are designated FL-D and FL-T, respectively.

Supplementary Lighting. In a scene that is lit primarily with fluorescent lamps, it is possible to add supplementary lighting to raise the illumination level and to ease color balancing. The specific type of lighting (tungsten lamps, flashbulbs, electronic flash, etc.) added to the scene, and the kind of film (tungsten or daylight) will determine whether or not filters are required, and if so, which ones. It is important to note that if the subject of the photograph is beyond the range of the supplementary lighting, the fluorescent lamps will be the light source on which the filter selection should be made.

Additional Tips. When exposing film under fluorescent lamps, all exposure times should be longer than 1/60 sec. (24 frames per second or slower when using movie cameras) in order to average variations in brightness and color that occur during a single alternating-current lamp cycle.

Fluorescent lamps change color as they warm up. They should be turned on at least 10 minutes before you start making exposures.

• *See also:* COLOR TEMPERATURE; FILTERS; LIGHTING.

f-Number

Historically, the relative apertures of various lens diaphragm settings have had a number of different measurement systems. The *f*-number system is practically the only one in use today.

The true *f*-number is the ratio of the diameter of the entrance pupil of the lens divided by the focal length at each setting. The entrance pupil is essentially the lens diaphragm as seen through the front elements of the lens. With most camera lenses, the entrance pupil is larger than the actual opening in the diaphragm because the front elements have a magnifying effect. In reverse telephoto wide-angle lenses, however, the front elements are negative in power, so the entrance pupil is smaller than the diaphragm opening.

For example, if the focal length is 200 mm and the entrance pupil diameter is 50 mm, the *f*-number is 50/200, which is 1/4, often written 1:4.

In common usage, however, the ratio is reversed; only the denominator of the *f*-number ratio is used. In the example above, the common usage *f*-number is 4, written *f*/4.

For the way *f*-numbers are usually used, then, the *f*-number is the focal length of the lens divided by the diameter of the diaphragm opening as seen through the front lens elements.

$$f = \frac{F}{d}$$

where:

F = focal length
d = diameter of aperture

$$f = \frac{200}{50} = 4$$

It is important to note two significant points concerning *f*-numbers:

1. As the actual size of the aperture in a given lens gets larger, the *f*-number (common use) gets smaller. Thus, *f*/2 indicates a relatively large opening, while *f*/32 indicates one that is relatively small.
2. When set at the same *f*-number, all lenses, regardless of focal length, create optical images of the same brightness. There are slight differences between lenses due to variations in glass transmission and lens coating, but these are small enough not to affect exposures.

• *See also:* APERTURE; DIAPHRAGM; FOCAL LENGTH; *f*-STOP, RELATIVE APERTURE.

Focal Frames

Focal frames are devices made for close-up photography with simple cameras. They consist of two parts. The first part is a frame that outlines the area covered, and determines the subject-to-camera distance. The second is a close-up lens that permits sharp focus at the close distance determined by the frame. The camera attaches to the frame in a position that centers the close-up lens in front of the camera lens. For more detail, and for information on constructing focal frames, see the article CLOSE-UP PHOTOGRAPHY.

Focal Length

Focal length is the distance between the optical center of the lens and the film when the lens is focused at infinity. The focal length of the lens of most adjustable cameras is marked on the lens barrel. The focal length is usually given in millimetres or inches.

There is a direct relationship between the focal length of a lens and the image size of the subject that is recorded on the film: The longer the focal length, the larger the image on the film. For example, in the accompanying diagram are two lenses: Lens A has a focal length of 2 inches, and lens B has a focal length of 6 inches. The subject is the same size and the same distance from the lens in both situations. However, the image produced by lens B is three times as large as the image produced by lens A because its focal length is three times as great.

The focal length of the lens is usually marked on the lens barrel. This lens has a focal length of 20 mm. Photo courtesy Ehrenreich Photo-Optical Industries, Inc.

Finding Lens Focal Length

Most lenses have the focal length printed on the front or side of the lens barrel. The focal length of a normal camera lens is equal to the distance from

A lens of long focal length produces a larger image than one of short focal length.

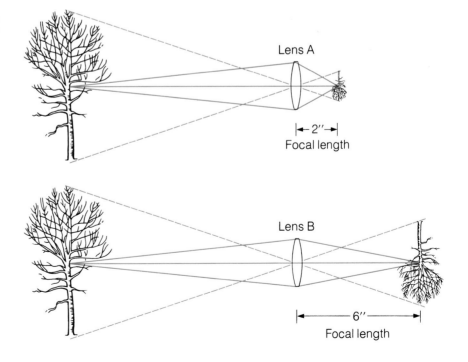

Lens A

|← 2″ →|
Focal length

Lens B

|←——— 6″ ———→|
Focal length

FOCAL LENGTH OF WIDE-ANGLE TO TELEPHOTO LENSES BY FILM FORMATS

Format		35 mm	6 × 6 cm	6 × 7 cm	4″ × 5″	8″ × 10″
Diagonal		44 mm	80 mm	90 mm	155 mm	305 mm
Lens Categories	Degrees					
Extreme Wide-Angle	110–90	12–22 mm	25–39 mm	30–42 mm	50–70 mm	95–150 mm
Medium Wide-Angle	89–72	23–29 mm	40–50 mm	43–55 mm	71–95 mm	151–200 mm
Moderate Wide-Angle	71–60	30–40 mm	51–69 mm	56–75 mm	96–127 mm	201–265 mm
Normal	59–47	41–55 mm	70–89 mm	76–109 mm	128–164 mm	266–355 mm
Moderate Telephoto	46–26	56–90 mm	90–159 mm	101–175 mm	165–305 mm	356–600 mm
Medium Telephoto	25–15	91–175 mm	160–299 mm	176–349 mm	306–550 mm	601–1200 mm
Extreme Telephoto	14–6	176–500 mm	300–700 mm	350–800 mm	551–1250 mm	1200–2500 mm

approximately the center of the lens to the image plane when the lens is focused on infinity. If you don't know the focal length of a normal lens, you can measure the approximate focal length from a point midway between the front element and the rear element of the lens.

You can determine the focal length of a lens more accurately by first focusing on an object at infinity, and then focusing on an object close to the camera to obtain a life-size image (unit magnification). Measure the lens-to-film distance at each setting. The difference between the two lens-to-film distances is equal to the focal length. When you use this technique to find the focal length, your camera must have a bellows or extension tubes that permit extending the lens to obtain an image the same size as the subject.

When the focal length of a lens is about the same as the diagonal of the film format, it is considered a normal-focal-length lens. When the focal length is considerably less than the diagonal, it is called a wide-angle lens. When it is considerably larger than the diagonal, it is called a narrow-angle or telephoto lens. The accompanying table gives the diagonals of some of the common still-camera formats and the range of lens focal lengths in a variety of normal, wide-angle, and telephoto categories.

• *See also:* LENSES; OPTICS.

Focal Range

When a lens is focused on a given subject, there is one lens-to-film distance where the image is the sharpest. As the lens is moved closer to the film or farther away from the film, the sharpness decreases. There is a small range of movement on either side of the position of best focus in which the degree of unsharpness is acceptable, and this total range is called the focal range or depth of focus.

Because the images that lenses form are only approximately flat, and because the degree of sharpness considered acceptable is a variable dependent on a number of factors, focal range is not an exact value. The most common way to calculate the focal range is with the following formula:

$$R = \frac{cvf}{F}$$

where:

R = the half of the focal range on one side of the focal plane;
c = the diameter of the acceptable circle of confusion;
v = the lens-to-image distance;
f = the *f*-number;
F = the focal length of the lens.

When the focal range is being calculated for infinity, the formula becomes:

$$R = cf$$

The total focal range is twice *R*, because the focal range is equal on both sides of the plane of best focus. However, the value of *R* is frequently of more interest: How far away from the plane of best focus can the film be and still produce an acceptable image? The main value of focal range is to camera manufacturers and not to photographers. It is used in assigning tolerances to lens mountings, film plane flatness, and focusing screen placement.

c VALUES			
	Format	c (millimetres)	c (inches)
Motion-Picture Cameras	Super 8	.012	.0005
	16 mm	.025	.001
	35 mm (single frame)	.025	.001
Still Cameras	110	.025	.001
	126	.050	.002
	35 mm (double frame)	.050	.002
	6 × 6 cm	.075	.003
	6 × 7 cm	.100	.004
	4″ × 5″	.150	.006
	8″ × 10″	.300	.012

The value of c commonly used is 1/1000 of the focal length of the normal focal length for the format, or the values in the accompanying table. For the most critical use, multiply table values by 0.6.
• *See also:* DEPTH OF FIELD; DEPTH OF FOCUS; LENSES; OPTICS.

Focusing Systems

The lens of a camera forms sharp images of various objects placed at differing distances in front of it at correspondingly different distances behind it. Thus, to secure a sharp image of an object at a given distance, you must adjust the lens to a certain distance from the film; this adjustment is called *focusing*. While there is a single, exact point of focus for an object at any given distance, there is some leeway allowable in focusing. This leeway is called "depth of focus" and refers to the permissible error in focusing; a similar latitude exists in the object space, so that objects at varying distances are, in certain cases, imaged with acceptable sharpness at a single focus setting. The latitude in subject distance, correspondingly, is called "depth of field." (*See:* DEPTH OF FIELD; DEPTH OF FOCUS.)

Because depth of field exists, it is possible to make certain simple cameras, such as "box" cameras, without any means of focusing at all. The lens in these cameras is focused at a distance corresponding to the "hyperfocal distance" for its focal length and aperture; then everything from half this distance

to infinity is reasonably sharp. As an example, a box camera making a 2¼″ × 3¼″ picture and equipped with a 4-inch lens of about *f*/11 aperture will have a hyperfocal distance of approximately 11 feet; hence everything from 5½ feet to infinity will be acceptably sharp.

Methods of Focusing

All other types of cameras require focusing. While in most cases, as mentioned, focusing is accomplished by adjusting the distance from lens to film plane, a few cameras have that distance fixed, and instead, adjust the focal length of the lens. The adjustment is accomplished by varying the spacing between the elements of the lens itself; such lenses are called "front-element-focusing" because, usually, the focusing method involves partly unscrewing the front element of the lens system to increase the size of the front air space in the lens.

This system has certain interesting properties; the movement of the front element for focusing at any given distance depends only upon the focal length of the front element itself, not of the entire lens. Thus, it is possible to make two lenses having different focal lengths, but in which the front element of each has the same focal length. Then, the movement of either front element for focusing will be exactly the same for any given distance, even though the two lenses differ in focal length. This makes it possible to manufacture a twin-lens reflex camera having the front elements of the two lenses coupled, even though the finder lens and taking lenses have different focal lengths.

There is some loss of correction in a lens when the distance between elements is varied; element spacing is usually critical in lens design. For this reason, the front-element-focusing system is used mainly in moderately priced cameras where the very highest image quality is not required.

Usually, then, focusing is accomplished by varying the distance from lens to film. It is quite immaterial which of the two is actually moved, and the method chosen depends upon the design of the camera. Thus, large view cameras are usually focused by moving the back to and from the lens. This is mainly a matter of convenience, since the back is closer to the operator. There is one other convenience: When the camera is used for close-ups and copying, it is easier to focus if the lens-to-subject distance remains unchanged. If the lens is moved for focusing, then both object and image distance are changing at the same time; and when working near a 1:1 ratio, it is exceedingly difficult to attain the exact distance for sharp focus.

In the case of smaller cameras, focusing is almost always accomplished by moving the lens closer to and farther away from the film plane. The lens may be mounted on a panel that moves in relation to the film plane on a track, the lighttight chamber being composed of a cloth or leather bellows. In most small cameras, though, the camera body is solid, and the lens is mounted in a threaded barrel that allows it to move in and out over a distance sufficient to focus the lens over its normal range.

Determining Focus

No matter what system of lens adjustment is used, there must be some means by which the photographer determines when the image is in focus. The simplest system, used on low-priced still cameras and most older movie cameras, is simply to have a scale of distances to which the lens is set. Such scales may be on the lens barrel or on the frame of the camera, depending upon the type of camera.

Scale focusing is used mainly with small-aperture lenses that have sufficient depth of field to overcome any small error in judging the camera-to-subject distance. Yet this is not always the case. For many years, professional motion-picture camera operators preferred to use the distance scale on the lens over visual focusing on a ground glass. There was, however, nothing approximate about the method. The lenses on these cameras were very accurately calibrated, and measurement of distance to the subject was made with a tape measure, to fractions of an inch, in close-ups.

In most cases, and especially with larger cameras, focusing was done by examining the image on a screen made of finely ground glass. Fairly critical focusing is attained this way, at least on large cameras. There is, though, some residual error. Because of the texture of the ground glass, the finest detail in the image cannot be resolved, and there is some latitude in focusing as a result. This takes the form of a small zone through which the lens can be moved without noticeably affecting the sharpness of the image. For critical focus, the camera operator can note the depth of this zone while moving the lens

back and forth, and then set the lens to the middle of the zone, considering this the sharpest point.

The drawback to the method is mainly that the focusing screen must be accurately installed so that its plane matches that of the emulsion side of the film in the holders. If this is accomplished, then ground-glass focusing can be very accurate.

Parallax Focusing

The ground surface of the glass is required to provide a definite point on which the eye can focus, but it does interfere with the precision of focusing, as has been pointed out. A clear glass would obviate this error, but some means is required to determine when the image is exactly in the plane of the glass. For very small images, this can be accomplished by engraving a cross on the front surface of the glass, and then focusing a fairly high-powered magnifier upon the cross. If the magnifier is about $20\times$ or stronger, it will have so little depth of focus that the eye will be forced to see the image formed by the camera lens in focus only when its image falls in the same plane as the cross. Such systems are used in certain motion-picture cameras, but have one disadvantage: A high-powered magnifier has a very small field, and you can only focus upon a single object in the center of the field.

There is a method of focusing on clear glass that obviates the necessity of using a strong magnifier. This depends upon the fact that unless the image formed by the camera lens is exactly in the plane of the cross on the glass, it will move at a different rate when the viewer's eye is moved from side to side.

With this method, a magnifier of about $6\times$ to $10\times$ is used. It is first focused on the cross marks, and adjusted so that it will stay in position. Then you move your head from side to side, while watching the image and the cross. If the image seen through the lens moves with respect to the cross, then it is out of focus. When cross and image move side to side at exactly the same rate, so there is no shift between them, the lens is in focus.

In any case, after focusing has been accomplished, the shutter must be closed, the ground-glass panel removed (or sprung backward), and a film holder inserted, to take the picture. This is time-consuming, especially where many pictures must be taken in rapid succession.

One way to avoid the problem was to make the camera double—a second camera built on top of the first, having a lens of exactly the same focal length. Then focusing could be carried out on the ground glass of the upper camera, while film was already loaded in the lower one, ready for exposure. A few such cameras were built in the early days, but they were large and clumsy and never attained much popularity, especially as the focusing image was still upside down, making composition difficult.

Reflex Cameras

The problem was solved by the reflex principle. In early forms such as the Graflex cameras, there was simply a large mirror, hinged so that in its normal, or down, position it reflected the rays of light from the lens upward to a focusing screen made of ground glass. The reflection served a second purpose; it turned the image right side up for easier composition. There was a focal-plane shutter directly behind the mirror, in front of the film. When the exposure button was pressed, the mirror swung up out of the way, and the shutter was tripped, taking the picture. The success of the entire system depended upon how accurately the distance from lens to film, and from lens to ground glass, could be matched for accurate focus.

One minor annoyance was that the mirror, which turned the image right side up, also reverted it left for right. Therefore, the image on the ground glass was not a true one but a mirror image. This was normally not very annoying, but could be a nuisance when trying to follow moving objects.

In the modern single-lens reflex camera, the same principle is used with refinements. The image on the ground glass is viewed by way of a pentaprism combined with a magnifier; thus the focusing is done at eye-level, rather than looking down into a hood. The pentaprism turns the image not only right side up, but right way around as well. The image is seen exactly as if one were looking directly at the subject, although it may have a different apparent size.

Focusing screens are quite varied in this type of camera. The most popular type has a small circle of "microprisms" in the center, which aid in critical focusing by visually shattering the image until it is exactly in focus, at which point the prisms seem to disappear and a smooth image is seen. Surrounding the microprism section is a "collar" of plain ground glass. This is useful for rough focusing, and, more important, for judgment of depth of field. The remainder of the screen is usually a clear Fresnel lens, providing a bright image right out to the corners of the screen, for easy composition.

(Left) One of the most popular types of focusing screen uses a small central circle of microprisms that visually shatters an out-of-focus image. (Right) When the image is exactly in focus, the prisms seem to disappear. Photos courtesy Petri International Corp.

Since focusing is most easily accomplished with the lens wide open, a mechanism is usually arranged to shut the lens to a predetermined aperture as the shutter release is set. This is often combined with some sort of exposure meter that automatically sets either the lens aperture or the shutter speed.

One final refinement: In the modern single-lens reflex, the mirror automatically returns as soon as the exposure has been made. Thus the composition and focus can be checked at once. Such cameras often have a depth-of-field preview control, allowing the lens to be stopped down to the shooting aperture.

Twin-Lens Reflexes

The system of focusing by means of matched lenses is still popular in such twin-lens reflex cameras as the Rolleiflex, Yashicaflex, Mamiyaflex, and others. These have the advantage of having no swinging mirror mechanism. The image is visible on the ground glass before, during, and after exposure. Like the earlier single-lens reflexes, the image in the focusing hood is right side up, but reversed left for right. There are accessory hoods, however, that contain either a pentaprism or a mirror system, so that the image can be viewed at eye level, right side up and right way around.

In the twin-lens system, the focusing lens is always wide open. This makes viewing and focusing easy, but it is not possible to judge depth of field in such a viewer. It does, however, eliminate the need for any kind of automatic diaphragm mechanism. Depth-of-field scales are usually provided on the lens or in connection with the focusing knob.

Most twin-lens reflex cameras have only a single matched pair of lenses; interchangeable lenses are usually not supplied. The exception, however, is the Mamiya camera, which has available matched pairs of lenses, each pair mounted on a lens board for easy changing. The cost of such matched pairs is necessarily higher than that of a single lens for an ordinary camera; but since no focusing mounts are required, and the viewing lens need not be fully corrected, the added cost is not as high as would be expected.

Rangefinder Focusing

Early miniature cameras, such as the Leica, were supplied with a separate rangefinder. This was of the mechanical type, where a mirror is tilted slightly by turning a wheel to bring two images into coincidence. The distance was then read off the rim of the wheel, and the camera lens was set to that distance.

Later miniature cameras had similar rangefinders built into the camera itself. The tilting device that moved the rangefinder mirror was a cam milled into the back of the lens mount; simply turning the focusing ring of the lens measured the distance and set the focus at the same time. Cameras of this type are still being made, though they are not as popular as they once were, because a separate viewfinder is needed for composition. Since the cam that operates the rangefinder is part of the lens mount, obviously any lens having a cam made to fit a particular camera will work with its rangefinder, regardless of the focal length of the lens. In some cameras, the coincident rangefinder is combined with the viewfinder. The rangefinder image is seen as a small colored area in the middle of the finder field.

There is another type of rangefinder that is purely optical; it has no moving parts. In effect, it is two small prisms, facing in opposite directions. The point at which they cross is level with the ground surface of the focusing screen, and the prisms themselves are usually made as part of the screen itself. If any part of the subject that is a straight line is viewed on the screen through the prisms, the line will be broken in two, exactly as in the usual split-image rangefinder. When the subject is exactly in focus, the parts join into a single straight line. Such rangefinders were built into the ground glass of a number of twin-lens reflex cameras. They are not as effective with lenses of short focal length, and are seldom found in 35 mm single-lens reflexes.

In single-lens reflexes, the microprism screen works in much the same way; but instead of a line being broken into two parts, it is broken into as many parts as there are prisms in the screen. The effect is to "shatter" the out-of-focus image. When it is in focus, it smooths out and the prisms themselves seem to disappear. This facilitates focusing greatly; there is a clear and definite point of correct focus for any subject distance.

There is only one problem with rangefinder focusing, a problem that also applies to any system of focusing by scale. Since you do not see the actual focused image, there is a question whether you really are in focus or not. This ambiguity comes about because the focusing scale (and the rangefinder) may be measuring distances from the front of the lens, or it may be calibrated from the plane of the film. For a distance of several feet out to infinity, the error is trifling, and may safely be ignored. For close-ups it must be taken into account. You may assume the rangefinder does, in fact, account for the difference, but if you are focusing by scale measurement, it is necessary to know from what point the scale is calibrated. Generally in cameras where the lens is calibrated from the film plane, there will be a mark on the camera body indicating the exact location of the film plane, and all measurements are made from this mark—a circle with a line through it ($\ominus$).

• *See also:* DEPTH OF FIELD; DEPTH OF FOCUS; HYPERFOCAL DISTANCE; VIEWING AND FOCUSING.

Fogging

Fog is any silver density occurring in a print or negative that was not intentionally put there by the photographer.

Fog in Black-and-White Materials

Two kinds of fog can appear in black-and-white materials. The first is light fog and is caused by an unintentional exposure to light of the sensitized material. The second, chemical fog, is the result of reduction of *unexposed* silver halide by the developer.

Light Fog. The causes of this kind of fog in a film or print are almost always obvious; it can be caused by a leaky camera back or bellows, malfunctioning film holders, or unsafe light conditions in the darkroom during loading or processing. In almost all cases, it is possible to deduce the cause of light fog by examination of the negative.

Careless Film Loading. In the case of roll films, fog at one end of the roll, fading out after a short distance, is the result of careless loading of the camera, during which too much of the protective paper is allowed to unroll before the camera back is closed. Obviously, the same effect at the opposite end of the roll is due to careless unloading of the camera, during which either the back is opened before all the paper is wound off or the paper is allowed to unroll

partly while the roll is being removed. Fog in the form of scallops along the edges of the film is usually due to loose winding that allows light to enter between the turns of paper at the ends of the spool.

Stray Light in Darkroom. Uniform gray fogging of a film over its entire length, as well as similar fog on sheet films, is usually caused by stray light in the darkroom, while loading or unloading; such fogging may also be caused by using a malfunctioning safelight or the wrong safelight for the film in question. With modern films, there is really no safelight that is safe for film in the dry state; loading and unloading of sheet-film holders, and loading of developing reels and film hangers should all be done in total darkness.

Faulty Film Holders. Although 35 mm cartridges are fairly safe when new, they should not be loaded into the camera in bright sunlight; some light can get past the velvet light-trap lips, causing fog on at least the first few frames of film. The ordinary metal cartridge supplied with 35 mm films is not intended for reuse, and there is always danger of leakage when such cartridges are reloaded.

Sheet-film holders, likewise, are safe when new, but the slide enters through a light trap, and when this becomes worn there is always the danger of light leaking through the slot when the slide is withdrawn. There is also a danger of light leakage at the opposite end, where the hinged flap may become worn and the tape forming the hinge may develop pinholes. It is well to keep a record of the individual holders used for given pictures; thus, if a fogged negative is encountered, one can usually tell in which holder it was made. Old and worn holders should be replaced at once, especially if they are old ones made of wood. The new plastic and metal types are far more rugged and reliable.

Light Leaks in Camera. Light leaks can also exist in the camera itself; the worst offender is usually the bellows of press-type and view cameras. Continual folding and unfolding of these bellows eventually cause the cloth and leather to wear thin; since this usually occurs first at the corners, those are the first places to look. One good way to check this is to place a small bulb on an extension cord inside the bellows in a dark room. By moving the light around and looking carefully, even tiny pinholes can be located. A temporary repair can be made with black masking tape.

Another point at which leakage often occurs is in the back, where the sheet-film holders slide into place. If fog occurs and cannot be traced to one defective holder, then the camera back should be examined to see if the holder fits tightly, and to make sure that the light-trap rib at the end of the holder slides into the groove provided for it. Dirt in the groove can keep the holder from seating properly, and fog can result.

Miniature cameras for 35 mm films and small roll-film cameras usually have hinged backs that are well trapped against light leakage, at least when new. A camera that has had heavy use, however, may have a bent or sprung back, which can cause light leakage and fog.

Faulty Shutter. In rare instances, fog results from a shutter not closing completely, thereby allowing a small amount of light to enter through the lens itself.

Unsafe Safelight. Fog on prints is usually the result of stray light in the darkroom, or, of course, an unsafe safelight. Safelight filters do tend to fade with time and use, and often cause fog on papers, especially when fast enlarging papers are used. (*See:* SAFELIGHTS.) Likewise, a wrong safelight can cause fog; for example, the Kodak safelight filter OA, while safe for all ordinary enlarging papers, will cause fog on variable-contrast papers such as Kodak Polycontrast paper and others. For these, only the Kodak safelight filter OC is safe, and since it is safe for ordinary papers as well, it should be used for all enlarging papers. The sole exception is the panchromatic type of paper used for making black-and-white prints from color negatives; this and, of course, color-print papers require special safelight filters.

Light Leaks in Enlarger. Another cause of fog on prints is leakage of white light from the enlarger lamphouse, possibly through the vents that are provided for escape of hot air from the lamp. Leakage can also occur around the negative carrier if the lamphouse does not fit tightly down upon it, or if the carrier does not close tightly upon the negative. There is a simple test for this form of leakage: Put a negative and carrier in the enlarger, place a cap over the lens, shut off the safelight, and turn on the enlarger lamp. There should be no light leakage visible from any part of the enlarger; if there is, the cure is to stop the leaks. Painting the wall behind the enlarger black helps reduce the effects of difficult leaks around the negative carrier.

Chemical Fog. Chemical fog is any fog on a negative or print that was not caused by exposure to light. It may, indeed, be a problem in the emulsion itself, resulting either from faulty manufacture, improper storage, or excessively old material.

Years ago, certain types of film and plate emulsions did have an appreciable fog level; this was especially noticeable in certain fast orthochromatic emulsions. Today, with improved sensitizers and methods of manufacture, all current films have fog levels so low as to be negligible under ordinary circumstances. (Note that the orange color in unexposed areas of a color negative is not fog; it is residual color coupler, deliberately left there to assist in color correction.)

Outdated Film. Most chemical fog, then, is due to development difficulties or to the age of the film. As far as age is concerned, there is little reason to use outdated film, and if the pictures are at all important, it is false economy to attempt to salvage old film. Where it is absolutely necessary, however, and if the fog level is not too high, addition of an organic antifoggant to the developer can produce fairly good negatives. The antifoggants usually used are either benzotriazole (Kodak anti-fog No. 1) or 6-nitrobenzimidazole nitrate (Kodak anti-fog No. 2). Both of these preparations reduce the speed of the film, so if you intend to use outdated film be sure to give considerable extra exposure—at least one full stop or more—and then process in a developer containing the antifoggant. No exact directions can be given; exposure and processing depend on how old the film is and the conditions under which it has been stored.

Push Processing. With reasonably fresh film and a normal developer, fog is seldom a problem. The exception comes about when one attempts to "push" film to a higher-than-normal speed; some pushing can be accomplished in Kodak D-76 developer or its equivalent without unduly raising the fog level of the film. But for extreme speed gains, it is necessary to use a film like Kodak Royal-X pan film, and to process it in a "maximum-energy" developer. This will necessarily result in an overall fog; if the development is curtailed to reduce the fog level, then little or no gain in emulsion speed is attained. The formula in question contains Kodak anti-fog No. 2;

if it did not, the fog level would be even worse. (*See:* PUSH PROCESSING.)

Dichroic Fog. Dichroic (two-colored) fog gets its name from the fact that it appears green when seen on the surface of the film or red when looking through the film. It is almost always the result of contamination, usually of developer by hypo or another silver solvent. In a few cases, it occurs in fixing bath that is exhausted or heavily contaminated with developer and lacking in acid.

Usually, dichroic fog occurs on slow, fine-grain, thin-emulsion films; it is less likely to occur on fast films with larger silver-grain structure. It is for this reason that one is warned against using fine-grain developers containing silver solvents (such as the discontinued Kodak developer DK-20, which contained sodium thiocyanate) with modern, fine-grain, thin-emulsion films. These fine-grain developers no longer have any real utility and should be avoided.

If dichroic fog is noted immediately after washing while the film is still wet, it can sometimes be removed by gently wiping the film with a chamois or a wad of wet cotton. Once it has dried on the film, the fog can no longer be wiped off but can usually be removed by a short treatment in Farmer's Reducer, or by a clearing bath such as the following:

Thiourea	10.0 g
Citric acid	10.0 g
Cold water to make	1.0 litre

Treat the negative only long enough to remove the fog, then wash it thoroughly, and dry as usual.

There is usually no reason to attempt to remove fog from a print; it is always preferable to make a new print rather than to waste time trying to salvage a bad one. Even with negatives, if the fog is mild and evenly distributed, it is best simply to proceed to print the negative without attempting to remove the fog. Generally, a satisfactory print can be made from a lightly fogged negative merely by using a higher-contrast grade of paper.

Fog on Color Materials

Many of the causes of fog on color films and papers are the same as the causes of fog on black-and-white materials.

Camera fog on color transparencies comes in positive rather than negative form—the fogged areas are light instead of dark. On color negatives, light fog darkens the film in streaks or overall. On prints made from transparencies by reversal, the fog lightens the image, while on color prints made from negatives, light fog darkens the image.

Chemical fog can come from a number of sources. See the tables on color processes given in the article ERRORS IN PROCESSING.

• *See also:* AERIAL FOG; ANTIFOGGANT; DICHROIC FOG; ERRORS IN PROCESSING; REDUCTION; STAINS, REMOVING.

Food Photography

The photography of food is one of the most highly specialized and challenging areas in the field of commercial photography. The art of photographing food products lies in the ability of the photographer to make the picture so appealing that the viewer will feel the urge to take a taste—or make a purchase—immediately. The basic problem facing the photographer is that the major appeals of food are aroma and taste, while photography is of course a visual medium. The usual solution is to photograph the product so that it appears even more realistic and more appetizing in the picture than it would in actuality, when a subjective factor such as its aroma is working on the viewer. To accomplish this, a great deal of careful preparation is required in addition to the use of visual imagination, knowledge of special techniques, and the ability to take technically excellent photographs.

The Food Studio

Food pictures are sometimes taken on location when a certain setting or background is required—a distinctive restaurant or a fish market, for example—or when a product such as ice cream can be kept in better condition in a location other than a studio. However, the vast majority of food photography is done in well-equipped studios. A studio offers controlled setup and lighting conditions, as well as the space to prepare the elements of the picture. It also permits the photographer to take as much time as required to get the desired results without interfer-

ing with other activity or business, which is often a source of pressure and distraction in location work.

In addition, a successful food studio requires a well-equipped kitchen and at least one home economist or food-preparation specialist on staff.

Facilities. The studio kitchen is used to prepare food for assignments, not as a shooting set. It must have facilities for broiling, roasting, baking, and stove-top cooking, all of which require efficient exhaust ventilation that removes steam and smoke immediately. Refrigerator and freezer capacity that is at least twice that of a household kitchen is essential to keep an ample supply of products and replacements ready for use.

Wheeled counter units or work tables make it easy to adjust to the job at hand. Most studios have an automatic dishwasher in addition to at least one double sink. As in any commercial studio, space for more than one setup is a great advantage in terms of both working convenience and economy. Ample shooting space allows one or more assignments to be prepared while another is being photographed and keeps delays caused by tearing down and setting up to a minimum.

Staff. Only a specially trained individual can adequately supervise food preparation and solve problems such as how to make souffles that will not collapse during shooting, or apple pies with fillings that do not run out when a slice is removed. Knowing how to cook green vegetables so they stay firm and colorful or roast a turkey so it does not overcook from its own retained heat is not something the photographer can take the time to learn.

In addition to the food and photographic personnel, other specialists may be kept on staff or hired as consultants when required. They generally include a designer-decorator to plan settings and decor; a stylist to obtain props and set up dressing, fruits, vegetables, flowers, and other accessories; and —when models are to be included in a picture—a wardrobe consultant and a make-up artist.

Sets and Props. There are few permanent sets in a food studio. Backgrounds, props, and arrangements are continually changed to suit the product presentation and to avoid a look of sameness from one assignment to another—an important factor in giving individual service to each client. When, for example, a kitchen set is needed, it is created by arranging appliances, cupboard units, wall flats, and accessories as required. This permits the photographer to vary the appearance of the sets and keep photographic activities out of the kitchen where the food must be prepared. On-camera appliances seldom have to be connected for practical operation; they are not used for actual preparation so that they

While most food photography is done in a studio, locations may be preferred in certain instances. Here, a wheatfield was chosen to emphasize the goodness and wholesomeness of the product. Photo by Phil Sidney.

remain new-looking. Although many props must be kept on hand to dress settings or solve photographic problems, major items such as furnishings and appliances are usually rented or obtained on loan.

Shooting Surface. One of the most useful items in a food studio is a readily available piece of equipment: an ordinary unmounted, flush-type wooden door. It can be used as a shooting surface for a wide variety of work. Background material is stretched across the top and pinned to the sides, out of camera view. If necessary, the material can be continued up in a sweep to form a seamless vertical background. The door is usually supported on 2 small sawhorses that place the entire setup about 20 inches above the floor. This permits high-angle and overhead vertical shots without the need for ladders or platforms, and makes it easy to set up the props. Background materials may also be placed on the studio floor for greater camera-to-subject distance.

Photographic Equipment

Cameras. Almost all food photography is done in color, usually on transparency films 4″ × 5″ or larger in order to obtain the highest quality images for reproduction. View cameras provide direct inspection of the picture composition and permit adjusting depth of field for maximum coverage of tabletop or countertop setups. Roll-film or 35 mm cameras may be used when rapid operation or quick position changes are essential, but even on location a tripod-mounted view camera is the rule.

The cameras and lenses used for the photographs in this article range from 35 mm single-lens reflex cameras with wide-angle lenses to studio cameras with 500 mm lenses. Some versatile studio view cameras can be changed from a 4″ × 5″ format to a 5″ × 7″ or 8″ × 10″ format by changing various components. Other lenses typically used with such

(Left) A food preparation specialist is essential for selection and preparation of the products to be photographed. This flaming cherries jubilee could not be created by the average cook to hold up under the conditions required in the studio. (Right) High angle shots such as this are set up on a platform approximately 20 inches from the floor. This eliminates the need for ladders or platforms, and facilitates arrangement of the props. Photos by Ted DeToy.

cameras are 300 mm (12″) and 375 mm (14¾″) in focal length.

Lighting. Both continuous-source lighting (floodlights and spotlights) and electronic flash are widely used. Continuous sources such as tungsten-halogen lamps make it easy to adjust lighting until a desired effect is obtained. Electronic flash avoids the problem of overheating the product, which can cause it to wilt, change color, or become otherwise useless. Whatever the lighting, stand-in preparations are used for the setting-up procedure and for test exposures with instant print films; a fresh product is used for the actual shooting. In fact, a number of fresh versions may be required during a session because certain foods lose their freshness—a steak quickly loses its just-sizzled look, ice cream rapidly glosses over and loses surface texture before it visibly begins to melt, and salad greens wilt quickly. The food preparation specialist is often busier than the photographer, providing ready-for-camera subjects one after another.

A commonly used light source is a single 1000-watt tungsten lamp aimed into a parabolic translucent silk umbrella reflector. The silk material is preferred to the more common reflective Mylar sheeting because, unlike the sheeting, it directs most of the light onto the subject while allowing some light through to bounce onto walls, floor area, and props. Fill lights used with such a unit are often also 1000-watt sources with umbrellas. However, with these the umbrella is placed so that light must pass through it before reaching the subject. This combination makes it easy to control the subject-lighting ratio while also illuminating the rest of the setup.

Gobos and scrims are used to control the placement and intensity of light. A gobo consists of a rectangular or otherwise-shaped piece of opaque material mounted on a gooseneck stand. It is used to block part of the light. Some gobos are fastened to a rod that clamps to a light stand for easy adjustment. Scrims are light diffusers that are made of mesh or other gauze-like materials. They too are mounted on light stands or other easily positioned supports to soften the light as required. A scrim of black net material can be rotated from a position perpendicular to the light beam to an angle of up to 45 degrees in order to obtain continuously variable light intensity. Excellent lighting can be created by covering the main light source with a scrim of glass-fiber diffusing material which has a hole about two inches in diameter cut out of the center. It diffuses all the light except that falling directly onto the central subject.

Information Sources. In addition to his or her own technical skill and the specialized knowledge of assistants and consultants, there is a book that an illustrative photographer will find invaluable: *Simon's Directory of Theatrical Materials, Services and Information,* published by Package Publications. This is an excellent source for locating products and services vital to studio and location photography. While the Yellow Pages of the local telephone directory may have some of the same information, the directory covers almost every state and can be extremely helpful in making advance arrangements for going to distant locations. Almost

Food Photography

Truth in advertising is a major consideration in the selection of foods to be photographed. Consequently, only a limited amount of picking and choosing of individual items may be permitted. A selection ratio of one item out of six is generally acceptable; arrangement of the items used may make the ratio appear higher. Photo by William R. Eastabrook.

any subject that comes to a working photographer's mind—acrobatic supplies, actors' agents, mock-up aircraft, costumes, cable, associations, unions—can be found in its table of contents.

Selecting Products

There was a time when the items of food used in advertising and display photographs were carefully hand-picked. For every single item used in the setup, perhaps 100 or more similar items were rejected. This was particularly true for fruits; only the largest items of best quality were chosen for a project. Such items necessarily gave a false impression.

Today, truth in advertising is a major consideration. As a result, a selection ratio of about 1:6 is the largest acceptable to most illustrative photographers. The food items depicted in most photographs are found at a local market after a minimum of searching and picking over.

Packaged products may be furnished by a distributor or manufacturer in order to avoid problems of shipping damage or shelf wear. Cooked items may be brought into the studio already prepared. This is usually the case when a certain type of preparation requires special equipment or techniques (special preparation is sometimes the very thing the client wants communicated). However, most cooked items are prepared in the studio kitchen immediately before they are photographed.

Techniques for Photographing Certain Foods

How the selected items are best photographed is something learned through practice and experience.

Food Photography

The rapid change in frozen dessert is illustrated in this series taken over a period of approximately 90 seconds. Dry-ice packing, where available, will retard the melting process. Photos by William R. Eastabrook.

The following problems and their photographic solutions illustrate a variety of useful techniques.

Frozen Confections. Among the food products most difficult to photograph are frozen confections like ice cream or yogurt. Such products have a very short "exposure time" before they begin to melt and must be discarded. Photography of this type of food is usually done on location in an ice-cream shop or at another source of direct supply. Many setups are made and passed to the shooting area as fast as the photographer can switch film holders and cock the shutter. If a 35 mm camera is used, the shooting resembles a rapid-fire sequence on a rifle range.

The three accompanying photographs illustrate frozen dessert. The first (above) shows the fresh dessert. Notice that it is dry and its surface texture is clearly rough. In the second photograph (above right), the confection has been exposed to lights for

about 45 seconds; the surface is slightly wet, and the texture is a bit smooth. The last picture was taken approximately 90 seconds after the initial positioning was made; in it, the surface of the yogurt is very wet, its texture has almost disappeared, and its tip in the cone is now rounded.

There are a few innovations associated with shooting frozen confections.

Use of Dry Ice. In the studio, ice cream should be packed in dry ice prior to being used. This makes it extra firm and as cold as possible. When on-location shooting is done, the dry-ice pack is not always available. In such situations, the photographer should make sure he has a supply of shaved or powdered ice that can be used to capture the desired surface texture.

If the confection comes out of a machine, it is used as "poured." Once it is in place on the shooting table, the photographer begins taking pictures as fast as possible. Between exposures, an assistant sprinkles a small amount of shaved or powdered dry ice onto the confection. This gives texture to its surface and makes it appear "normal." A firm confection such as ice cream may be spooned from a container with an ordinary teaspoon. Each spooned portion is carefully placed into a cone, dish, or other container until the desired shape is obtained. Dry-ice shavings may then be sprinkled over the ice cream in order to give it as natural a surface texture as possible.

Support Device. The ice-cream cone in the accompanying photograph is supported in a unique manner. A 12d (12 penny) nail and metal disk per-

This ice-cream cone appears to be standing with no means of support. The diagram at right illustrates the technique used for setting up such a shot. Photo by William R. Eastabrook.

Food Photography

Lighting and composition are the key techniques used for this arrangement of fruit with ceramics and glass. The lighting method used is discussed in the text. Photo by William R. Eastabrook.

form this function. A wire coat hanger can also be used, with several props obtainable from one hanger. For the disk, a cover removed from a can or a scrap of tin or galvanized metal can be used—as long as it will take solder. The nail head is then soldered to the metal. If a wire is used, it can be bent at a right angle and placed through a hole drilled in the base disk (see the accompanying diagram).

The cone is prepared by pushing an ice pick, or similar instrument, through the cone (from the open end) and puncturing the tip. The cone is then placed on the support, and a quantity of modeling clay is packed around the nail inside the cone. The clay serves two purposes: It steadies the cone on the support and also prevents the ice cream from running through the hole onto the shooting surface.

If a prop, such as a dish of ice cream, is placed in front of the cone to hide the base, then the cone can be placed directly on top of the shooting surface. If there is to be nothing in the foreground, the base can be hidden by pushing the nail, or wire, up through a piece of material that then becomes the shooting surface.

Supporting a machine-filled cone can be a problem. One solution is to place a large metal washer into the cone and then pack some modeling clay on top of the washer. If the hole in the washer is just large enough to pass the nail shank, it can be positioned by feel as the filled cone is placed onto the support. The result is a seemingly self-supported ice cream cone.

Fruit and Glass. Picture composition and control of light are the major techniques used for the picture of the fruit on the hutch. A single 1000-watt tungsten lamp was the light source. A scrim with a hole in the center directed the primary light onto the fruit. Some reflector cards and additional scrims and gobos were used to control bounce light. The highlights seen in the brandy bottle were made by placing a wrinkled piece of aluminum foil behind the bottle. The foil was tilted to pick up light from the main source and to transmit it through the bottle. The star-shaped light seen in the glass door is a low-wattage ceiling fixture hanging in the studio. It adds some warmth and depth to the photograph.

(Left) Photographs of iced drinks require special techniques, described in the text, to simulate condensation on the glass. (Right) The appearance of crushed ice was created by substituting crumpled plastic wrap for the actual ice. Photos by William R. Eastabrook.

Ice and Moisture. In the accompanying photograph of an iced drink, some things are real and some have been created. The glass was one of a dozen placed in the freezer compartment of a refrigerator until needed for the shot. Upon removal from the freezer, the glass was inverted. Large drops of clear corn syrup were then placed on the bottom rim and carefully brushed down to simulate water run marks. An artist's brush was used for this operation. The glass was righted and the surface sprayed with a mist of glycerine and water from an ordinary spray bottle with an adjustable nozzle. The glass was then placed in position on the shooting table and filled with the required contents. Besides the glass, the straw, or mixing rod, and liquid are real. The ice cubes may or may not be real.

Plastic "ice" cubes are manufactured expressly for this type of photographic use. They are made of acrylic material and come in various sizes, shapes, and colors. Synthetic ice cubes are used for most pictures that require ice cubes. For iced tea the cubes may be slightly tinted towards the color of the liquid. This gives a "truer" appearance to the overall scene. A real ice cube, or a colorless plastic one, would detract from the tea color, and the photo would look a little false. There is also another color factor to ice cubes. Ice from an ordinary home refrigerator freezer has a whitish color pattern, while commercially made cubes are clear. Real ice is more often used in close shooting, while the plastic variety does a better job in open shots, where the accent is not on a single item.

Real ice floats to the top of a drink, but many of the plastic substitutes sink. One way to solve this problem is to fill the glass with enough plastic cubes so that some reach up to the surface of the liquid.

Food Photography

Apparent water drops on fruits and vegetables add to the impression of freshness. Actually, the "water" is clear corn syrup, which does not evaporate as quickly under studio lights. Modeling clay has been used to make this celery stalk stand upright. Photo by William R. Eastabrook.

Another way is to invest in much more expensive plastic cubes, which do float.

To simulate a glass of water and crushed ice, wrinkle up some plastic wrap, place it in a glass, and fill the glass with water.

The lighting in this photograph was achieved by using a Mole-Richardson Dinky-Inkie spotlight with a 125-watt lamp placed directly behind the glass. It was positioned so that an imaginary straight line from the spotlight to the camera lens axis would pass directly through the center of the glass. Reflector cards were used to direct some of the light that came from the fill-in flash, which was a 1000-watt tungsten lamp/umbrella unit placed at a 45-degree angle above and to the right of the camera.

The water drops in the photograph of a bunch of celery are actually drops of clear corn syrup. The celery is supported by modeling clay, which is hidden from the camera view. A special type of modeling clay made specifically for photographic prop work is manufactured by ESP Products, a firm based in Hollywood, CA. Although this clay basically resembles that used by florists, it contains an adhesive that is helpful in prop work.

The Pour. One of the most difficult things to recreate in a photograph is a pour. A special technique is needed to show liquids like oil or milk being poured from their containers. It is not as simple as removing a bottle cap or making a hole in a can, and then pouring. In fact, none of these things are done. In order to photographically capture a pour, the photographer must simulate one. This requires a degree of control not possible with an actual pour, in which the liquid often runs back along the surface of the container. Props of some kind must be used.

An actual can of the product is used for the mock-up. A hole is made at the pouring "spout" position, the contents are removed, and the can is thoroughly cleaned internally and externally. Another hole is made—this time in the side of the can that will be away from the camera view. A hollow rod is inserted into the second hole, and the assembly is soldered. Care must be taken so that the axis

Pouring prop. The can that appears here is modified with a metal tube soldered in place. Flexible hose connects the tube to the liquid reservoir for controlled flow. Assembly is supported by clamping the rigid tube to a convenient stand. When the source of power is not included in the picture, only a tube is required, without the can.

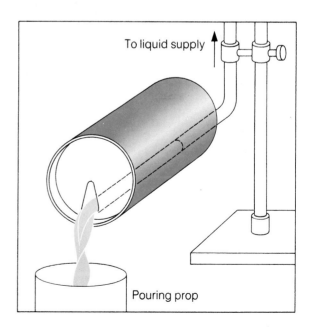

To liquid supply

Pouring prop

of the rod is at right angles to the axis of the can and the pour hole. The rod is positioned in a holder that is fastened to a sturdy stand. The can is turned to the desired pouring angle, and a flexible tube is attached to the metal tube. The other end of the flexible tube (or hose) is connected to a reservoir containing the liquid product that is to be poured and photographed. Naturally, a catch basin must be provided under the pour spout.

With camera and lights ready for the first exposure, the liquid is allowed to run out of the reservoir, through the tubes, into the can, and out of the pour hole. The resulting photos will indeed look as though the container has been punctured and held in a pouring position. With controlled pouring there is no back splashing of liquid. Everything flows out of the pour hole directly down into the catch basin.

The accompanying photographs of cream and coffee illustrate a bad pour and a good one. The cream used here was purchased and then kept in the special pour container in the refrigerator until ready for use. If cream is too warm and on the verge of turning sour, it will curdle as soon as it touches the surface of a hot liquid such as coffee.

About 12 clean, dry mugs were readied for this shooting. Used cups cannot be used without being thoroughly washed in soap and water, and dried. Plastic locating blocks, which were removed and replaced during cup changes, aided in the placement of cups on the shooting table. This kept camera and

To create a pour, control is necessary to avoid back splashing of liquid. Photograph at left demonstrates an unsuccessful pour; photograph at right has desired results. Photos by William R. Eastabrook.

Food Photography

Luster in a beer pour is created by use of a small silver reflector placed behind the glass and tilted up to an overhead light. Photo by William R. Eastabrook.

lighting adjustments to a minimum. Shooting was done very rapidly, and exposures were bracketed.

Photographing Beer. In order to create and capture an appealing beer pour and subsequent head, you must start with about 12 or more glasses or steins that have been thoroughly washed in soap and water, and thoroughly dried. There must not be even a minute amount of moisture in the glass. The beer is brought to a temperature slightly above room temperature (starting at 80 F, the temperature can be raised by heating the beer). At this point, the beer is poured, and several shots are made in rapid succession. The next glass or stein is put into place and the process repeated. After several pours the correct temperature will be achieved. If a particular pour is unsatisfactory, do not dump out the beer and reuse the same glass or stein without washing and drying it. You cannot raise a satisfactory head on beer in a glass or stein that is wet with beer.

There is one prop that is essential for creating luster in a beer pour—a small piece of silver reflector material. This is placed behind the glass and tilted up toward a single light directly overhead.

Electronic flash is used to photograph pours. For the accompanying photo of a stein and beer, a 2000-watt-second electronic flash unit was aimed into an umbrella. A reflecting opaque material placed over the silk umbrella reflected most of the light onto the subject. The secondary cover is approximately three-fourths the diameter of the umbrella and thus permits some light to spill through and illuminate surrounding areas.

(Above) Meats that appear grilled are rarely cooked by that method; they are pan broiled to a uniform color and then placed in a pan of brown butter. (Left) Grill marks are added with the tip of an electric soldering gun. Photos by William R. Eastabrook.

Many photographers who are unfamiliar with illustrative photography attempt to photograph bottles and other containers of liquid by throwing large amounts of light on the front, or camera side, of the container. No matter how much light is directed in this manner, the object looks dark and lacks luster. By simply placing a small silver reflector in back of the subject—as just described—all of the necessary light is picked up from the main light. (*See:* GLASS, PHOTOGRAPHING.)

Grill Marks on Meat. The grill marks you see on the steaks in the accompanying photos did not come from a grill. In fact, photographing actual grill marks produces very unsightly lines. To avoid this, some photographers draw a hot poker across the surface of steaks, chops, and hamburgers to simulate grill marks; others prefer the alternative method.

Most of the steaks or hamburgers used in food photography never see a grill. They are pan-broiled for uniform surface color, and then placed in a fry pan with some cooking oil. Once the desired color is reached, the meat is removed and placed in another fry pan, which contains butter that has been heated until it has turned brown. The hot, brown butter imparts a dark brown color to the meat that resembles a "done" surface.

At this point, grill marks are created with the wide tip of an electric soldering gun. The hot tip is carefully drawn across the surfaces of the steaks or hamburgers. Small amounts of cooking oil brushed across the burnt surfaces darken the apparent grill marks. Hot dogs are given a grilled appearance by using the knife edge of the soldering tip.

Froth. Often, props are needed to show a product in a manner that will be familiar to the viewer. For example, a beverage such as hot chocolate that contains a frothy substance may not photograph satisfactorily because of the froth itself. You can beat hot chocolate in a blender, but it will not look normal in a photograph because the froth will not remain long enough to be photographed.

Hot chocolate has a peculiar surface. It is higher in the center of the cup, then dips slightly, and finally rises where it meets the sides of the cup. This curvature must be maintained. The solution is to pour specially prepared "froth" into a cup that is almost filled with hot chocolate. Such froth is made by mixing a small amount of liquid soap and hot chocolate in a blender, or by beating these substances together with a spoon. The results are evident in the accompanying photo. Again, use a clean, dry cup for each setup.

"Leftovers." One may wonder what happens to all the luscious food used in photography sessions. In arranging food, various positioning aides—mod-

(Above right) Froth on hot chocolate can be created by mixing liquid soap and chocolate in a blender. (Below) Unfortunately, it is unsafe to eat the leftovers from a shooting session. Once the photographer and his assistants had completed setting up and photographing this elaborate arrangement, the food was discarded. Photos by William R. Eastabrook.

Food Photography

Food Photography

◀ *Setting up a shot such as this required hours of planning and preparation. The different temperatures and states of doneness called for almost split-second timing. Photo by Phil Sidney.*

eling clay, pins, nails, wood dowels, pieces of metal, etc.—must be used. Consequently, the food becomes contaminated and must be discarded. While some meats and cheeses can remain out of refrigeration for periods of time without visibly spoiling, harmful bacteria may begin to form after the product reaches room temperature. The accompanying photograph took several hours to set up. After the shooting, all of the pictured food had to be discarded.

• *See also:* ADVERTISING PHOTOGRAPHY; COMMERCIAL PHOTOGRAPHY; GLASS, PHOTOGRAPHING; PRODUCT PHOTOGRAPHY.

Further Reading: Bennett, E. *Tabletop and Still Life Photography,* 2nd ed. Garden City, NY: Amphoto, 1970; Croy, O.R. *Graphic Effects by Photography.* (Visual Communications Books) New York, NY: Hastings House Publishers, Inc., 1973; Eastman Kodak Co. *Indoor Picture-Taking,* pub. No. AC-31. Rochester, NY: Eastman Kodak Co., 1974; Life Library of Photography. *Studio.* New York, NY: Time-Life Books, Division of Time, Inc., 1971; Simon, Bernard, ed. *Simon's Directory of Theatrical Materials, Services and Information,* 5th ed. New York, NY: Package Publications, 1975.

  Formats

The term "format" refers, basically, to the size and shape of the image area of a given camera, which is generally smaller than the size of the film or plate the camera takes. The nominal size of the camera is usually that of the film itself. A 2¼″ × 3¼″ roll-film camera produces an image 2¼″ × 3¼″ on film that is about 2½″ wide, but a 2¼″ × 3¼″ sheet-film camera takes film less than 2¼″ × 3¼″ overall, while the image size is more nearly 2″ × 3″.

Still-Camera Formats

When photography first began, each photographer built his or her own camera and adopted an arbitrary size for his negative material. However, as photography became commercialized, some standardization became necessary.

Format Standardization. The first example of this was the silver-coated copper plate that was designed for daguerreotype operators. It appears that the standard size for such copper plates was 6½″ × 8½″. Some photographers bought them at this size and cut them down to a smaller size. Eventually, suppliers began making copper plates in not only the "whole plate" size of 6½″ × 8½″, but also as "half plates" (4¼″ × 6½″) and "quarter plates" (3¼″ × 4¼″).

In England, this terminology continues to this day, with one curious variation. The English "whole plate" is still 6½″ × 8½″, and the "quarter plate" is still 3¼″ × 4¼″; but the "half plate," for reasons unknown, is 4¾″ × 6½″ instead of 4¼″ × 6½″. This latter size is sometimes referred to as "double quarter plate" but is not commercially made.

In the United States, glass plates were made to the same formats and to a new set of formats that included a smaller size, 2¼″ × 3¼″, intermediate sizes, 4″ × 5″ and 5″ × 7″, and bigger sizes, 8″ × 10″ and 11″ × 14″.

European sizes, naturally, were made to metric measure and were fairly systematic. Again, though, there were unexplained irregularities: The most popular size was 9 × 12 cm, but the half size of this, 6 × 9 cm, was made only in roll films; the plate size was, for some unknown reason, 6.5 × 9 cm. Larger sizes, obviously, could be made by doubling the previous ones, and there was, indeed, a 12 × 18 cm size (roughly equal to our 5″ × 7″ plate). Again, there was an intermediate size between these, 10 × 15 cm, which was popular for making postcards; it was about 4″ × 6″, and allowing for the edge area covered by the plateholder, it printed without borders on a standard 3½″ × 5½″ postcard.

The greatest proliferation of sizes came with the introduction of the daylight loading roll film; this film ranged from the tiny No. 100 roll to a huge-size roll for 5″ × 7″ cameras of normal format. Even larger rolls were made for the 8 × 10 cameras with Cirkut attachments.

The development of formats occurred in two ways: Some designers built a camera and then demanded that a roll film be made available to fit it. Others, not having access to film-manufacturing facilities, produced cameras with non-standard formats on standard roll films. The latter accounts for the variety of image sizes made by different cameras, all of which use the standard No. 120 roll film.

Shown here actual size are five popular film formats. Top row: (Left) 4″×5″ sheet film. (Right) 2¼″×2¾″ roll film. Bottom row: (Left) 35 mm full-frame roll film. (Center) 35 mm half-frame roll film. (Right) 2¼″×2¼″ roll film.

Formats

Many of the roll-film formats remained in vogue for short periods, and then disappeared from the market; there is still some simplification occurring.

Format Aspect Ratio. Because negatives taken in still cameras are often enlarged onto standard sizes of photographic paper, the format ratio of length to width has an importance. For example, the ratio of 5:4, or 1.25:1, is sometimes called "ideal" because 8″ × 10″ paper has that ratio. Higher as-pect ratio negatives must be cropped at the ends to be printed on paper of this format, while lower ratio negatives must be cropped at the sides. The following comparisons of format aspect ratios have been prepared so that the ratios of different camera formats can be compared.

Roll-Film Image Formats. The accompanying illustration and corresponding chart show nominal negative image sizes on standard roll films.

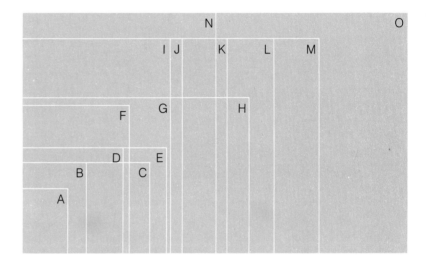

Illustrated at right are nominal negative image sizes on standard roll films. The table below gives corresponding data.

STANDARD NEGATIVE IMAGE SIZES

Image Size*	Film Size Designation	No. of Exposures per Standard-Length Roll	Format Aspect Ratio
13 × 17 mm (A)	110	12, 20	1.33:1
18 × 24 mm (B)	135 (35 mm half-frame)	40, 48, 72	1.36:1
24 × 36 mm (C)	135 (35 mm full-frame)	20, 24, 36	1.48:1
28 × 28 mm (D)	126	12, 20	1.10:1
28 × 40 mm (E)	828 (Bantam)	8	1.40:1
1³/₁₆″ × 1⁹/₁₆″ (F)	127	16	1.33:1
1⅝″ × 1⅝″ (G)	127	12	1.00:1
1⅝″ × 2½″ (H)	127	8	1.54:1
1⅝″ × 2¼″ (I)	120, 620	16	1.38:1
2¼″ × 1¾″ (J)	120, 220, 70 mm†	15 (120), 20 (220)	1.29:1
2¼″ × 2¼″ (K)	120, 620, 220, 70 mm†	12, 24, (220)	1.00:1
2¼″ × 2¾″ (L)	120, 220, 70 mm†	10 (120), 20 (220)	1.22:1
2¼″ × 3¼″ (M)	120, 620, 220, 70 mm†	8, 16 (220)	1.44:1
2⅛″ × 2½″ (N)	616	16	1.17:1
2½″ × 4¼″ (O)	116, 616	8	1.65:1
4″ × 5″ (—)	Sheet film	1	1.27:1
5″ × 7″ (—)	Sheet film	1	1.41:1
8″ × 10″ (—)	Sheet film	1	1.26:1

*Letters in parentheses indicate image sizes as shown in corresponding diagram.
†The number of exposures on 70 mm film is determined by the length of film that a given roll-film holder accepts.

Sheet-Film Formats. Sheet films are designated by the nominal outside measurements of the sheet itself. Standard sizes are:

9 × 12 cm	8″ × 10″
2¼″ × 3¼″	10″ × 12″
3¼″ × 4¼″	11″ × 14″
4″ × 5″	16″ × 20″
5″ × 7″	20″ × 24″

The image size obtained on a sheet film is determined by the amount that the retaining lips overlap the film edges in a given holder. To obtain approximate maximum image sizes:

	Subtract:	
	(For short	*(For long*
	film	*film*
For these	*dimension)*	*dimension)*
sheet sizes:		
Up to 4″ × 5″	¼″	5⁄16″
5″ × 7″ and larger	⅜″	7⁄16″

Motion-Picture Formats

Early motion-picture experimenters used a variety of film sizes, some of them as wide as 2½″. A strange coincidence marked the development of the first commercial motion-picture films. In the United States, Thomas Edison designed a film format by working up from the size of the image area and then devised a camera and projector using this film. In order to achieve a pleasing height-to-weight ratio, he established a 1″ image width and a ¾″ image height. A film with sixteen frames per foot of film was thus produced. Edison added 3⁄16″ on each edge of the film for the perforations and spaced the perforations 3⁄16″ apart so that each edge of each frame would contain four perforations. The film thus had an overall width of 1⅜″, with sixty-four perforations for each foot on each edge.

In France, Louis Lumière developed a film with an 18 × 24 mm image area and an overall width of 35 mm; he likewise designed four perforations per frame on each edge. These metric dimensions corresponded quite closely to Edison's figures, and with the inaccuracy of the machines of the time, either film would run on either manufacturer's machinery. The result was that this film became a world-wide standard and remains so to this day. There have been minor changes, mainly in the dimensions and shapes of the perforations, but today's 35 mm film will operate on an original Edison machine and on an original Lumière machine.

Of course, other formats were also devised. Charles Pathé, for instance, conceived of a home-movie system as early as 1912; he realized that a nonflammable film would be essential to the success of any such system and succeeded in producing safety base at that time. To avoid the obvious danger that would occur if people tried to use the highly inflammable nitrate film in home projectors, he made his home-movie system (the "KOK" camera and projector, known in the United States as the Pathescope) for a film 28 mm wide, with one perforation per frame at the left side of each image, and three perforations per frame on the right side; this made it impossible to put the film in the machine backwards and also provided automatic framing of the image.

A number of inventors in the United States worked on home-movie systems using films 11 mm wide and 17.5 mm wide, as well as others. None of these achieved any great success, though the Movette with its 17.5 mm film did sell fairly well for a while.

In 1923, Kodak introduced 16 mm safety-base film that had forty frames per foot and one perforation per frame on each edge. At the same time, Pathé, in France, introduced the 9.5 mm film that had a picture area almost as large; this was accomplished by having a single perforation per frame, in the middle of the film, in the frame line between pictures. The latter format attained considerable popularity in England and on the European continent, but never became established in the United States.

By the 1930s, sound had been added to the 16 mm film. It appeared that this format had professional advantages. A still smaller safety-film format 8 mm in width was introduced for home use.

More recently, development has proceeded in two directions: an 8 mm film for home use, known as super 8, and films of much larger formats for theatrical spectaculars. The larger-format innovations include 65 mm, 70 mm, and some multi-film,

MOTION-PICTURE CAMERA AND PROJECTOR PICTURE DIMENSIONS

Film	Description	Height (in.)	Width (in.)	Semi-diagonal (in.)	Height (mm)	Width (mm)	Semi-diagonal (mm)
8 mm	Camera	0.145	0.192	0.120	3.68	4.88	3.06
8 mm	Projector	0.130	0.172	0.108	3.30	4.37	2.74
8 mm	(Super 8) camera	0.163	0.228	0.140	4.14	5.79	3.56
8 mm	(Super 8) projector	0.158	0.209	0.131	4.01	5.31	3.33
16 mm	Camera	0.295	0.404	0.250	7.49	10.26	6.35
16 mm	Projector	0.286	0.380	0.238	7.26	9.65	6.04
16 mm	Video recording camera*	0.285	0.380	0.237	7.24	9.65	6.03
16 mm	Video reproducing‡	0.276	0.368	0.230	7.01	9.35	5.84
35 mm	(Sound) camera	0.631	0.868	0.537	16.03	22.05	13.63
35 mm	(Sound) projector	0.602†	0.825	0.511	15.29	20.95	12.97
35 mm	Video recording camera*	0.612	0.816	0.510	15.54	20.73	12.96
35 mm	Video reproduction‡	0.594	0.792	0.495	15.09	20.12	12.57
35 mm	Instrumentation camera§	0.735	0.980	0.6125	18.67	24.89	15.56
35 mm	*Cinemascope* or *Panavision* camera‖	0.735	0.870	0.569	18.67	22.10	14.46
35 mm	*Cinemascope* or *Panavision* projector‖	0.700	0.838	0.546	17.78	21.29	13.91
35 mm	Original *Cinerama* camera¶	1.116	0.997	0.748	28.35	25.32	19.00
35 mm	Original *Cinerama* projector¶	1.088	0.985	0.734	27.64	25.02	18.64
65 mm	*Todd-AO* or *Ultra-Panavision* camera**	0.906	2.072	1.131	23.01	52.63	28.72
70 mm	*Todd-AO* or *Ultra-Panavision* projector††	0.870	1.912	1.050	22.10	48.56	26.68

*For subsequent television reproduction only.
†Height of 35 mm projected image may vary from 0.602 to 0.446 in.
‡Portion of motion-picture film image reproduced on television.
§ANSI Standard PH 22.59—1966.
‖Projected aspect ratio 2.35:1, anamorphic squeeze ratio 2:1.
¶Originally three cameras and three projectors. *Cinerama* now uses *Ultra-Panavision* camera lenses. Projector now uses "rectified" prints on 70 mm film and lenses designed for a curved screen.
**Ultra-Panavision* camera lenses employ an anamorphic squeeze ratio 1.25:1, giving a taking aspect ratio of 2.86:1.
††*Ultra-Panavision* prints are released on 35 and 70 mm film for a variety of projected aspect ratios, up to 2.7:1.

multi-projector systems. The present state of motion-picture systems for home use is listed in the accompanying table.

• *See also:* CAMERAS; FILMS AND PLATES; NOTCH CODES.

Formulas for Black-and-White Processing

Developers, stop baths, and fixers for black-and-white films are available in proprietary form, both solid and liquid. Under ordinary circumstances, it is not worthwhile to mix processing solutions from bulk chemicals. Because the amateur uses relatively small amounts of chemicals, any savings he or she might gain by mixing solutions from such chemicals would be small. It is true that a professional might find some savings in buying large quantities of bulk chemicals, but because his or her time represents earnings, the savings in chemicals would be largely offset by the labor cost of mixing them. Another advantage of proprietary products is that they often contain small amounts of special additives that increase their capacity or life span over that of similar solutions mixed from chemicals.

The only advantage to mixing solutions from scratch is that such mixing is likely to be educational. For the beginner, it is good to know what goes into a developer or other processing solutions. But for the professional, the only time it pays to mix from bulk chemicals is when a special solution is needed, probably for one-time use only, in which case it would not pay to stock a large amount of a ready-mixed formula that would rarely be used.

Mixing Chemicals

Every chemical in a processing solution has a function; some are there to do the actual job, others for protection. Thus, a developer usually contains, along with water, one or two developing agents that do the work of development, an alkali that serves as accelerator or activator of the developing agents, a bromide or other restrainer that serves as an antifoggant, and a preservative that protects the developing agents from oxidation by the air.

For a number of reasons, there is always a definite order in which a developer (or other formula) must be mixed. For instance, if the developing agents and accelerator are mixed first, severe oxidation will take place and the developer will be ruined. The basic order to follow, then, is: (1) preservative, (2) developing agents, (3) accelerator, and (4) restrainer.

This order cannot always be followed. For example, the preservative generally used is sodium sulfite, but Kodak Elon developing agent does not dissolve in solutions of sodium sulfite. It is usually safe to dissolve the Elon agent in plain water if the sodium sulfite is added immediately after the Elon agent is dissolved; little oxidation will take place. Therefore, the usual order of mixing a developer is: (1) Kodak Elon developing agent, (2) sodium sulfite, (3) hydroquinone, (4) sodium carbonate, and (5) potassium bromide.

You will note that the ingredients of the developer formulas given in this article are named in this order. Some very meticulous workers like to add just a pinch of the sodium sulfite to the water before dissolving the Elon agent, but it is doubtful whether this is really necessary. A different order is sometimes used for developers containing phenidone in place of Elon agent.

For different reasons, a particular order is also necessary when mixing fixing baths. The fixing baths discussed here each contain a fixing agent (sodium thiosulfate), an acid (sometimes two acids), a preservative, and a hardening agent (generally potassium alum). This combination of chemicals complicates matters. If the hypo and alum are mixed, they will react with each other and form a milky precipitate of aluminum sulfite. However, if the hypo and acid are mixed, they will decompose to form a milky mass of colloidal sulfur. Thus, there is only one order for mixing a fixing bath: (1) sodium thiosulfate, (2) sodium sulfite, (3) acetic acid (and boric acid if called for), and (4) potassium alum.

The sodium sulfite protects the hypo from the acid, and the acid, in turn, protects the alum from the sulfite. You will find that the following fixing-bath formulas are arranged in this order. When using published formulas, always mix a bath in the order in which the ingredients are named in the formula. But read the instructions first; now and then there is a special technique required for mixing.

Dissolving Chemicals

Most chemicals are more soluble in hot water than in cold, but some are decomposed by excessively hot water. The usual compromise is to mix chemicals in moderately warm water. For developer solutions, use water that is about 50 C (120 F). Fixing baths require some care; even moderately warm water may be too hot. On the other hand, hypo cools the water while it is dissolving; thus, if you start to mix a fixing bath in water at 50 C (120 F), by the time the hypo is fully dissolved, the water will have cooled a good deal. Even so, it is best to wait until the solution is down to about 27 C or 28 C (80 to 82 F) before adding the remaining chemicals. If this is done, any slight milkiness in the final solution will probably clear up when the solution has stood overnight.

Chemicals should always be weighed out on clean pieces of paper placed on the scale pans; this avoids contamination. It is best to weigh out all the chemicals for a given formula, each on a separate piece of paper that is marked with its name and weight, before dissolving any. Using a mixing vessel partly filled with warm water, start sifting the first chemical into the water from its paper while stirring the solution. Be sure each chemical is fully dissolved before adding the next.

It will be noted that the following formulas require that about ¾ of the final volume of warm water be placed in the mixing vessel; the remainder of the water is added after all chemicals have been dissolved. The reason for this is that the chemicals take up room in the solution even though they seem to disappear when dissolved. If you were to start with the final volume of water, you would have more than the right amount of solution after the chemicals were dissolved. The solution would necessarily be somewhat weaker than it should be.

Careful mixing of chemicals is essential for the processing of high-quality black-and-white photographs. Photo by Jan Lukas for Editorial Photocolor Archives.

Formulas for Black-and-White Processing

Meticulous care in measurement of chemicals, preferably using metric quantities, will result in negatives and prints of exactly the desired contrast and general quality. Photo by Raimondo Borea for Editorial Photocolor Archives.

Formulas for Black-and-White Processing

For this reason, the final listing is always given as "Add cold water to make . . . ," meaning simply that, after all chemicals are dissolved, you should add cold water slowly until you have the exact final amount indicated. The final addition is always cold water; it aids in cooling the final solution to room temperature for use. Be sure, however, that you bring the solution to its proper working temperature before using it. For black-and-white processing, this is usually 20 C (68 F).

A clean bottle or jug should be ready for the solution; label it at once to prevent any possibility of mixing up solutions. Developers should be in dark bottles because light can hasten oxidation. Labels are best made of waterproof adhesive tape and marked with a "permanent" Magic Marker or other felt-tip pen. Dymo type labels are also excellent.

Weights and Measures

To avoid confusion, and also to promote accuracy in mixing, it is recommended that you do all your chemical mixing in metric measures. The following formulas are given in metric measure only. If you have only an avoirdupois balance, it is best to buy a set of metric weights for it; this will save a great deal of time that would otherwise be wasted in translating from one system to another. In addition, it will avoid the arithmetic errors that often occur in such conversions.

Negative Developers

Kodak developer D-8

Water, about 32 C (90 F). . .	750.0 ml
Sodium sulfite (anhydrous). .	90.0 g
Hydroquinone	45.0 g
Sodium hydroxide (granular)	37.5 g
Potassium bromide (anhydrous)	30.0 g
Water to make	1.0 litre

Kodak developer D-8 is a fast-acting film-and-plate developer for continuous-tone or line work requiring *very high* contrast and density (D-11 is recommended for general high-contrast work).

Development recommendations: For use, mix 2 parts of stock solution with 1 part of water. Develop about 2 minutes in a tray at 20 C (68 F). This developer has a short tray life, and must be used immediately after mixing.

Kodak developer D-11

Water, about 50 C (125 F) . .	500.0 ml
Kodak Elon developing agent	1.0 g
Sodium sulfite (anhydrous) . .	75.0 g
Hydroquinone	9.0 g
Sodium carbonate (monohydrated)	30.0 g
Potassium bromide (anhydrous)	5.0 g
Cold water to make	1.0 litre

Kodak developer D-11 is a vigorous film-and-plate developer with good keeping properties, for general use where high contrast is desired. When very high contrast is desirable, use Kodak developer D-8. D-11 is recommended for use with high-contrast films for reproducing written or printed matter, line drawings, and similar material.

Development recommendations: For line subjects, use without dilution. For development of copies of continuous-tone subjects, dilute with an equal volume of water. Develop about 5 minutes in a tank or 4 minutes in a tray at 20 C (68 F).

Kodak developer DK-15
(tropical developer)

This developer is intended for film and plate developing under tropical conditions.

Water, about 50 C (125 F) . .	750.0 ml
Kodak Elon developing agent	5.7 g
Sodium sulfite (anhydrous) . .	90.0 g
Kodalk balanced alkali	22.5 g
Potassium bromide (anhydrous)	1.9 g
Sodium sulfate (anhydrous)*	45.0 g
Cold water to make	1.0 litre

The average time for tank development is about 10 minutes at 20 C (68 F) and 2 to 3 minutes at 32 C (90 F). These times apply when the developer is fresh. Vary the time to produce the desired contrast.

When you are working at temperatures below 24 C (75 F), you may omit the sodium sulfate in order to obtain a more rapidly acting developer. The development time *without* the sodium sulfate is approximately 6 minutes at 20 C (68 F).

---

*If crystalline sodium sulfate is preferred to the anhydrous form, use 105.0 grams instead of the 45.0 grams listed.

When you are developing film in trays, shorten the developing times given above by about 20 percent.

When development is complete, rinse the film or plate for just 1 or 2 seconds, and then immerse it in Kodak hardening bath SB-4 for 3 minutes. Omit the rinse if you find that the film tends to soften. Fix the film for at least 10 minutes in an acid hardening fixing bath, such as Kodak fixing bath F-5, and wash for 10 to 15 minutes in water not over 35 C (95 F).

Gas blisters will not form when this developer is used; Kodalk balanced alkali does not generate a gas when it is treated with an acid. This is a distinct advantage when processing work must be done at high temperatures.

Kodak developer D-19

Water, about 50 C (125 F) ..	500.0 ml
Kodak Elon developing agent	2.0 g
Sodium sulfite (anhydrous) ..	90.0 g
Hydroquinone	8.0 g
Sodium carbonate (monohydrated)	52.5 g
Potassium bromide (anhydrous)	5.0 g
Cold water to make	1.0 litre

A high-contrast, clean-working developer, Kodak developer D-19 produces brilliant negatives with short development times. It has good keeping properties and high capacity. D-19 is recommended especially for continuous-tone work that requires higher-than-normal contrast.

Development recommendations: Develop about 6 minutes in a tank or 5 minutes in a tray at 20 C (68 F).

Kodak replenisher D-19R

Water, about 50 C (125 F) ..	500.0 ml
Kodak Elon developing agent	4.5 g
Sodium sulfite (anhydrous) ..	90.0 g
Hydroquinone	17.5 g
Sodium carbonate (monohydrated)	52.5 g
Sodium hydroxide (granular)	7.5 g
Water to make	1.0 litre

Use this replenisher undiluted. After each 8″ × 10″ (20 × 25 centimetre) film or its equivalent developed, add to the developer 25 millilitres of replenisher solution (1 fluidounce for each 100 square inches of film). The total volume of replenisher added should not exceed the original volume of the developer.

Kodak developer D-23

This is a slow-working developer that will not produce high contrast even with extended developing times. Use it when a low density range is desired.

Water, about 50 C (125 F) ..	750.0 ml
Kodak Elon developing agent	7.5 g
Sodium sulfite (anhydrous) ..	100.0 g
Cold water to make	1.0 litre

Average development time is about 12 minutes in a tank or 10 minutes in a tray at 20 C (68 F).

The life of the developer can be extended by using Kodak replenisher DK-25R. Add the replenisher at the rate of 23 millilitres per roll developed (¾ fluidounce per roll). Discard the developer after about 26 rolls (13,420 square centimetres or 2,080 square inches) of film per 946 millilitres (1 quart).

Kodak developer D-25

Water, about 50 C (125 F) ..	750.0 ml
Kodak Elon developing agent	7.5 g
Sodium sulfite (anhydrous) ..	100.0 g
Sodium bisulfite (anhydrous)	15.0 g
Cold water to make	1.0 litre

Most Kodak roll films should be developed in a tank for approximately 20 minutes at 20 C (68 F), or for approximately 11 minutes at 25 C (77 F). If the developer is used at 25 C (77 F), the results will be similar to those obtained by using Kodak developer DK-20* at 20 C (68 F). The grain resembles that obtained with the popular paraphenylenediamine type of developer, but Kodak developer D-25 is nontoxic and nonstaining.

---

*NOTE: The formula for Kodak developer DK-20 is not given here because it does not produce satisfactory results on most modern thin-emulsion films; solvent developers of this type often produce dichroic fog, and their use should be avoided.

Formulas for Black-and-White Processing

If it is not essential to obtain minimum graininess, or if it is not convenient to work at the higher temperature, use half the specified quantity of sodium bisulfite. The development time will then be approximately 14 minutes at 20 C (68 F). The graininess will usually be intermediate between that for Kodak developer D-23 and that for Kodak developer D-25.

Replenishment: Add Kodak replenisher DK-25R at the rate of 38 millilitres per 946 millilitres of solution (1¼ fluidounces per quart) for each roll developed, for the first 13 rolls, and at the rate of 23 millilitres per 946 millilitres of solution (¾ fluidounce per quart) for each of the following 13 rolls. Then replace the developer with a fresh solution.

Kodak replenisher DK-25R

Water, about 50 C (125 F). .	750.0 ml
Kodak Elon developing agent	10.0 g
Sodium sulfite (anhydrous) . .	100.0 g
Kodalk balanced alkali	20.0 g
Cold water to make	1.0 litre

Kodak developer DK-50 stock solution

Water, about 50 C (125 F) . .	500.0 ml
Kodak Elon developing agent	2.5 g
Sodium sulfite (anhydrous) . .	30.0 g
Hydroquinone	2.5 g
Kodalk balanced alkali	10.0 g
Potassium bromide (anhydrous)	0.5 g
Water to make	1.0 litre

Clean-working and moderately fast, Kodak developer DK-50 is extremely popular with commercial and portrait photographers. It can be used with or without dilution, in a tank or tray, to produce crisp-looking negatives with all types of subjects. DK-50 developer is highly recommended for portraiture.

Development recommendations: For tank development of portrait negatives, dilute with an equal volume of water; develop about 10 minutes at 20 C (68 F). For tray development, use without dilution; develop about 6 minutes at 20 C (68 F).

For commercial work, use without dilution. Develop about 6 minutes in a tank or 4½ minutes in a tray at 20 C (68 F).

Replenishment: Add 30 millilitres (1 fluidounce) of Kodak replenisher DK-50R per 8″ × 10″ (20 × 25 centimetre) sheet or equivalent (516 square centimetres or 80 square inches) processed. If the developer is diluted 1:1 for use, the replenisher should be diluted in the same proportion.

Kodak replenisher DK-50R

Water, about 50 C (125 F) . .	750.0 ml
Kodak Elon developing agent	5.0 g
Sodium sulfite (anhydrous) . .	30.0 g
Hydroquinone	10.0 g
Kodalk balanced alkali	40.0 g
Water to make	1.0 litre

Kodak developer DK-60a

Water, about 50 C (125 F) . .	750.0 ml
Kodak Elon developing agent	2.5 g
Sodium sulfite (anhydrous) . .	50.0 g
Hydroquinone	2.5 g
Kodalk balanced alkali	20.0 g
Potassium bromide (anhydrous)	0.5 g
Water to make	1.0 litre

Kodak developer DK-60a is a fast-acting developer for general, large-negative use. It has relatively short developing times (4 minutes in a tray, 5 minutes in a tank) and produces negatives with moderate grain characteristics, high brilliancy, and low fog levels. To replenish, add 30 millilitres of Kodak replenisher DK-60aTR per 516 square centimetres (80 square inches) of film.

Kodak replenisher DK-60aTR

Water, about 50 C (125 F) . .	750.0 ml
Kodak Elon developing agent	5.0 g
Sodium sulfite (anhydrous) . .	50.0 g
Hydroquinone	10.0 g
Kodalk balanced alkali	40.0 g
Cold water to make	1.0 litre

Kodak developer D-61a

This developer is recommended for tank or tray use with professional films and plates.

Water, about 50 C (125 F) ..	500.0 ml
Kodak Elon developing agent	3.0 g
Sodium sulfite (anhydrous) . .	90.0 g
Sodium bisulfite (anhydrous)	2.0 g
Hydroquinone	6.0 g
Sodium carbonate (monohydrated)	14.0 g
Potassium bromide (anhydrous)	2.0 g
Cold water to make	1.0 litre

For tray use, dilute 1 part of stock solution with 1 part of water. Develop for about 6 minutes at 20 C (68 F).

For tank use, dilute 1 part of stock solution with 3 parts of water. Develop for about 12 minutes at 20 C (68 F). Add stock solution (diluted 1:3) at intervals to maintain the volume, or use Kodak replenisher D-61R to maintain the strength of the tank solution.

Kodak replenisher D-61R

This formula is designed to replenish the *tank* dilution of Kodak developer D-61a.

Stock solution A

Water, about 50 C (125 F) ..	3.0 litres
Kodak Elon developing agent	6.0 g
Sodium sulfite (anhydrous) . .	180.0 g
Sodium bisulfite (anhydrous)	4.0 g
Hydroquinone	12.0 g
Potassium bromide (anhydrous)	3.0 g
Cold water to make	6.0 litres

Stock solution B

Sodium carbonate (monohydrated)	280.0 g
Water to make	2.0 litres

To use: Take 3 parts of Stock solution A and 1 part of Stock solution B, and add to the tank dilution of developer as needed. Do not mix solutions A and B until you are ready to use them.

Kodak developer D-76

Water, about 50 C (125 F) ..	750.0 ml
Kodak Elon developing agent	2.0 g
Sodium sulfite (anhydrous) . .	100.0 g
Hydroquinone	5.0 g
Borax (decahydrated)	2.0 g
Water to make	1.0 litre

Kodak developer D-76 is unsurpassed by any other Kodak developer in ordinary use for its ability to give full emulsion speed and maximum shadow detail with normal contrast. Films developed in D-76 developer have excellent grain characteristics. For greater sharpness, but with a slight sacrifice in grain characteristics, dilute the developer 1:1. D-76 has excellent development latitude, and produces relatively low fog on forced development. This particular developer has long been a favorite of pictorial photographers.

Development recommendations: For sheet films, the average development time is about 9 minutes in a tray or 11 minutes in a tank at 20 C (68 F).

Replenishment: Add 30 millilitres (1. fluid-ounce) of Kodak replenisher D-76R per 8″ × 10″ (20 × 25 centimetre) sheet or equivalent (516 square centimetres or 80 square inches) processed.

Kodak replenisher D-76R

Water, about 50 C (125 F) ..	750.0 ml
Kodak Elon developing agent	3.0 g
Sodium sulfite (anhydrous) . .	100.0 g
Hydroquinone	7.5 g
Borax (decahydrated)	20.0 g
Water to make	1.0 litre

Kodak developer D-78
(glycin negative developer)

Water	750.0 ml
Sodium sulfite (anhydrous) . .	3.0 g
Glycin (athenon) (*p*-hydroxy-phenylaminoacetic acid) . .	3.0 g
Sodium carbonate (monohydrated)	7.2 g
Water to make	1.0 litre

The average development time, using D-78, is 15 to 25 minutes at 18.5 C (65 F).

Kodak developer D-79
(pyro tank developer)

Water . . . . 750.0 ml
Sodium sulfite (anhydrous). . 25.0 g
Pyrogallol . . . . 2.5 g
Sodium carbonate
(monohydrated) . . . . 6.0 g
Potassium bromide
(anhydrous) . . . . 0.5 g
Water to make . . . . 1.0 litre

The average development time with D-79 is 9 to 12 minutes at 18.5 C (65 F). This solution oxidizes rapidly; use it within one hour after mixing.

Kodak developer D-82
(maximum-energy developer)

This developer is intended for use with badly underexposed films.

Water, about 50 C (125 F). . 750.0 ml
Methyl alcohol . . . . 48.0 ml
Kodak Elon developing
agent . . . . 14.0 g
Sodium sulfite (anhydrous). . 52.5 g
Hydroquinone . . . . 14.0 g
Sodium hydroxide (granular) 8.8 g
Potassium bromide
(anhydrous) . . . . 8.8 g
Cold water to make . . . . 1.0 litre

Use without dilution. Develop for 4 to 5 minutes in a tray at 18.5 C (65 F). The prepared developer does not keep for more than a few days. If methyl alcohol is not added, and the developer is diluted, the solution is not as active as in the concentrated form.

Paper Developers

Kodak developer D-51 (amidol developer
for bromide papers) stock solution

Water, about 50 C (125 F). . 750.0 ml
Sodium sulfite (anhydrous). . 120.0 g
Diaminophenol hydro-
chloride (amidol) . . . . 37.5 g
Cold water to make . . . . . . 1.0 litre

To use: Take 180 millilitres of stock solution, 3 millilitres of 10% potassium bromide solution, and

750 millilitres of water. Develop for 1½ to 3 minutes at 21 C (70 F). The solution must be used immediately after the water is added; it oxidizes rapidly on exposure to air.

Kodak developer D-52 stock solution

Water, about 50 C (125 F). . 500.0 ml
Kodak Elon developing
agent . . . . 1.5 g
Sodium sulfite (anhydrous). . 22.5 g
Hydroquinone . . . . 6.0 g
Sodium carbonate
(monohydrated) . . . . 17.0 g
Potassium bromide
(anhydrous) . . . . 1.5 g
Cold water to make . . . . 1.0 litre

Kodak developer D-52 embodies all the latest improvements and offers ease of preparation. A long-life developer specially designed for the development of warm-tone papers, it produces a pleasing image tone and contrast, remains clear during use, and has high development capacity and good keeping properties. Since development activity decreases only very slowly with use, constant image tone is easy to maintain. Kodak Selectol developer is a packaged preparation with properties similar to those of D-52.

Development recommendations: Dilute 1 part of stock solution with 1 part of water. For average results, develop 2 minutes at 20 C (68 F). For slightly warmer image tone, develop 90 seconds. Contrast can be increased slightly with some papers by developing up to 4 minutes. Increased development times will produce colder image tones.

Kodak developer D-72

Water, about 50 C (125 F). . 500.0 ml
Kodak Elon developing
agent . . . . 3.0 g
Sodium sulfite (anhydrous). . 45.0 g
Hydroquinone . . . . 12.0 g
Sodium carbonate
(monohydrated) . . . . 80.0 g
Potassium bromide
(anhydrous) . . . . 2.0 g
Water to make . . . . 1.0 litre

Kodak developer D-72 embodies all the latest improvements, and offers ease of preparation. Solutions mixed from D-72 remain unusually free from muddiness, sludge, precipitation, and discoloration throughout the normal solution life. Kodak Dektol developer is a packaged preparation that has properties similar to those of D-72.

Development recommendations: Dilute 1 part of stock solution with 2 parts of water. Average development times for recommended papers range from 1 to 1½ minutes at 20 C (68 F).

Stop Baths, Fixing Baths, and Hardeners

Kodak stop bath SB-1

Water . . . . 1.0 litre
Acetic acid, 28%* . . . . 48.0 ml

Rinse prints for 5 to 10 seconds with agitation.

Kodak stop bath SB-1a

Water . . . . 1.0 litre
Acetic acid, 28%* . . . . 125.0 ml

This bath is recommended for use after highly alkaline developers, such as those used with line materials.

Kodak hardening bath SB-4

This solution is recommended for use in conjunction with developers containing sodium sulfate. It is used at temperatures above 24 C (75 F).

Water . . . . 1.0 litre
Potassium chrome alum,
   crystals (dodecahydrated).. 30.0 g
Sodium sulfate (anhydrous)† 60.0 g

Agitate the negatives for 30 to 45 seconds when they are first immersed in the hardener, or streakiness will result. Leave them in the bath for at least 3 minutes between development and fixing. If the temperature is below 29.5 C (85 F), rinse the negatives for 1 to 2 seconds in water before immersing them in the hardener bath.

The hardening bath is a violet-blue color by tungsten light when freshly mixed, but it ultimately turns a yellow-green with use; it then ceases to harden and should be replaced with a fresh bath. The hardening bath should never be overworked. An unused bath will keep indefinitely, but the hardening power of a partially used bath decreases rapidly on standing for a few days.

Kodak stop bath SB-5

Water . . . . 500.0 ml
Acetic acid, 28%* . . . . 32.0 ml
Sodium sulfate (anhydrous).. 45.0 g
Cold water to make . . . . 1.0 litre

This is a non-hardening stop bath for use at temperatures up to 26.5 C (80 F).

Treat the films or plates in this bath for about 30 seconds with agitation at 18 to 21 C (65 to 70 F) between developing and fixing.

This bath should be replaced after approximately 13 rolls have been processed per litre (quart).

Kodak stop bath SB-5a

For photofinishing, use double the quantities of 28% acetic acid indicated for Kodak stop bath SB-5.

Kodak fixing bath F-5

Kodak fixing bath F-5 is recommended for general use. This bath has the advantage over the older type of fixing baths, (which did not contain boric acid) of giving much better hardening and having less tendency to precipitate a sludge of aluminum sulfite.

Water, about 50 C (125 F) .. 600.0 ml
Sodium thiosulfate
   (pentahydrated) . . . . 240.0 g
Sodium sulfite (anhydrous) .. 15.0 g
Acetic acid, 28%* . . . . 48.0 ml
Boric acid, crystals‡ . . . . 7.5 g
Potassium alum, fine granular
   (dodecahydrated) . . . . 15.0 g
Cold water to make . . . . 1.0 litre

---

*To make approximately 28% acetic acid from glacial acetic acid, add 3 parts of glacial acetic acid to 8 parts of water.
†If crystalline sodium sulfate is preferred to the anhydrous form, use 2¼ times the quantity listed.

---

‡Crystalline boric acid should be used as specified. Powdered boric acid dissolves only with great difficulty, and its use should be avoided.

Films or plates should be fixed properly in 5 to 10 minutes in a freshly prepared bath. The bath need not be discarded until the fixing time becomes excessive; that is, over 10 minutes. Fix prints 5 to 10 minutes.

The hardener can also be mixed separately as a stock solution as follows:

Kodak hardener F-5a

Water, about 50 C (125 F)	600.0 ml
Sodium sulfite (anhydrous)	75.0 g
Acetic acid, 28%*	235.0 ml
Boric acid, crystals†	37.5 g
Potassium alum, fine granular (dodecahydrated)	75.0 g
Cold water to make	1.0 litre

Slowly add 1 part of the cool stock hardener solution to 4 parts of cool 30% hypo solution (300 grams of sodium thiosulfate per litre of water), while stirring the hypo rapidly.

Kodak fixing bath F-6

In warm weather and in inadequately ventilated darkrooms, the odor of sulfur dioxide given off by the Kodak fixing bath F-5 may be objectionable. This can be eliminated almost entirely by omitting the boric acid and substituting twice its weight in Kodalk balanced alkali. This modification, which is known as Kodak fixing bath F-6, can also be used to advantage for fixing prints, since it washes out of photographic papers more rapidly than the baths that have a greater hardening action. It should be used in conjunction with a stop bath such as Kodak indicator stop bath or Kodak stop bath SB-1 to obtain the full useful life.

Kodak rapid fixing bath F-7

This bath fixes much more rapidly than Kodak fixing bath F-5 or F-6, and its useful fixing capacity is considerably greater.

---

*To make approximately 28% acetic acid from glacial acetic acid, add 3 parts of glacial acetic acid to 8 parts of water.
†Use crystalline boric acid as specified. Powdered boric acid dissolves only with great difficulty, and its use should be avoided.
CAUTION: With rapid fixing baths, do not prolong the fixing time for fine-grain film or plate emulsions or for *any* paper prints; with prolonged fixing, the image may have a tendency to bleach, especially at temperatures higher than 20 C (68 F). This caution applies particularly to warm-tone papers.

Water, about 50 C (125 F)	600.0 ml
Sodium thiosulfate (pentahydrated)	360.0 g
Ammonium chloride	50.0 g
Sodium sulfite (anhydrous)	15.0 g
Acetic acid, 28%*	48.0 ml
Boric acid, crystals†	7.5 g
Potassium alum, fine granular (dodecahydrated)	15.0 g
Cold water to make	1.0 litre

Kodak rapid fixing bath F-9

If corrosion is encountered when Kodak rapid fixing bath F-7 is used in stainless steel containers, it can be minimized by substituting 60 grams of ammonium sulfate for the 50 grams of ammonium chloride in each litre (quart) of solution. When this change is made, the resultant formula is known as Kodak rapid fixing bath F-9.

Kodak fixing bath F-24

This bath can be used for films, plates, or papers when no hardening is desired. For satisfactory use, the temperature of the developer, rinse bath, and wash water should not be higher than 20 C (68 F).

Water, about 50 C (125 F)	500.0 ml
Sodium thiosulfate (pentahydrated)	240.0 g
Sodium sulfite (anhydrous)	10.0 g
Sodium bisulfite (anhydrous)	25.0 g
Cold water to make	1.0 litre

• *See also:* COMPENSATING DEVELOPER; DEVELOPERS AND DEVELOPING; DIRECT POSITIVE PROCESSING; INTENSIFICATION; REDUCTION; REVERSAL PROCESSING OF FILMS; TONING.

Further Reading: Carroll, John S. *Photographic Lab Handbook,* 4th ed. Garden City, NY: Amphoto, 1977; Eaton, George T. *Photographic Chemistry.* Dobbs Ferry, NY: Morgan & Morgan, Inc., 1965; Jacobson, C.I. *Developing: The Technique of the Negative.* 18th rev. ed. Garden City, NY: Amphoto, 1972; Lyalikov, K. *The Chemistry of Photographic Mechanisms.* (Focal Library Books) Belmont, CA: Pitman Publishing Corp., 1967; Mason, L.F. *Photographic Processing Chemistry.* New York, NY: Halstead Press, Division of John Wiley & Sons, Inc., 1975; Russell, G. *Chemical Analysis in Photography.* (Focal Library Books) Belmont, CA: Pitman Publishing Corp., 1965; Sheppard, S.E. and C.E. Mees. *Theory of the Photographic Process.* (Focal Library Books) Belmont, CA: Pitman Publishing Corp., 1969 (reprint of 1907 ed.).

Freelance Photography

A freelance photographer offers photographic services for hire on a job-by-job basis. He or she operates as an independent, one-person business, usually unencumbered by a studio, assistants, or even darkroom facilities. The business is simply taking pictures to order or on speculation.

Although the concept of freelance work was first established in journalistic photography, there are freelance photographers of all kinds. The greatest amount of freelance activity is in the areas of publicity and public relations, sports, advertising illustration, weddings and similar events, and feature coverage for specialized or limited-circulation publications. There are also successful freelance photographers who work in the areas of architecture, industrial photography, and fashion illustration, as well as in many other specialized fields, but their numbers are relatively few.

Advantages of Hiring on a Freelance Basis

This type of arrangement offers many features that are valuable to clients:

Photographic Expertise and Experience. Most freelance photographers are specialists who can handle assignments beyond the capabilities of the general studio or staff photographer (underwater pictures, and photographs from light planes or helicopters are just two examples of specialized work). However, wide professional experience with more common kinds of photography is equally important.

Geographic Location or Experience. Most freelance work is done on location, at the scene of the event or subject action. Often a freelance photographer is hired because he or she is located where the picture must be taken. This consideration may save the client a good deal in travel expense. Or, he or she may be familiar with working in an unusual locale. Experience in jungle or desert photography, with the language and customs of a foreign people, or with the layout and transportation facilities of a distant city can save many days on an assignment.

Many sports assignments are done on a freelance basis, especially in connection with less publicized athletic events such as dirt-bike racing. This photograph was made for a magazine directed at motorcycle buffs. Photo by Paul J. Bereswill.

(Above) Many freelance photographers, although capable of general work, may be particularly proficient in certain areas such as underwater photography. Specialized equipment is, of course, necessary for such work. (Right) Most freelance work is done on location, and much of a freelance photographer's success depends upon being on-the-spot, or the ability to get to a location quickly. Photos by Herb Taylor.

Freelance Photography

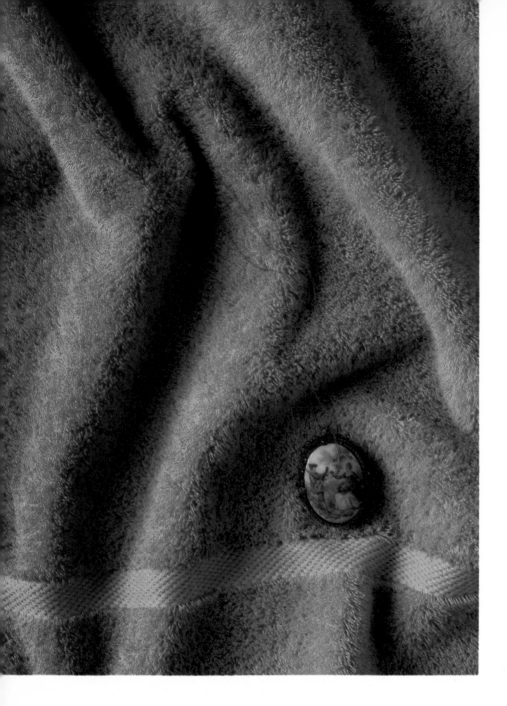

Product photography employs many freelance photographers. While the client supplies the product itself, obtaining props and other equipment or personnel directly related to the job is the responsibility of the photographer. Expenses incurred are charged to the client. Photo by Stephen Stuart.

Availability. Clients generally want immediate service. A freelance photographer is free of the routine and prescheduled work that occupy a staff photographer most of the time. A successful freelance photographer always keeps equipment, passport, and other necessities ready and up-to-date. The ability to respond immediately makes it possible to handle more assignments in any year and helps increase repeat business from clients.

Lower Cost. Freelance photographers should not work more cheaply than others—satisfactory work is worth a certain basic payment no matter who does it—but they can offer overall economy for a client. Because the photographer maintains neither studio nor staff, and often not even a darkroom, little overhead must be included in the day rate or fee charged. When special facilities or pieces of equipment are required, they are rented and charged directly to the job along with lab fees and expenses for models and assistants, costumes, props, and similar items. Although the total billing for the job may be substantial, it is far cheaper than the client's having to carry the cost of a staff photographer and facilities within his or her own organization. These are points the free-lance photographer should always stress in discussions with potential clients.

Getting Assignments

Most freelance photographers obtain their first assignments by showing samples of their work to possible clients. The client may be the picture editor of a publication, the art director or public-relations officer of an agency or corporation, the owner or manager of a business, the parent of a bride-to-be, or one of many other kinds of people. The important point is that the pictures shown a client must be of the type that interest him or her, and they must be of the best possible quality.

It does no good to show sports photographs to a corporate officer who wants a photographer to do work for an annual report. An editor of a nature publication wants to see nature and outdoor pictures, and people with a wedding to be photographed want to see examples of wedding pictures.

In approaching publications, timing is important. Monthly magazines work about three months ahead of publication. Editors begin to look for winter pictures in September, and first-robin-of-spring pictures in December or January. Seasonal pictures are usually the product of a previous year's work.

(Top right) Corporate officers seeking photographs to illustrate brochures or annual reports want to see how a photographer deals with difficult subjects such as industrial products or processes. The photographer should be prepared with samples of work that will be of pertinent interest to prospective clients. Photo by William Rivelli. (Right) When showing photographs of a seasonal theme, the photographer should be aware of publications working schedules. This autumn scene would probably be selected by an editor in early summer, and obviously had to have been taken during the a previous autumn. Photo by Herb Taylor.

Freelance Photography

The purpose of showing photographs is not to sell those particular pictures, but to indicate the range of the photographer's capabilities in a specific area and perhaps in some closely related areas. Only the best finished work should be shown. Near misses, unsharp or poorly exposed images, and unspotted or old prints do not show potential; they show ineptness and disregard for standards of quality. Well-composed, technically excellent pictures of interesting subjects and picture situations are required. If any work has been published, tear sheets or other reproductions should be included. Clients will be impressed by any evidence that a freelance photographer is an experienced professional; they do not give assignments for purposes of on-the-job training.

A maximum of two dozen prints, neatly presented in a presentation book with plastic-sleeve pages or in an album similar to those designed to hold wedding photographs, should be sufficient. Slides are best presented in plastic sheets that have individual pockets and hold up to twenty slides. In this form the slides can easily be examined over a light box or illuminator, thus avoiding not only the inconvenience of setting up a projector and darkening the location—something that is often difficult in

Well composed, technically excellent photographs of subjects that will be of interest to the individual client will be the most successful selling point. A client interviewing a photographer for a travel assignment, for example, will want to see how the photographer deals with such a story. Small details can be just as expressive of a particular location as larger subjects such as monuments, crowd scenes, or scenic pictures, and should be included in the portfolio. Photo by Herb Taylor.

Freelance Photography

offices—but also potential damage from repeated handling and projection of the images. The photographer's name, address, and telephone number should be clearly marked on every photograph.

Presenting a portfolio of pictures in person is by far the most effective method of obtaining assignments. A telephone call or a brief letter will determine who the photographer is to see; then a direct inquiry, by name, can set up an appointment. If work must be submitted by mail to a distant client, or must be left for examination without an interview, it should be addressed to the target individual by name and position, not vaguely to an anonymous Picture Editor or Public Relations Director. It is essential to include return postage and address labels, or to arrange to pick up the work.

During the conversation at the time of presentation, or in the accompanying letter, the photographer should indicate the following:

1. That he or she is a freelance photographer.
2. The specific area in which he or she has special abilities or experience.
3. The clients for whom he or she has photographed, and the publications in which his or her work has appeared.
4. That the pictures being presented are examples of the kind of work he or she can do for the client.
5. Specific project ideas that he or she feels would be valuable to the client. (A brief outline of these ideas is optional but sometimes recommended because it shows that thought has been given to the client's individual needs. It may even spark some ideas in return. In many situations, however, it is not necessary or even applicable.)
6. That he or she would be pleased to carry out an assignment that the client feels he or she can do.

If the photographer has an established payment rate, he may mention it during the presentation. Most freelance fees, however, are negotiated according to the project budget and the estimated amount of work required. For this reason it may be best to leave financial matters until a definite assignment offer is received, especially at the time of first contact with a potential client.

Equipment

The equipment that the freelance photographer has available to him helps determine the type of picture assignments he can successfully undertake. Some publications will accept 35 mm color transparencies for illustrations, while many require larger sizes. If the photographer has only 35 mm equipment, he will not be able to accept assignments from all potential clients. Medium- and large-format cameras are essential for some types of picture-taking. A variety of lens focal lengths for each camera provides the freelance photographer with the ability to expand the range of his picture-taking.

Portability of equipment is essential to the freelance photographer. Moderate-size equipment cases that are well-padded to protect the equipment from damage are desirable. Small but powerful electronic flash units equipped with slave units for convenient multiple light setups extend the picture-taking range. If the photographer expands into motion pictures, portable floodlights may be necessary. Exposure meters, tripods, filters, etc., are all desirable additions to the equipment inventory of the freelance photographer.

Accepting Assignments

When an assignment is offered, it should usually be accepted; after one or two refusals, for whatever reasons, a client will look elsewhere. But if the job is beyond the photographer's experience or abilities, or if the payment offered is too low, a polite refusal and explanation should be given. If it is possible to recommend another photographer for the job, it may create good will to do so.

Speculative Assignments. A freelance photographer may often work for himself, speculatively photographing a subject or event in the hope of selling some pictures of it. Assignments, however, should not be accepted on speculation—that is, on the basis that the client may or may not make a purchase after seeing the finished pictures. An assignment that does not include a stated minimum fee is not an assignment at all; it is usually an attempt to get something for nothing, or for much less than it is worth. The photographer bears all the risk and expense of a speculative assignment; he or she can

Many photographers take photographs for themselves on the chance that they will be able to sell them later. This picture was taken by a newspaper staff reporter on his day off. Photo by Jim Peppler.

afford to do that only for himself, with subjects of special personal interest or commercial potential.

Many freelance photographers place photographs in agents' files on speculation. A potential client may then see and purchase these photographs for publication. (*See:* AGENCIES, PICTURE.) Other experienced photographers who are also writers may freelance articles and send them to magazines on speculation.

The Assignment Agreement. Discussion of the various aspects of an assignment should be put into written form, either as a purchase order or a letter of agreement. This is the only way to minimize misunderstanding at a later time, and to be certain that the job delivered meets the client's specifications. The written document is a contract that protects both the photographer and the client; it should cover the following points:

1. The kind of work to be done: scouting or inspecting locations; taking prelimi-nary pictures for go-ahead approval; taking final pictures.
2. How much work is to be done: how many pictures, or how many days' work; the scope of the coverage; the minimum number of usable pictures.
3. Where the work is to be done; the starting date; the completion or delivery date.
4. The fee to be paid for the photographer's services.
5. The expenses and other costs to be covered: travel, lodging, and meals; equipment rental; materials and processing; shipping costs.
6. How payment is to be made: the number of installments; when payment is to be made; the advance payment for travel and preparation costs; the period for final payment after delivery of the job.

Freelance Photography

7. Ownership of pictures: whether the client has all rights to all pictures, or only to those finally used. (This determines whether the photographer can subsequently make stock sales of unused pictures from the assignment.)

8. Cancellation: what payment is to be made, or how payment is to be determined, if the client should cancel the assignment before the work is completed. Full payment should be stipulated for a satisfactorily completed assignment, even if the client may ultimately decide not to use the pictures.

A number of additional points should be discussed and thoroughly understood by both photographer and client before the assignment begins. It is of primary importance to get as much information as possible about what the client wants: the kind of pictures, the specific coverage required, the tone or mood of expression. A thorough understanding of how the pictures are to be used will help keep the photographer working along the desired lines. It is also important to know whom to contact and report to at the photographic location as well as at the client's headquarters. Procedural matters should be discussed: how to submit bills or invoices, to whom they should be submitted, and what documentation of expenses (such as receipts) should be included.

Other Considerations

Freelance photography is not a guaranteed road to success. Until a photographer is well-established with a sizable list of clients, he or she is unlikely to be able to live on the income from photography alone. The majority of freelance photographers probably have other jobs as well during at least part of the year; even so, most who try freelance work give it up within two or three years. There is no way

Some photographs taken on assignment for a specific client but not used by the client may revert to the photographer for possible sale elsewhere. Questions of ownership of pictures made under circumstances should be covered in a written agreement between photographer and the client. Photo by Michael Fairchild.

(Left) Interesting landscape photographs may be purchased by a variety of publications or agencies serving widely differing clients. Photo by Michael Fairchild. (Right) Freelance photographers with a specialized knowledge of food photography are in considerable demand. Photo by Viles Studio Inc. for Editorial Photocolor Archives.

Freelance Photography

Freelance Photography

Weddings and other social events may supply work for many freelance photographers. However, such work is often seasonal and can rarely be relied upon as a steady source of income. Since most large weddings take place on weekends, the timing may work out nicely by not causing conflict with other, more regular work.

to guarantee a steady flow of work month after month; virtually every area has cycles of activity that produce periods of feast and famine for the freelance worker. There are thousands of weddings in June for every wedding in January; most corporations issue their annual reports at the same time of year; and the largest volume of consumer goods is sold from September through December. The examples are endless.

When there are no assignments, the freelance photographer must create some in order to produce pictures and articles that can be submitted to new

Freelance Photography

markets. Often, affiliation with a stock picture agency will provide some income from unused photographs from previous assignments or from self-assignments.

In spite of these drawbacks, freelance photography can be immensely rewarding and satisfying. Many people prefer work that has no set hours, involves travel and new experiences, and constantly poses new challenges. It is a field ideally suited to those who are talented, energetic, and self-reliant.

• *See also:* ADVERTISING AGENCIES; ADVERTISING PHOTOGRAPHY; AGENCIES, PICTURE; BUSINESS METHODS IN PHOTOGRAPHY; CAREERS IN PHOTOGRAPHY; COMMERCIAL PHOTOGRAPHY; COPYRIGHT; LEGAL ASPECTS OF PHOTOGRAPHY; MODEL RELEASE; MODELS AND MODELING; NEWS PHOTOGRAPHY; RIGHTS; SELLING PICTURES; SPORTS PHOTOGRAPHY.

Further Reading: Ahlers, Arvel W. *Where & How to Sell Your Photographs,* 8th ed. Garden City, NY: Amphoto, 1977; Holden, Stan. *Twenty Ways to Make Money in Photography.* Garden City, NY: Amphoto, 1977; Miller, Gary E. *Freelance Photography.* (Petersen's How-to PhotoGraphic Library) Los Angeles, CA: Petersen Publishing Co., 1975; *Photo Market Survey.* Little Falls, NJ: Career Institute, Inc., Division of Singer Communications Corp., 1976.

Fresnel Lenses

For many purposes where good image-formation is unnecessary, such as in condensers, spotlights, and field lenses, it is possible to collapse a lens into a flat plane in small steps, as shown in the accompanying illustration. In this diagram, the part *ab* of the original thick lens has been stepped into *a′b′*, in order to reduce the mass of the lens and to prevent it from becoming too thick. Similarly the part *bc* is stepped into *b′c′*, and so on across the entire lens. Lenses of this type were suggested by the French physicist A. J. Fresnel in 1822, and have long been used for lighthouses and for ship lanterns, and so forth. More recently, they have become familiar to the photographer in spotlight condensers. In this case, the lens is molded in glass without any very great precision, the steps being bold and few in number.

However, for field lenses it is possible to mold a Fresnel lens in a transparent plastic, with a very large number of minute steps so close together that the steps themselves can scarcely be seen without a magnifier. In this form, we have a thin sheet lens that can be cut out with scissors and mounted in any convenient way. An excellent application is to place such a lens close to the ground glass of a view camera or a translucent projection screen to increase the brightness of the corners of the picture. Once a suitable (and costly) mold has been made, the lenses themselves are not nearly as expensive as the familiar ground and polished glass lenses. Many single-lens reflex 35 mm cameras have modified Fresnel field lenses with molded microprisms in a circular area in the center, a clear circular ring area around this, and a Fresnel lens pattern around the circular ring that extends to the corners of the field. Combined with the ground glass, this provides two types of focusing, as well as an image that is bright to the corners for framing.

Nearly all currently made twin-lens and single-lens reflex cameras have Fresnel field lenses next to the ground-glass focusing screen.

The most perfectly diffuse material for a focusing or projection screen is opal glass, but its transmittance is so low that the image is likely to be too dim for comfortable observation. Some successful

Fresnel lens. Part ab *of the original thick lens has been stepped in to* a′b′ *to reduce the mass of the lens. In the same manner, part* bc *has been stepped in to* b′c′, *and so across the lens.*

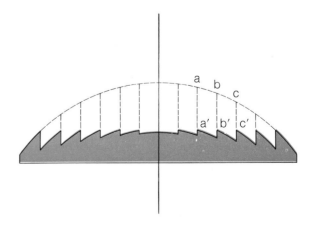

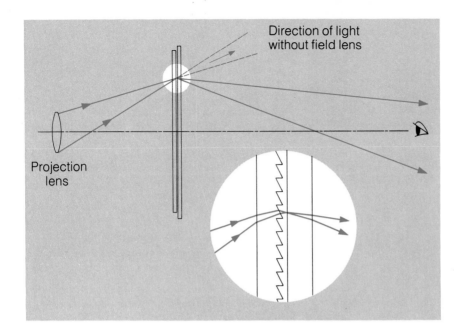

The Ektalite field lens behind a ground-glass screen.

diffusing screens have been made by depositing chemical substances on glass. Plain ground glass is more common, but its diffusing properties are often insufficient to cause the more oblique incident light to be scattered towards the observer's eye. (See the accompanying illustration.) The result is the formation of a bright "hot spot" surrounding the point on the screen where it is pierced by a line joining the projection lens to the observer's eye, and as the observer moves his or her head laterally, the hot spot follows him or her around. Outside the bright hot spot, the screen appears relatively dim.

In the limit, of course, if *all* diffusion were removed and the screen were replaced by a clear glass sheet, the hot spot would become nothing but the projection lens aperture, and its brightness with no slide in the projector would be equal to the brightness of the projection lamp itself. Diffusion, then, increases the size of the hot spot at the expense of image brightness.

As was mentioned above, it is possible to increase the size of the hot spot very materially by the addition of a field lens to the ordinary ground-glass screen. A convenient lens is the flat plastic Ektalite Fresnel lens originally introduced by Kodak. If the eye is correctly located within the image of the projection lens aperture formed by the field lens, the diffusion can be dispensed with altogether to give a fully specular system. This results in an astonishing increase in the picture brightness, and the entire field will appear as bright as the lamp filament itself. However, the latitude in eye position is then likely to be too small for convenient observation, and some diffusion must be employed to make a satisfactory system.

• *See also:* FIELD LENS; FOCUSING SYSTEMS; LENSES; OPTICS; VIEWING AND FOCUSING.

Friese-Green, William

(1855–1921)
English photographer

William Friese-Green was claimed by the English to be the real inventor of the motion picture. In 1889, he patented a camera that took instantaneous photographs in rapid succession, and in some ways this could indeed be considered a motion-picture camera. He was an inventor of note; he patented a two-color additive system of color photography, as one of his many inventions.

Front Projection

Backgrounds for studio photographs can be created by erecting sets, by hanging painted drops or various materials, or by projecting images from slides or transparencies onto a suitable screen. Although projected backgrounds may be solid colors, abstract designs, or patterns of light and color, their greatest value is to produce surroundings that appear realistic, so that photographs taken in locations anywhere in the world can in fact be produced under controlled conditions in the studio.

An Early Method of Projection

The first widely used method for creating such backgrounds was to project an image onto the rear of a translucent screen; the photograph was made from the other side with the subject positioned in front of the transmitted image. There are several drawbacks to this method. A considerable amount of extra studio space is needed to locate the projector the required distance behind the screen. Light falls off rapidly toward the edges of the projected image, creating a "hot spot" of brightness at the center. The translucent screen material reduces the brightness of the transmitted image considerably, but more importantly it reduces contrast and color saturation. It may also affect sharpness and the resolution of fine detail. Frontal lighting on the subject must not fall onto the rear-projection screen or the image will be washed out. This means that the subject must be placed a good distance in front of the screen so that spill light will fall on the floor or out of camera range on the screen. Because broad, general lighting cannot be used, the subject is confined to a single position or to an extremely limited area of movement. In addition to increasing the requirement for studio

The greatest value of front-projected backgrounds is their ability to offer an unlimited variety of realistic-looking backdrops for studio use. By simply changing slides and adjusting the lighting appropriately, the photographer can reproduce locations from anywhere in the world without leaving the controlled conditions of the studio. Photos courtesy Lumi-Tek.

This front-projection setup shows the tripod-mounted projector at center of photograph with camera mounted on top. Whatever image may be projected onto the subject himself will be washed out with subject lighting from the large reflector at right of picture. Photo courtesy Lumi-Tek.

depth, the necessary subject-screen separation increases the screen size required to fill the camera's field of view. This in turn amplifies the problem of even illumination on the screen. Further, it necessitates a very high-powered projector.

Modern Projection

These disadvantages are largely overcome by modern front-screen projection. As the name indicates, the background image is projected from the camera and subject side of the screen. This technique produces images of great brightness with full contrast and color saturation. Frontal subject lighting can easily be arranged so that spill onto the screen does not greatly affect the background image quality; and lighting can be established over the entire camera field to permit virtually unrestricted subject movement. Because the projector is in front of the screen rather than behind it, extra studio depth

is not necessary; set-up space is about the same as that required with a seamless paper background of standard width. In addition, it is easy to change slides or make other projector adjustments without an assistant or the need to go back and forth between the camera and a distant projector.

Principles of Front Projection

In a front-projection setup, an image is projected onto a background screen from the camera position. The image also falls on the subject in front of the screen; but because of the screen characteristics, the intensity of the image on the subject is insignificant compared to the background intensity. It can be washed out with subject lighting that does not affect the background image. The camera position is related to the projector position in such a way that wherever the subject moves, it conceals its own shadow on the screen from view.

Front-projection apparatus has three major components:

1. A screen of highly directional reflective material.
2. A beam-splitting mirror to place the projector and the camera on a common optical axis.
3. A high-efficiency projector that produces even illumination over its entire field.

A still camera using any size film, a motion-picture camera, or a television camera can be used in conjunction with front-projection components.

Front-Projection Screen

The reflection screens commonly used to view slides and movies have surfaces that reflect light out over a useful viewing angle of up to about 45 degrees to each side of the screen. This makes it easy to accommodate large audiences, but limits maximum image intensity as viewed from any given position.

Screens for front-projection photography are made from a special material that reflects virtually all light back along its original path, to the source. As a result, the image, as viewed from the source position, is as much as 850 times brighter than it would be on a matte-surface white screen. The image is visible at full or nearly full intensity only when viewed precisely on the camera/projector optical axis. At about 20 degrees from the camera/projector axis, the intensity falls off so drastically that the image is virtually invisible. This narrow reflection angle is not a drawback, however, because only one viewer must be accommodated: the camera. In fact, high-efficiency light reflection within a very narrow angle is the key to front-projection photography.

As discussed in the section on lighting, light from instruments placed outside the narrow angle will not be reflected to the camera; therefore the screen permits virtually unlimited subject-lighting techniques to be used. Although the most common setup places the camera and projector axis at a right angle to the screen, successful results can be obtained from anywhere within the reflection angle. As the projector is moved farther from the perpendicular to the screen, keystoning and oval distortion of rectangular and circular shapes in the projected image may become noticeable. If necessary this can be eliminated by using a background transparency taken with an appropriate amount of distortion in the opposite direction.

(A) An ordinary screen scatters light as much as 45° from perpendicular at any point in order to permit viewing over a wide area. (B) A screen for front-projection photography directs almost all light back toward the point source. An intense image is visible when viewed from the perpendicular; virtually nothing can be seen on the screen from about 20° off the perpendicular. Photographs are taken from the position along the axis to the center of the screen.

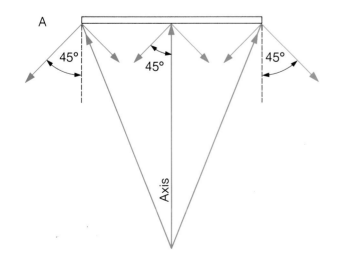

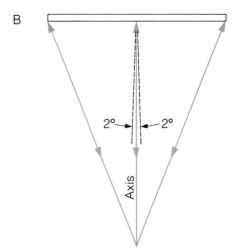

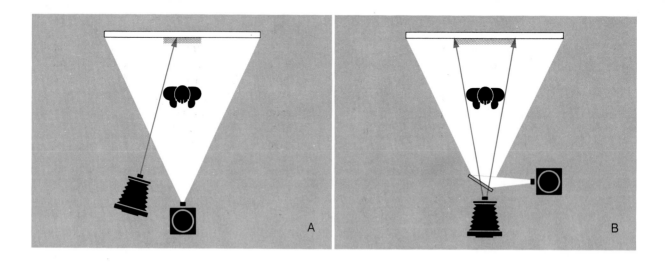

(A) When the camera is not on the axis of the projected image, it can see subject shadow on the background screen. (B) A beam splitter combines the projected image and the camera view on the same optical axis. Wherever the subject is located within the field of view, it hides its own shadow from the camera.

Beam Splitter

If the camera is not on the optical axis of the projected image, it can see past one edge of the subject to the shadow on the screen caused by the subject blocking the projected illumination. A beam-splitting mirror—a partially reflective, "see-through" mirror—is used to give the camera and projector a common optical axis. The beam splitter is usually placed at an angle of 45 degrees, close in front of the camera lens; other angles can be used for special purposes, but with reduced efficiency. The camera lens "looks" through the beam splitter at the subject and screen. The projector may be located at either side of, above, or below the beam splitter, which reflects the projected beam toward the screen. Light loss through the beam splitter is not significant; in a precisely aligned setup with a high-quality beam splitter, the loss may be as little as the equivalent of ¼ stop of exposure.

The angle of view of the camera lens should be the same or nearly the same as that of the projector lens to avoid size distortion. Because the projected image size and the camera field of view may not be the same size, the two lenses will not necessarily match in focal length; it is their comparative fields of view and the alignment of the setup that count.

Projector

In theory, any projector that will accept the desired transparency or slide can be used for front-projection photography. However, the projected image must have an even intensity over its entire field. Many ordinary projectors do not provide uniform enough illumination for this purpose. While the lack of uniformity is not noticeable with normal screens under common viewing conditions, it may be very evident when a highly directional front-projection screen is used. Accordingly, projectors for front-projection photography have high efficiency and very even illumination over the entire field.

The most versatile projectors accept a variety of transparency sizes and formats. They also have built-in adjustable masking blades to limit the projected area, and permit the transparency to be moved in the focal plane of the projector so the background can be shifted without changing the projector position.

Projector illumination must match the color balance of the film in use, or corrective filtration must be placed in the projection beam. Projectors with continuous light sources must have highly efficient heat-absorption and cooling systems, since color transparencies fade at an accelerated rate when projected for long periods, as is common in studio background work. Some projectors can be fitted with an electronic flash tube to match the subject illumination. A continuous light lamp in the projector is used for setup and alignment, just as modeling lights are used with electronic flash units. The projector flash tube can be synchronized with the camera shutter and subject-lighting units for simultaneous operation.

Lighting

The projected image falls on both the subject and the screen. The diffuse surface characteristics of ordinary subjects scatter so much light that only a small portion is reflected back toward the camera, whereas virtually all the light striking the screen reaches the camera. As a result, the subject is so much darker that it would register as a black silhou-

A photograph taken only by the projector illumination registers the subject as a black silhouette. Subject lighting must be added to bring the subject brightness to the exposure level of the background. Photo courtesy Lumi-Tek.

Front Projection

For realistic effects, it is necessary to be sure the quality of the light falling on the subject is in keeping with the type of background projected. Direction of the main light must also relate appropriately. Photo courtesy Lumi-Tek.

ette if a photograph were taken by only the projector illumination. Lighting is added to raise the subject brightness to the exposure level of the background. Under most circumstances, subject lighting and color is not affected by the projected background image.

There are three exceptions to this:

1. The retinas of animals' eyes have reflective characteristics similar to the background screen; at certain angles the projected image will be visible in their eyes, and must be retouched out of the finished photographs.

2. Under some circumstances, shiny curved areas of products being photographed will reflect portions of the image; this can usually be corrected by turning the subject slightly to a different reflective angle.

3. When a clear white light or a very light color is projected at high intensity and at close range—approximately 45 cm (18 inches) or less—subject contrast and color saturation may be reduced. The solution is to move farther from the subject and use a longer-focal-length lens to achieve the same image size and field of view.

Any kind of light source can be used, as long as its illumination is compatible with the projector illumination and the color balance of the film emulsion. Because of the narrow reflective angle of the screen, light from instruments placed outside that angle cannot be reflected to the camera and therefore will not reduce the contrast or desaturate the colors of the background image. In addition, shadows caused by the subject lighting that falls on the screen cannot be seen. For this reason, it is often easier to achieve shadowless product photographs by using white or single-color light in a front-projection setup than by using diffuse light and a white paper background.

Lighting arrangements of any kind can be used. However, it is necessary to stay outside the screen's reflective angle (otherwise, background desaturation may occur); and it is necessary to make sure that the quality of the light on the subject fits in with that of the background image. If a realistic effect is desired, it is especially important that the main light come from the same direction in all areas of the picture.

Because the background intensity is often great enough to permit use of an aperture of $f/16$ or even $f/22$ with a medium-speed film, a great deal of light may be required to bring the subject up to the required exposure level. For this reason, high-intensity electronic flash units are often preferred. They are compact, easy to put into position, and avoid the discomfort or possible product damage that can be caused by the heat of continuous light sources.

Illumination levels can be balanced by taking alternate readings of the background and of the subject as the lighting is adjusted. Incident-light readings of the subject should be taken with the background projector turned off. Reflected-light readings of the background must be made on or parallel to the camera-subject axis, but for perfect balance of subject and background, test exposures must be made.

Background Slides

Any transparent or translucent material that can be put in the projector can be used to create a background, but slides or transparencies of actual scenes, miniature setups, or other prints are commonly used. There are a number of things to consider when making slides for background use.

The background lighting should be easy to duplicate on the subject in the studio; for this reason,

overhead, midday sunlight is seldom suitable. The directionless illumination of a bright, overcast day produces suitable backgrounds for almost any kind of subject lighting.

If the screen is normally used at a 90-degree angle to the camera, the background should be photographed head-on to avoid distortion. The camera lens and location for the background shot should preserve perspective and proportions that will be appropriate to the subject size and distance from the camera in the studio. If the finished photograph is to have great depth of field, the background slide must be made with maximum depth of field.

The composition of the background shot must be carefully thought out to insure that trees, posts, or other objects will not appear to be growing out of the subject in the studio setup.

When a particular subject is to be shown in front of a particular background, the best approach is to take the subject or a stand-in on location in order to line up the composition exactly as desired. Then the subject is removed and the background photographed in a series of bracketed exposures to insure the most useful image. Back in the studio, the setup can be recreated with other foreground elements or props added as required, under controlled conditions where lighting and effects impossible to achieve on location can easily be obtained.

Full-Length Pictures

When only a background screen is used, full-length front-projection photographs are not possible; the floor under the subject and the bottom edge of the screen destroy the illusion. It is possible to raise the subject on a pedestal, steps, or other object appropriate to the setting in order to include the feet or the bottom of the product; but in any case the bottom of the camera field must not go below the bottom edge of the projected image. It is not feasible to pull the screen material down onto the floor in a continuous sweep as is commonly done with rolls of background paper, because the narrow angle of reflection is then directed vertically rather than horizontally.

However, special floor material is available that will reflect the projected image at the proper angle. It must be carefully placed with relation to the background screen, and changes in lighting technique are

Full-length photographs require use of a special floor material to reflect the projected image at the proper angle. Once the special techniques of placement and lighting required for use of this material are understood, the process becomes simple and economical to use. Photo courtesy Lumi-Tek.

required. In addition, great care must be taken in walking or moving objects around on the floor material. Once the basic principles of its use are mastered, it makes full-length pictures with completely projected settings easy and economical to achieve.
• *See also:* BACKGROUNDS; BACKGROUNDS, ELIMINATING; BEAM SPLITTER; LIGHTING; REAR PROJECTION.

  ƒ-Stop

The term "ƒ-stop" refers to the lens opening (usually called aperture) that lets light through the lens to expose the film. The sizes of lens openings are usually expressed in terms of ƒ-numbers, for example,

$f/2.8$ and $f/4$. These are determined simply by dividing the focal length of the lens by the diameter of the aperture. For example, if the focal length of the lens is 4 inches and the aperture is 1 inch, the f-number is $f/4$ ($\frac{4}{1}=4$). So with a lens opening of $f/4$, the aperture is only ¼ of the focal length. Similarly, $f/8$ means that the aperture is ⅛ of focal length, $f/11$ means the aperture is $\frac{1}{11}$ of the focal length, and so forth. Once it is understood that f-numbers indicate the size of the aperture as a fraction of the focal length, it is easier to understand that the smaller the f-number, the larger the lens opening. Technically, the f-number is a fraction; for example, what is commonly called $f/16$ is really

$f/1/16$. This is found by inverting the division given above, that is:

$$f\text{-number} = \frac{\text{aperture diameter}}{\text{focal length}}$$

If all lenses had the same transmission, the images formed of the same subject by any lens at a given f-number setting would all have the same brightness. In practice, variations between lenses in the number of elements, types of glass, thickness of the elements, and lens coating does cause some variation in image brightness between lenses at the same

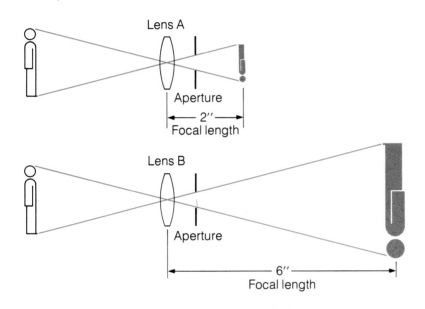

Both Lens A and Lens B have a 1-inch aperture and are focused on the same subject. Lens A has a focal length of 2 inches, and Lens B has a focal length of 6 inches. The image produced on the film is three times larger with the 6-inch lens than with the 2-inch lens, and the image made on the film by the 6-inch lens is less bright. The longer-focal-length lens has a smaller relative aperture.

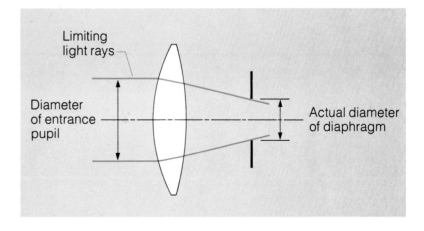

The aperture referred to by the term "f-stop" is the diameter of the entrance pupil, that is, the diameter of the diaphragm as seen through the front element of the lens. As the diagram shows, the actual diameter of the diaphragm is considerably smaller.

aperture. Where exposure is critical, this factor may have to be considered.

The aperture referred to is not the actual diameter of the lens diaphragm, but rather the diameter of the entrance pupil, which is the diameter of the diaphragm as seen through the front element of the lens (see illustration on previous page).

Because the focal length is measured with the subjects at infinity, *f*-numbers are valid for distant subjects, but use of uncorrected *f*-numbers at close distances (less than eight times the focal length) can result in underexposure. For close distance photography, the effective *f*-number is useful.

$$\text{Effective } f\text{-number} = \frac{\text{lens-to-film distance}}{\text{focal length}} \times \text{marked } f\text{-number}$$

OR

$$\text{Effective } f\text{-number} = \text{marked } f\text{-number} \times \text{magnification} + 1$$

Relative Aperture

Take, for instance, two lenses, each with a 1-inch aperture and focused on the same man. Both lenses transmit the same amount of light, but lens A has a focal length of 2 inches and lens B has a focal length of 6 inches. With the 6-inch lens, the image of the man produced on the film will be three times as large as the image produced with the 2-inch lens. While both lenses transmit the same amount of light reflected from the man, the light is spread over an

This series of photographs illustrates the variations in exposure resulting from changes in f-stops by half-stop increments from f/4 through f/16. Shutter speed was constant. Photos by John Menihan.

f-Stop

area nine times as large with the 6-inch lens. For this reason the image made on the film by the 6-inch lens is less bright. So while both lenses have a physical aperture of 1 inch, the longer-focal-length lens has a smaller *relative* aperture.

It would be difficult to take properly exposed pictures if, for example, *f*/8 on a long-focal-length lens and *f*/8 on a short-focal-length lens didn't mean the same thing from an exposure point of view. Fortunately they do—but for this to be true, the *f*/8 on the long-focal-length lens must be a physically larger opening than the opening of *f*/8 on the shorter-focal-length lens. Both lenses have the same-size *relative* aperture, but their *physical* apertures are of different sizes.

Lens Diaphragms and Their Markings

Simple lenses in inexpensive cameras have a fixed lens opening or a series of apertures in a movable slide or disk. More complex lenses have an adjustable lens opening, called a lens diaphragm, that varies the amount of light that passes through the lens. The size of this opening is indicated by a lens-opening (lens-aperture) scale that is marked in *f*-numbers.

The *f*-numbers *f*/1, *f*/1.4, *f*/2, *f*/2.8, *f*/4, *f*/5.6, *f*/8, *f*/11, *f*/16, *f*/22, *f*/32, *f*/45, and *f*/64 are full-stop increments. Each lens opening in the series transmits one-half as much light as the preceding lens opening; for example, *f*/5.6 transmits half as much light as *f*/4. Most lenses do not have a range of openings this great. Sometimes the largest opening for a lens is less than one full *f*-stop from the next marked lens opening. Examples are *f*/3.5, *f*/4.5, and *f*/6.3. Most lens diaphragms are continuously variable so that the lens opening can be set at intermediate *f*-numbers for small changes in exposure. Some lenses have click stops, which makes it easier to locate the aperture settings exactly. These clicks are at the full-stop settings; some have half-stop click settings as well.

In the above series, each full stop varies from the next by a factor of $\sqrt{2}$, or 1.414. It can be seen that every other number is an abbreviation of the true stop value. The accompanying list of full stops, half stops, and third stops, is accurate to three decimal places.

• *See also:* APERTURE; DIAPHRAGM; *f*-NUMBER; RELATIVE APERTURE; U.S. STOPS.

LENS DIAPHRAGM SETTINGS		
	f-Numbers	Marked
Full	1.000	1.0
1/3	1.122	
1/2	1.189	
2/3	1.260	
Full	1.414	1.4
1/3	1.587	
1/2	1.682	
2/3	1.782	
Full	2.000	2
1/3	2.245	
1/2	2.378	
2/3	2.520	
Full	2.828	2.8
1/3	3.175	
1/2	3.364	
2/3	3.564	
Full	4.000	4
1/3	4.490	
1/2	4.757	
2/3	5.040	
Full	5.657	5.6
1/3	6.350	
1/2	6.727	
2/3	7.127	
Full	8.000	8
1/3	8.980	
1/2	9.514	
2/3	10.079	
Full	11.314	11
1/3	12.699	
1/2	13.454	
2/3	14.254	
Full	16.000	16.0
1/3	17.959	
1/2	19.027	
2/3	20.159	
Full	22.627	22
1/3	25.398	
1/2	26.909	
2/3	28.509	
Full	32.000	32
1/3	35.919	
1/2	38.055	
2/3	40.318	
Full	45.255	45
1/3	50.797	
1/2	53.817	
2/3	57.018	
Full	64.000	64

Fungus on Films

When photographic films or prints are stored or kept for any length of time in an atmosphere having a relative humidity above 60 percent, there is a tendency for fungus (often called "mold" or "mildew") to grow on either the emulsion surface or the back of the film. Humidity of 60 percent and higher is quite common in tropical countries; but it is also frequently encountered in other areas, including many sections of the United States, especially during the warm summer months. High temperature alone, without accompanying high humidity, will not cause trouble from fungus.

Fungus spores are found in the air everywhere, regardless of temperature and humidity. There are a great many varieties of fungi, and like other plant seeds, the spores will germinate and grow whenever conditions permit.

Whether or not anything can be done to correct for the effects of fungus depends upon the degree of the growth and whether it started to grow before or after exposure and processing.

Unexposed Films

You cannot correct for fungus damage when it occurs on unexposed or unprocessed film. A pattern of fungus filaments is formed that shows up later in the processed image. The areas where fungus grew will show a change in density on black-and-white films and a change in color on color films.

The danger of fungus damage on unexposed films can be reduced by keeping the moistureproof packaging sealed or intact until you are ready to use the film. Opening the packaging will make it easier for fungus to grow on the film. Also, have the film processed as soon as possible after exposure. Fungus can attack unprotected exposed film inside or outside the camera.

Processed Films

When fungus occurs on processed films, the damage to the image is not immediate; in fact, if the fungus is discovered in time, some steps can be taken to remove it and to prevent its recurrence. If the growth proceeds too far, however, it may cause per-manent damage to the image. This is likely to be more serious with color film, because the growth of fungus may liberate substances that affect the dyes. With either black-and-white or color film, fungus growth may also etch or distort the gelatin of the emulsion or the backing.

Prevention of Fungus Growth

The best method of protecting processed films against fungus growth is to store them in a cabinet or container in which the relative humidity can be kept below 50 percent. This can best be accomplished by using a desiccating agent, such as activated silica gel, placed in a moistureproof package such as an airtight can, polyethylene bag, or cannister along with the film. One inexpensive, convenient drying unit is the Davison Silica Gel Air Dryer, available from Hunt Sales Company. This is a small perforated metal container holding 43 grams (1½ ounces) of silica gel and a color indicator that changes from blue to pink when the desiccant needs reactivation. Silica gel lasts indefinitely, but it must be reactivated periodically to remove the absorbed moisture. Heat it to 121–144.5 C (250–300 F) in a vented oven until the color indicator turns deep blue. Heating for about 30 minutes is sufficient to reactivate small quantities of silica gel; larger quantities require two or three hours.

One ounce of silica gel is sufficient to protect approximately fifty 35 mm transparencies in cardboard mounts, about 400 feet of super 8 film, 200 feet of 16 mm film, or a total weight of about 4 ounces of negatives plus their storage envelopes.

The relative humidity can be lowewed in a metal cabinet of the type used for office supplies by burning electric light bulbs continuously in the lower part of the cabinet. The number of lamps should be adjusted to keep the temperature at about 5.5 C (10 F) above that outside the cabinet. Small holes or ventilating louvers should be provided at top and bottom to allow a slow but constant change of air through the cabinet.

When desiccation is not convenient, you can provide considerable protection against fungus attack by storing your processed films so that they are protected from dirt and dust. There is some advantage in using storage boxes of metal, polyethylene, or styrene rather than wood or cardboard, as the latter tend to absorb and hold moisture. One way to dry slides that are stored without desiccation is to project them occasionally.

Any form of surface contamination is likely to promote the growth of fungus. When handling films, therefore, make every effort to avoid leaving fingerprints on the surfaces. Remove any fingerprints immediately with Kodak film cleaner or equivalent.*

Store films in negative envelopes, available at photo stores. These envelopes are designed to protect film from dirt and moisture.

Use of *Kodak* Film Lacquer. Coating miniature-camera films with Kodak film lacquer† offers considerable protection against fungus growth, as shown by tests at a tropical test center. The lacquer contains a fungicide, and also offers mechanical protection so that if fungus does grow, it is kept on the surface and prevented from attacking the film for a considerable time. If fungus growth is discovered before it has penetrated the lacquer coating, it can be removed along with the lacquer by the treatment described in the following section. After thorough drying, the clean emulsion can be relacquered.

To apply Kodak film lacquer to the cleaned transparencies, first place the film, emulsion side up, on a flat surface, preferably a sheet of glass. Fasten the edges of the film to the glass with masking tape, taking care to cover the perforations, because the solvents in the film lacquer will attack the back of the film. Pour a small quantity of the film lacquer into a small, clean receptacle, and apply it with a camel's-hair brush. Allow the transparency to dry for 10 minutes in a dust-free location. Discard the unused film lacquer; do *not* return it to the bottle. Clean the brush with a 1-percent solution of sodium carbonate (washing soda) or sodium bicarbonate (baking soda). Rinse the brush well and dry it before using it again.

No films or slides are lacquered by Kodak at the time of processing.

---

*Some film cleaners may remove the protective lacquer that some processors apply to films. Therefore, if any cleaner is used other than Kodak film cleaner, first make a test on an unimportant piece of film.
†Kodak film lacquer is not recommended for relacquering roll-film or sheet-film transparencies because of the risk of streaking or uneven application. It is not adapted to dipping methods and cannot be used for motion-picture film. Those who want lacquer protection for their 16 mm films should contact commercial 16 mm laboratories, a number of which are equipped to apply a Kodak lacquer specially developed for motion-picture use.

Removal of Fungus

It is not safe to use water for removing fungus from color or black-and-white films, because fungus growth on the emulsion usually makes the gelatin soluble in water. The use of water or water solutions will therefore damage the image.

You can remove most surface fungus from negatives and slides by wiping them with soft plush, absorbent cotton, or chamois skin moistened with Kodak film cleaner. Remove slides from their cardboard mounts before cleaning, and use new mounts after cleaning.

In the case of films that have been protected with Kodak film lacquer, if the fungus growth has not penetrated to the emulsion, the lacquer can be removed by soaking the film in a dilute solution of sodium bicarbonate (baking soda). Dissolve a level tablespoon of soda in 475 ml (1 pint) of water at 15.5–21 C (60–70 F). Agitate the film in the solution for 1 minute and rinse it for 1 minute in water at 15.5–21 C (60–70 F), preferably about 15.5 C (60 F). Bathe the film in Kodak Photo-Flo 200 or 600 solution diluted according to the directions on the label, and hang the film up to dry in a dust-free place. Thorough drying will usually require several hours.

CAUTION: Do not use this treatment if the fungus growth is at all extensive. As mentioned, if the fungus has penetrated the emulsion, some of the emulsion may be removed by any treatment with water. Make a test with the least important slide or section of film before treating the more valuable ones.

To remove Kodak film lacquer from films that have been damaged by fungus, treat them with a solution of denatured alcohol and household ammonia (1 tablespoon of ammonia to 237 ml [1 cup] of alcohol). The alcohol should be of the type sold by paint and hardware stores for thinning shellac—*do not use rubbing alcohol.* Any ordinary household ammonia, either cloudy or clear, can be used if it is reasonably fresh and strong. Clean miniature-camera negatives or Kodachrome or Kodak Ektachrome slides by wiping their surfaces with absorbent cotton saturated with the alcohol-ammonia mixture. Support the film, emulsion side up, on a smooth nonporous surface, such as glass, to avoid scratching or marking the film base. Kodacolor negatives can be cleaned by dipping and agitating them in the solution at room temperature for no longer than 2 minutes. Dry the transparencies thoroughly before remounting them.

No satisfactory method is known for complete restoration when the gelatin has become etched or distorted by fungus. If the fungus is in the gelatin backing only, the backing can be removed, but the film may curl excessively as a result.

Miniature-camera slides from which fungus growths have been removed should *not* be remounted in their original holders. After being dried thoroughly, the slides can be remounted in new cardboard mounts or between glass. Take care to avoid touching the film surfaces, either by wearing clean cotton gloves or by using a clean lintless tissue between your fingers and the film.

Experience in the tropics with large numbers of glass-mounted, tape-bound slides has shown very little evidence of trouble, although there may be a tendency for fungus to grow on the inside surface of the glass. When slides are bound in glass, it is important to have both the film and the glass dry. Warming the slide glass and film to about 5.5 C (10 F) above room temperature for 5 to 10 minutes before assembly is generally sufficient. This can be done by placing the materials on a piece of window glass mounted a few inches above a lighted electric lamp. If slides are mounted in glass binders with metal frames, they should be stored in a dry place. In damp locations, moisture condensation and ferrotyping can occur on metal-bound transparencies. Cementing or laminating a slide to a single piece of glass will help prevent fungus.

Fungus on Prints

Photographic prints stored under conditions of high humidity are also subject to damage by fungus. The growth of fungus colonies on a print surface can cause dull spots on an otherwise glossy print. Fungus can degrade the gelatin in the emulsion layer to such an extent that localized stripping will occur, removing the image and exposing the baryta layer or the paper base. Insects are attracted to fungus and may damage the emulsion layer. Furthermore, certain chemicals present in insect excretions may fade or bleach the image in localized areas.

Black-and-white prints processed in hardening fixing baths are more resistant to fungus attack than those processed in non-hardening baths. Hypo-alum toning of prints also provides some protection against deterioration from fungus, as well as from residual processing chemicals. Other toning procedures, such as selenium and gold toning, are much less effective. Treating the prints with a fungicide and storing them properly in albums will provide considerable protection.

Fungicide Treatment. Black-and-white prints can be protected by treatment with a fungicide, such as Hyamine 1622.* For example, after thorough washing, soak the prints for 3 to 5 minutes at room temperature (not below 21 C [70 F]) with occasional agitation, in a 1-percent aqueous solution of Hyamine 1622. This treatment is suitable for both contact prints and enlargements and is excellent for large display prints. Hyamine treatment may produce a very slight coloration with some photographic papers, although it is not detectable with the majority of Kodak papers. In any case this hue is less objectionable than the fading, the yellowing, and the fungus damage likely to occur on untreated papers. Correctly processed black-and-white prints treated in this way have remained for seven years in tropical testing locations with no serious yellowing or fungus growth. Untreated prints disintegrated badly in the same test.

At the present time, no satisfactory fungicidal treatment for color prints is known.

Prints in Albums. Some additional protection will be afforded by mounting the prints in albums. For best results, the album leaves should be of high-grade paper. Do not mount the prints on opposite pages since this would press them together face-to-face when the book is closed. Also, prints should not be mounted on the first page of an album with glued covers. Most paste adhesives are hygroscopic and should not be used in very humid climates. Kodak dry mounting tissue or Kodak rapid mounting cement is satisfactory.

Modern albums in which prints are placed on self-adhesive papers and covered with thin acetate overlays provide a generally acceptable way to store prints. The acetate adds physical protection and does not contribute to fading.

• *See also:* FILING AND STORING NEGATIVES, PRINTS, AND TRANSPARENCIES; STORAGE OF SENSITIZED MATERIALS AND PROCESSING SOLUTIONS.

---

*Available from Rohm & Haas Co., Philadelphia, Pa.

Gamma

Emulsion response to exposure results in various silver or dye deposits upon processing. For a given kind and degree of processing, the density of each deposit is related to the amount of exposure received. Thus, response can be graphed in terms of density—which is a logarithmic quantity—and the logarithm of exposure. The resultant graph usually has an S-shape composed of a toe, a straight-line portion, and a shoulder (see the article CHARACTERISTIC CURVE). The upward slant or slope of the curve is related to the contrast characteristic of the emulsion response; a steep slope indicates higher contrast response than a less steep slope does. When slope is determined from the straight-line portion of the curve, as shown in the accompanying diagram, it is called *gamma.*

Gamma indicates how much tone compression occurred between the optical image and the finished image in the range indicated by the straight-line portion of the curve. An image with a gamma of 0.6 has a compression of 6/10 in the tones that record on the straight line. That is, if two tones in the optical image that exposes the film have a density difference of 1.0, and the film is developed to a gamma of 0.6, the density difference between those two tones as recorded in the image will be 0.60—indicating how much the tones were compressed.

Gamma is now primarily used to measure the effect of development on contrast in aerial photography and in motion-picture processing. However, because it is concerned only with the straight-line portion of the curve, gamma is only a partial indication of the printing characteristics of a negative. Modern emulsions are exposed and processed so that a significant number of dark tones are recorded on the

Gamma is the tangent of the angle θ formed when the straight-line portion of a characteristic curve is extended to meet the log-exposure baseline. In practice, it is most easily determined by selecting two points (a, b) on the straight line. The slope, or gamma, is equal to the density difference between the points divided by the log-exposure difference, or rise ÷ run.

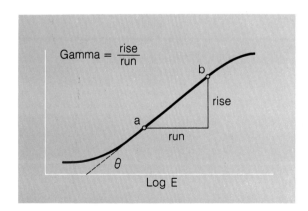

toe of the curve. The printing contrast characteristics of such negatives are more accurately indicated by the slope of a line drawn to join the points of minimum and maximum printable density. One such measure is *contrast index*.

• *See also:* CHARACTERISTIC CURVE; CONTRAST; CONTRAST INDEX; DENSITOMETRY; SENSITOMETRY.

Gaseous-Burst Agitation

Many approaches have been made to the problems of agitation. The gaseous-burst method introduced by Kodak has come closest to providing the best means for practical photographic service. It is applicable to many films and papers, is reasonably economical to install and operate, and, because it is automatic, does not require the full-time attention of a darkroom technician.

Gaseous-burst agitation consists of releasing bursts of gas, at controlled intervals, through many small holes in a distributor at the bottom of a processing tank. When first released, the bursts impart a sharp displacement pulse, or piston action, to the entire volume of solution; and then, as the bubbles make their way to the surface, they provide a localized agitation around each small bubble. The great number of bubbles and the random character of their paths to the surface provide effective agitation at the vertical surfaces of films or papers hanging in the solution.

If the gas were released continuously, rather than in bursts, constant flow patterns would be set up from the bottom to the top of the tank and cause uneven development. These flow patterns are not encountered, however, when the gas is introduced in short bursts, with an interval between bursts to allow the solution to settle down.

Equipment

The Gas. Nitrogen, because of its inert chemical character and low cost, is the best gas to use. It is obtainable in compressed form in large, cylindrical tanks, about 1.5 metres (5 feet) high by 0.3 metres (1 foot) in diameter, from local suppliers of compressed gases, who can be located by consulting the classified telephone directory under such categories as "Gas, Compressed" or "Oxygen." For photographic purposes, "water-pumped nitrogen" is recommended.

Experience has shown that one cylinder, operating at an output pressure of 103.5 kPa (15 pounds per square inch [psi]) and with a burst duration of 1 second and an interval between bursts of 10 seconds, will feed a distributor in a 13.2-litre (3½-gallon) tank 7 hours a day for 4 or 5 days. Longer intervals between bursts naturally extend the life of the cylinder.

Compressed air cannot be used as the agitating gas in developer solutions because it contains oxygen. Compressed air can be used with all other processing solutions, however, since they are not harmed by oxygen. The only consideration here is that the compressed air must be free of oil. This means that an oil-free air-compression system should be used, since most regular compressors inject a slight oil mist into the air as they compress it.

Pressure Control Valve. Nitrogen in cylinders is under an initial pressure of 13,800 kPa (2000 psi). To reduce this pressure to the 103.5 kPa (15 psi) desirable for release in a 13.2-litre (3½-gallon) tank, a gas-pressure control valve of the type shown in the accompanying figure should be obtained from the gas supplier. It provides an adjustable pressure-reducing valve and two pressure gauges. The gauge on the tank side indicates the amount of gas remaining in the cylinder, while the one on the line side shows the static output pressure.

Burst Valve. To provide automatic control of the flow of nitrogen to the gas distributor in the tank, a unit such as an intermittent gaseous-burst valve, shown in the accompanying illustration, is recommended. This model consists of an electronic control unit and solenoid valve. Basically, it provides for varying the duration of bursts from 0.4 second to 3 seconds, and the interval between bursts from 8 seconds to 90 seconds. In addition, it includes a gas-bleed valve that bypasses the solenoid. When opened and properly regulated, the gas-bleed valve maintains a standby pressure in the gas lines to prevent processing solutions from entering the gas distributor. The gas-bleed valve is especially useful in a system that is not free from gas leaks. It may not be required in a leak-free system. Read the section "Pressure and Leaks" in this article for details concerning the elimination of leaks.

A pressure-reducing valve such as this should be purchased from the local supplier of nitrogen gas. It allows the tank pressure to be reduced to the proper value for introduction of the gas into the solution.

The Gas Distributor. To provide uniform distribution of the gas bubbles across a horizontal cross-section at the bottom of the tank, a suitable gas distributor is needed. The plastic gas distributor, shown in the accompanying illustration, provides an ideal distribution pattern in 13.2-litre (3½-gallon) tanks, provided the tank and distributor are properly leveled.

Installation

To equip a darkroom for nitrogen-burst agitation, the equipment just described, plus interconnecting pipe and tubing needed to suit the individual installation, must be obtained.

An adjustable intermittent gaseous burst valve provides accurately spaced and timed intervals for controlling the program of gas bursts.

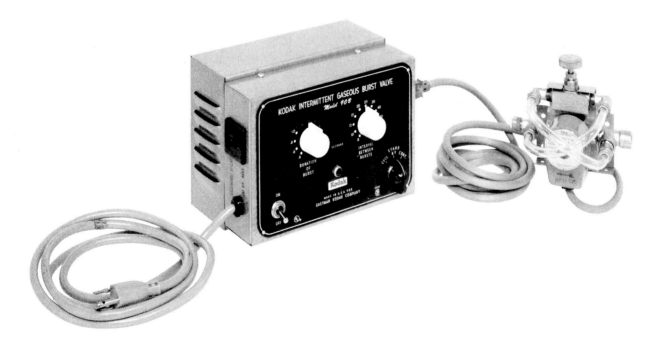

Gaseous-Burst Agitation

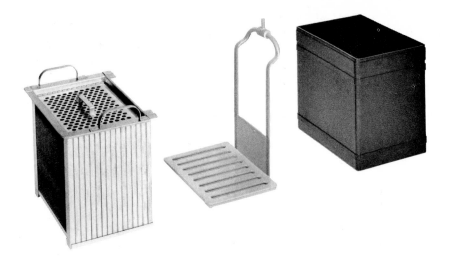

(Left to right) A processing basket (for Kodak Ektachrome or Kodak Ektacolor professional paper in sheets); a gas distributor; and an 8"×10" hard rubber tank.

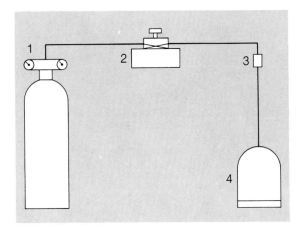

This schematic diagram shows the tubing connections between the gas cylinders, pressure-reducing valve (1), intermittent gaseous-burst valve (2), header (3), and gas distributor (4).

The gas cylinder should be mounted firmly in an upright position so that it cannot be knocked over accidentally. The mounting should be easily disconnectable to facilitate the changing of cylinders when they have been exhausted. A chain around the cylinder and attached to the wall with open screw eyes or hooks is a simple mounting method. The cylinder should be accessible for convenience in checking and adjusting the reducer valve and its gauges. (See the accompanying diagram.)

Either hose or pipe can be used to handle the flow of gas through the system. However, since a flexible connection facilitates changing the cylinder, it is desirable to use hose from the pressure control valve to the distributor solenoid valve.

From the solenoid valve, the piping should lead to a header located above the tanks. The header can be equipped with turncocks and conical slip-on hose fittings, or quick-disconnect air-hose fittings of the snap-in type. From this point, use flexible ⅜-inch I.D. × ½-inch O.D. tubing to connect the gas header to the nipple on the gas distributor. To avoid tubing kinks at the nipple, a stiffener, consisting of a 6-inch length of ¼-inch I.D. × ⅜-inch O.D. tubing, can be inserted into the end of the ⅜-inch I.D. supply tubing. To facilitate assembly, apply talcum powder to the tubing as a dry lubricant.

Mount the intermittent gaseous-burst valve in a convenient, accessible position, reasonably close to the tanks so that the controls can be reached easily.

It is very important that the tanks and gas distributor be level. If they are not, more of the gas will tend to rise on one side of the tank than on the other, and uneven agitation will result. A quick check for misalignment is to observe the pattern of bubbles on the surface of the tank. If there are more bubbles on one side of the tank than on the other, the distributor

Gaseous-Burst Agitation

needs leveling or the tank and distributor need to be leveled as a unit until a uniform pattern is achieved over the entire surface of the solution. (See the accompanying illustrations.)

When several solutions are being agitated simultaneously in a processing line, the degree of turbulence in the various tanks can be standardized by the use of turncocks installed at each take-off on the gas header. With more than one distributor in use, it will usually be necessary to increase the setting of the gas-pressure control valve.

Pressure and Leaks

Gas Pressure. The static gas pressure, as shown on the gauge on the line side of the pressure control valve, should be adjusted initially to about 103.5 kPa (15 psi) when the gas distributor is used in a standard 13.2-litre (3½-gallon) tank. This initial pressure setting can be varied in individual cases to give the desired degree of agitation, yet not cause difficulties by foaming the solutions over the tops of the tanks.

Some of the factors that may necessitate adjustment of the setting are:

1. Size and length of the gas line between the pressure control valve and the solenoid valve.
2. The number of gas distributors in use on the same solenoid valve.
3. The depth of the solutions (hydrostatic head pressure).
4. The orifice size of the solenoid valve.
5. The gas distributor.

An experimental clear-plastic tank is used here to show the effect of a distributor which is not level. (Left) Note that the bubbles are concentrated on the right-hand side of the tank. (Right) When the distributor is properly leveled, the bubbles of gas cover the surface of the solution evenly, and provide uniform agitation, as shown here.

The ideal pressure setting will cause a burst to raise the solution level in the tank by 15.9 millimetres (⅝ inch). A ruler can be used to measure the amount by which the solution is raised just before the gas bubbles burst at the surface.

Gas Leakage. Optimum agitation is obtained only when the system is completely tight. If leakage is suspected or determined as described in the next section, check the union of tubing to the intermittent gaseous-burst valve and the distributor nipple, quick-disconnect air-hose fittings, and any other fittings in the gas piping. These are the most common places for leakage to occur.

Even a small leak in the system can cause the gas pressure to be reduced sufficiently between bursts so that processing solution enters the gas-outlet orifices in the distributor. When this occurs, the next burst of nitrogen forces most of the gas out at those points nearest the intake of the distributor. Although the solution in the distributor is usually expelled during the burst, the amount of gas ejected at the orifices farthest from the intake may be reduced significantly, and agitation of film or paper on that side may be lessened appreciably.

Only a leakproof system will retain pressure in the gas lines between bursts and prevent processing solution from entering the gas distributor.

Just before the processing, the gas distributor should be cleared of developer by adjusting the gas so that it will flow continuously for several seconds or by effecting several closely spaced intermittent bursts. When the gas distributor is disconnected and moved to another tank during processing, it will lose its pressure and, when submerged, will fill with solution. However, in processing solutions after the developer, agitation is not usually so critical, and, in a leakproof system, the distributor will normally be cleared of solution during the initial burst.

Determining Gas Leakage. To determine the amount of gas leakage in the system, place the distributor in a tank of water and adjust the gas so that it flows continuously for several seconds or allow several closely spaced intermittent bursts to discharge completely any water that may be in the gas distributor. Turn off the gas so that no further bursts can follow; wait 1 minute; then withdraw the distributor quickly from the tank and tilt it so that any water in the distributor will drain into the gas-supply tubing. If this tubing is transparent, the water will be visible. Disconnect the tubing and drain all of the water into a graduate. If more than 10 millilitres (⅓ ounce) of water is drained from the tubing of a system utilizing a gas distributor in a 13.2-litre (3½-gallon) tank, corrective measures should be taken to seal leaks in the system. The factors affecting the setting of the static gas pressure can result in a greater or smaller quantity of water drained from the tubing.

Eliminating Leaks. Leaks that develop in the gas distributor—for example, at the union of the gas-supply tube and the distributor nipple—can be repaired by applying a cement to the broken parts.

Plastic tubing that is heavy and somewhat inflexible can cause strains, cracks, and finally, leaks at unions, such as the juncture of the gas-supply tube and the distributor nipple. Therefore, a very flexible plastic tubing should be selected, and it should be held snugly in place by tubing clamps. Satisfactory brands of vinyl plastic tubing can be obtained from laboratory supply houses.

Frequently, leaks in quick-disconnect fittings can be reduced greatly or eliminated by applying a thin film of an inert grease, such as stopcock grease or Vaseline, to the face of the fittings.

In cases where it is difficult to eliminate leakage, a standby pressure can be introduced in the gaseous-burst system. The pressure should not be sufficient to cause a release of bubbles, but should maintain enough pressure at the gas distributor to prevent the processing solutions from entering the distributor. To effect such a standby pressure, install a bypass gas-bleed valve across the solenoid valve. The Kodak intermittent gaseous-burst valve, model 90B, comes already equipped with a bypass gas-bleed valve.

Operation

The objective of a gaseous-burst system is to match or improve the results obtainable by processing the film or print material by hand in accordance with recommended procedures. The criterion for judging the effectiveness of nitrogen agitation is the uniformity of development in the picture area.

In the case of black-and-white materials, the variables that can be adjusted to achieve this end are burst duration, interval between bursts, and total time of immersion of the film in the developer.

A gas distributor is secured to a processing basket with stainless steel clips. The basket and distributor can be transferred as a single unit from one solution tank to another.

Burst Duration. The optimum length of the gas burst has been found to lie within the rather narrow range of ½ second to 2 seconds. A shorter burst may be ineffective, and a longer one results in channelization of the bubbles, with consequent nonuniformity.

Burst Interval. Longer intervals give less agitation and less development, while shorter intervals give more agitation and greater development in the same time. It is desirable to make any necessary adjustment by varying the burst interval rather than the burst duration, because of the narrow range over which the duration of burst can be regulated.

Development Time. With black-and-white sheet films, adjusting the development time is an alternative to varying the burst interval in order to increase or decrease the development level. A change from the time recommended for hand agitation is often necessary for satisfactory contrast. Note also that two films having the same time recommended for hand agitation may require different development times when gaseous-burst agitation is used.

In general, development times of less than about 5 minutes should be avoided. When very short development times are used, the wetting time of the film becomes a significant fraction of the total time, and nonuniformity can become a problem.

Transferring the Distributor and Basket. With the aid of processing basket clips, the gas distributor and the processing basket can be transferred together from one solution to the next (see the accompanying illustration), provided the gas is turned off just prior to the draining period. *This precaution will prevent injury to the eyes or skin from solution being sprayed into the room during the draining and transfer period.* After the distributor and basket are immersed in the next solution, the gas can be turned on again.

Notes on Film Hangers and Tank Loading. It is important that the film hanging in the tank not be too close to the distributor, or uneven development will occur near the gas orifices. For this reason, sheet-film hangers should not be hung in a tank without using a developing hanger rack. When 8″ × 10″ or multiple film hangers are used, hanger separators, sold in sets of two, are recommended to provide equal top-to-bottom spacing of the hangers in the rack. The separators hold the hangers in position vertically, thereby preventing film contact and aiding uniformity in a gaseous-burst agitation system.

If films of different sizes are developed at the same time in a tank, a spacer sheet of discarded film or acetate sheeting should be loaded in a hanger and placed between the groups of different-sized hangers. For example, 4″ × 5″ and 5″ × 7″ hangers in the same tank should be separated by a 5″ × 7″ hanger loaded with an old negative or a sheet of blank film, and 4″ × 5″ multiple hangers in the same tank with 8″ × 10″ film should have an 8″ × 10″ separator between the two sizes. Otherwise, the slight turbulence around the frame members of the smaller-size hanger will cause differential development on the larger sheet developing next to it.

It is important to agitate the film hangers by hand for about 15 seconds when they are first placed in each bath. This should be done in accordance with the instruction included with the packaged chemicals. The purpose is, of course, to dislodge any air bubbles that may have been trapped in the hanger channels or on the film surface and to get uniform chemical action started rapidly.

Preventing Plugged Nitrogen Distributors. Plugged orifices in the gas distributors disrupt the uniform flow pattern of the bubbles, causing variable and uneven development of sensitized photographic products. The plugging is usually caused by a buildup of developer products inside the distributor at the gas-release points. *Dry* nitrogen causes this condition by allowing evaporation of the developer solution to take place at the distributor orifices. Thus, small amounts of developer solution become crystalline deposits around the orifices. Once the crystals begin to form, they seed the developer, and plugging of the hole proceeds rather rapidly. Adding moisture to the dry nitrogen (humidification) prevents evaporation of the developer solution.

The method of humidifying the nitrogen is relatively simple. A filter housing containing a filter cartridge and water can serve as a "nitrogen humidifier." It is installed between the pressure-reducing valve and the line leading to the gas-burst valve. The accompanying schematic diagram shows the installation of a nitrogen humidifier in a processor that does not contain a nitrogen canister or surge tank. A second filter housing with no filter cartridge will serve as both a surge tank and a trap to prevent water from entering the developer solution. The pressure-relief valve should be located as shown in the diagram.

Cleaning Distributors. Unless humidified nitrogen is used, gas-distributor orifices may require

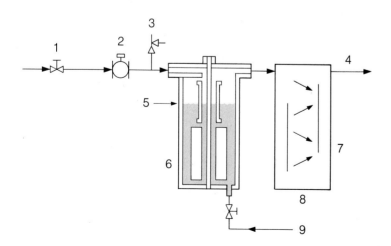

This schematic drawing shows a nitrogen-humidifier setup for use with a gas distributor in a 3½-gallon tank system. Shown here are the following: dry-nitrogen supply (1), pressure reducer (2), pressure-relief valve (3), moist nitrogen to gas burst valve and nitrogen distributor (4), water level (5), filter housing made of clear plastic (6), filter housing (7), nitrogen surge tank (8), and water supply (9).

Gaseous-Burst Agitation

occasional cleaning by soaking them for about 15 minutes in methyl alcohol and then wiping them thoroughly with a clean cloth. If at any time it is noticed that gas is not issuing from a few holes, these holes can be opened by inserting a No. 73, or smaller, size drill into them; however, be careful not to enlarge the diameter of the holes. After opening the holes, place the distributor in a tank of clean water and siphon water out through the intake tube for 2 or 3 minutes. This procedure will wash out foreign particles that might otherwise clog the holes again.

Whenever the tank is emptied of solution or a distributor is removed from the tank, it is a good practice to run a few bursts of gas through the system to clean the holes of solution that might otherwise dry and restrict or clog the orifices.

• *See also:* AGITATION; DARKROOM, PROFESSIONAL; DEVELOPERS AND DEVELOPING.

Gaumont, Léon

(1863–1946)
French motion-picture pioneer

Gaumont was responsible for marketing the Demeny Chronophotographe, which was an early form of motion-picture camera and projector. Subsequently, he produced and marketed a wide variety of motion-picture equipment, including cameras, projectors, printing machines, developing machines, and some early attempts at sound motion-picture equipment. Practical sound systems were eventually developed from the latter. Gaumont was also a film producer of considerable note.

Gauss, Karl F.

(1777–1855)
German astronomer and optician

Gauss was director of the observatory at Göttingen and did considerable work on the theory and design of telescope objectives. The so-called Gauss Objective, which contains two separate elements, allows correction not only for spherical and chromatic aberration, but also for the variation of spherical aberration in different colors (sphero-chromatism). From this simple telescope objective, a series of camera lenses that consist of two sets of separated elements in symmetrical form has been developed; the "double Gauss" objective is the basis of many of today's fast anastigmats. In optics, the two principal points of a lens are called Gauss points (another term used is nodal points). The focal length of a lens is measured from the rear Gauss point.

Gelatin

Gelatin is a glutinous material used as carrier for the light-sensitive salts in photographic emulsions. Dr. R. L. Maddox is generally credited with having invented the gelatin silver-halide emulsions in 1871. Gelatin is made from the hides, bones, and by-products of animals. Its exact composition is unknown, and depending upon various impurities present (primarily sulfur salts), one obtains either a photographically active gelatin or an inert type. Its prime chemical constituents are carbon, hydrogen, nitrogen, and oxygen. Photographically, the most valuable property of gelatin is its ability to absorb from five to ten times its weight in water, without dissolving, at ordinary temperatures, while it can easily be dissolved by hot water, glycerin, acetic acid, etc.

It is used in adhesives and for making light filters, but its primary use is in emulsions. Bichromated gelatin (gelatin sensitized with potassium, ammonium, or sodium bichromate) is light-sensitive. Exposure to light causes the gelatin to harden. When an image is exposed on a bichromated gelatin surface, the gelatin hardens in proportion to the amount of exposure. The image is washed in hot water and the unexposed gelatin washes away while the hardened gelatin remains fixed. This effort serves as the basis for a number of photographic pigment processes. Included among them are carbon, carbro, and bromoil.

Glamour Photography

Glamour photographs emphasize and enhance the attractive appearance of their subjects. While portraits reveal something of character or inner personality, glamour pictures concentrate on the outward handsomeness or loveliness of the subject.

Such photographs are widely used for illustrative and publicity purposes. They are the photographs that performers send to agents, producers, and fans. Models include them in the sample portfolios they show to agencies, clients, and photographers. These pictures are the editorial and advertising illustrations that say, "Here is a desirable person, one with an extra degree of intangible appeal and beauty." It is exactly this extra quality that the glamour photograph is intended to bring out.

Beauty pictures concentrate on showing how cosmetics and hair styling can be used to create a beautiful appearance; fashion photographs emphasize the role of the subject's clothes or costume. Although these elements may be part of a successful glamour picture, they are subordinate; the point of the glamour picture is to show a beautiful person, not a beautifying technique. Similarly, in the language of the product-illustration studio, a "nuts and bolts" picture shows details of construction, materials, controls, and the like; a "glamour shot" concentrates on the styling and eye-appeal of the product.

The term "glamour picture" is almost automatically taken to mean a picture of a pretty girl. But men can be glamour subjects as easily as women can; the determining factor is the style and intention of the photograph, not the sex of the subject. At one time glamour photography consisted almost entirely of artificial poses, exaggerated lighting, and plenty of

Unlike beauty or fashion photographs, which are made to sell products, glamour photographs are made to sell the model: the model is the product. Such photographs are used by models in their sample portfolios, and are used in advertisements and publications when the message is "This person is attractive, desirable, appealing." Photo at left by Judith Gefter; photo at right by Bob Clemens.

A few props and simple settings can do much to create different glamour photographs of the same model. The photographer's skill and the model's ability to interpret the photographer's concepts are the most essential ingredients in good glamour photography. Photos by Bob Clemens.

clichés: slit skirts, black slinky evening gowns, shirts unbuttoned to show a hairy male chest, white top hat and tails, and of course "cheesecake" and "beefcake" pictures of models in bikinis or swimming trunks, showing lots of female anatomy or rippling muscles.

Today, such pictures are a small part of glamour photography. A more modern approach is to emphasize the natural beauty of the subject by the use of unobtrusive lighting and relaxed, natural poses, expressions, and picture situations. Because the artificial and contrived are out of place, most anyone can learn to take successful glamour photographs—it is not necessary to be a professional photographer with a studio, lots of equipment, and a large stock of costumes and props.

It is not necessary to use professional models, either. There are a great number of men and women who are excellent potential subjects for glamour pic-

tures but who have little or no experience in modeling or posing. In fact, almost all of the subjects in the pictures accompanying this article are amateur models who pose only occasionally for photographs.

In working with non-professionals, the photographer's job is to recognize the potential in a subject, and to coax and coach him or her into a relaxed, appealing mood, expression, and pose. Of course the photographer must also know how to take technically excellent pictures in order to make the most of the subject's qualities, but that can be done with quite ordinary equipment, lights, and accessories. It is the photographer's skill and knowledge that makes the difference between a snapshot and a successful glamour picture.

Equipment

The following equipment and accessories will help make it easy to take a wide variety of glamour

(Right)A simple, graceful pose is complimented by a carefully arranged composition in color and form. Note how hairstyle, makeup, and gown combine to give a contemporary rendition of a 1930's look. Photo by Norman Mosallem for Editorial Photocolor Archives.

(Above) Some models have particularly good features that should be emphasized. This model's long, beautiful legs are shown to best advantage by a lighting arrangement which immediately draws the eye to the lower part of the picture, and by the unobtrusive color of the clothing and background. Photo by Robert Farber. (Right) The warm colors which give this picture its pinkish tone are particularly flattering to any model. Photo by Norman Mosallem for Editorial Photocolor Archives.

A standard table lamp can create the natural lighting of a comfortable room. The camera must be mounted on a tripod and a cable release used to trigger the shutter. Photo by Bob Clemens.

pictures; all the photographs in this article were made with similar items.

A Dependable Camera. You will need a camera in good working condition with which you are thoroughly familiar. Film size is not important. However, 35 mm or roll films make it possible to take many poses and variations without having to interrupt the mood by changing film after each shot. A camera that accepts interchangeable lenses provides increased versatility. The ability to manually adjust the exposure settings makes it possible to obtain controlled exposure effects.

A Steady Tripod. Many glamour pictures are made under low-level lighting conditions that require slow shutter speeds, so a camera cannot be hand-held. This is especially true when using slower-speed films. A tripod that is easy to adjust, but that is sturdy enough to withstand mirror and shutter vibration in the camera is essential for high-quality

pictures. By having the camera on a tripod, the photographer is freer to capture the best poses and expressions.

A Cable Release. This inexpensive accessory goes hand in hand with a tripod. It permits tripping the shutter smoothly, without the danger of moving the camera by finger pressure. A long cable release allows the photographer to move around so that he or she can direct the model to look in the right direction.

An Accurate Exposure Meter. A meter is necessary with manually controlled cameras, of course. But even when the camera has a built-in metering system, a separate meter is valuable for taking close-up readings of specific areas, and for accurately determining light balance and subject contrast range.

An Efficient Reflector. This valuable aid conveniently controls lighting contrast by bouncing light into shadow areas of the subject, particularly

Reflectors are invaluable in controlling lighting. (Above) In photo taken without a reflector, too much of the girl's face is in shadow. (Right) A reflector is placed to catch the window light and bounce it onto the model's face. (Below right) Window light bounced off a white card adds more flattering lighting, especially to the model's eyes. Photos by Bob Clemens.

the eyes. Using a reflector is especially important when using sidelighting and backlighting, two very flattering types of lighting for models.

Reflectors come in many shapes and sizes. An especially useful type is a commercially made unit that resembles a small square umbrella with white fabric on one side and silver foil on the other. It measures about 33 inches on each side, and can be mounted on a portable light stand by means of an adjustable bracket.

To make a reflector, use a large sheet of white cardboard, a white bed sheet, or a sheet of lightweight plywood sprayed with white enamel or aluminum paint. Another very workable reflector is a home-movie screen that has its own tripod stand.

A Flash Unit. Light from a flash unit can also be used to fill in shadows when working with backlighting or sidelighting, indoors or out. Like a reflector, the flash fill reduces contrast, but it tends to be harsher in appearance. And, unless a particular

setup has been tested in advance, balancing the light from fill-in flash against the main light can be a little tricky. It is not possible to make a visual check of its effect on the subject before taking the picture as is the case when using a reflector. However, bounce flash is convenient to use in certain situations. Reflected from a wall, ceiling, or reflector indoors, it can help augment or boost the existing light and provide soft, pleasing lighting. (*See:* BOUNCE LIGHT; FLASH PHOTOGRAPHY.)

A Soft-Focus or Diffusion-Type Lens Attachment. These attachments take the sharp edge off the focus, giving a misty, pleasingly soft look to the picture. This subtle quality is particularly welcome in close-ups of girls, in which the sharpness of modern lenses can be quite unflattering: Few models have flawless skin and facial features.

A soft-focus attachment can also enhance the romanticism in a given scene where a more literal (perfectly sharp and crisp) rendering would not be appropriate or desirable.

A Medium-Focal-Length Telephoto Lens. If the camera will accept interchangeable lenses, this one will prove extremely valuable. While it is possible to make facial close-ups with a normal lens, the nose and other features closest to the lens can be distorted by appearing out of proportion to the rest of the face. A telephoto lens of moderate focal length (85 mm to 135 mm on a 35 mm or 126 camera, 150 mm to 250 mm on a 2¼″ × 2¼″ camera) will fill the frame with just the model's head or even just the face without producing unflattering distortion.

A Working Philosophy

Especially when working with inexperienced models, it is best to take a straightforward approach. Avoid cheesecake clichés and a stilted, contrived style. Overly meticulous lighting arrangements and

(Left) Soft focus gives a misty, romantic look and diminishes any flaws in the model's skin or features. (Right) However, if the model has good skin, teeth, and hair, sharp focus may result in an equally pleasing photograph. Photos by Bob Clemens.

Honesty and spontaneity are more appealing than the unnatural or bizarre. However, poise and grace are still essential: note the delicate line of the model's fingers, the raised knee, and the pointed toes—all necessary for the woman to look her most glamourous. Photo by Bob Clemens.

unnatural posing can render the subject as lifeless as a mannequin. Props and costumes that are dated in style will make the pictures look dated as well. Contemporary, candid approaches to glamour photography do not have to be bound by rules such as the one that says a subject should never look directly into the camera.

Make it your objective to create an honest image of a woman looking lovely—or a man looking handsome—showing poise and self-confidence in a pictorially interesting framework. And, make sure your

subject enjoys the entire experience, for that will communicate itself in the picture.

Some work may be done indoors in a studio-like setup where conditions can be carefully controlled. But working outdoors or in an interesting location often will lead to more relaxed and more interesting pictures. For natural-looking results, try to use the natural lighting present in the scene; augment its effect on the subject by using a reflector. Open or deep shade outside, or indirect sunlight coming through a window, provides especially pleasant illu-

(Left) Props can suggest moods to model and photographer. Here, a stuffed leopard suggests a sultry, exotic pose. (Right) Sometimes the model's coloring clearly demands other dramatic colors. The brilliant scarlet clothing is a striking foil to the dark complexions of this handsome couple. Photos by Norman Mosallem for Editorial Photocolor Archives.

(Left) Many moods can be elicited from responsive models. When using more than one model, the permutations are almost endless. Photo by Norman Mosallem for Editorial Photocolor Archives.

Mood and meaning can be easily altered, even with the same model. The photograph at left was taken in midsummer, with the model sitting demurely on top of the tree-stump, in a halter-neck dress. The focus is soft and the feeling is innocent. The photo at right, of the same woman, was taken in late summer. In a more assertive pose, wearing a low-cut, light-colored dress that emphasizes her figure against the dark background, the model shows a rather different aspect of her personality. Obviously, a single shooting session is not enough to bring out all the possible facets of the model–photographer working relationship. Photos by Bob Clemens.

Glamour Photography

mination for glamour pictures. It is most enjoyable to work in settings that offer flattering, interesting light combined with an attractive physical setting such as trees, water, architectural details, or furniture.

Above all, do not expect the best results in just one session. An amateur model has to gain some experience in working for a photographer, and the photographer has to have time to see the model under working conditions. Both are partners in a picture-making experience, and the first shooting session—like a first date—is primarily a means of getting to know one another better. After that, there can be significant results.

Helping the Model

Rapport is a relationship marked by harmony, accord, or affinity; it is the key to a successful photographer/model collaboration. Without rapport, everything else—attractive model, the right clothes, fine equipment, appropriate setting and lighting—can be virtually wasted. Rapport is an elusive ingredient that must be present for a successful shooting session.

Rapport begins when both the photographer and the model *want* to produce good pictures, and are willing to cooperate and work hard to do so. Rapport develops and grows as the model and photographer gain mutual confidence in the other's intentions and abilities.

A warm sense of humor certainly helps set the emotional stage and seldom fails to relax a model. A photographer who is too somber or is taking either himself or the shooting session too seriously cannot expect to get the best from his model.

A model—especially an amateur—needs appreciation and reassurance. Compliments on how well things are going throughout the session, frequent remarks about how attractive he or she looks through the camera, and other attentive comments will please and relax the model. Freer, more spontaneous expressions and poses will result.

It helps the model a great deal to receive specific directions and suggestions, so he or she may know what is wanted in each picture. Most people who are likely to be chosen for glamour pictures probably have a latent ability to pose reasonably well, but they need direction, especially if they have not worked with the photographer before. The more the model understands just how he or she is going to be portrayed on film, the better the performance will be in front of the camera. Some ideas for directions are included in the section of hints on posing; more ideas are given in the article MODELS AND MODELING.

The photographer should enjoy the picture-making experience, and should make that obvious to the model. The feeling will be infectious, which will bring about better poses and better pictures.

Makeup

The use of makeup is especially important in photographs of women. Often, makeup can make the difference between a so-so picture of a woman and one that almost demands attention—and admiration. Never has there been a wider selection of makeups, colors, or possible "looks" that can be produced.

A cream or liquid base is first applied to the face, matched as nearly as possible with the model's natural skin color. To keep a smooth, natural look, do not powder over this base application.

A blusher is sparingly applied to the cheeks to shape and accent them, and to add a touch of color to the face.

Lips are outlined and lightly filled in with lipstick, using a lip brush. Avoid too thick an application; put on just a film of color. To add sheen to the lips, use lip gloss over the color.

Skin blemishes, lines, and dark areas under the eyes can be concealed or minimized with a lipstick-like cosmetic such as "Erace," by Max Factor. Use it over these areas before applying regular makeup. Most such products are available in a wide range of skin tones.

The eyes are the most important part of all. Start making up the eyes by outlining the upper lash line with an eyebrow pencil or with liquid eye liner. For a more dramatic effect, the bottom !ash line can be outlined, too. The upper lash line should be extended slightly beyond the outside edge of each eye, and curved upward slightly. Underlining tends to decrease the "openness" of the eyes, so work carefully.

Eyelashes are emphasized by using mascara, applying it twice to build the desired effect. A third application is made on the outer lashes to give a wide-open impression. False eyelashes can be used instead, if preferred.

The softness and luxury of fur is always flattering to a woman's face, and gives an especially appealing contrast to the high cheekbones and angular facial planes so highly prized for photographic modeling. Photo by Norman Mosallem for Editorial Photocolor Archives.

Glamour Photography

Eye shadow should be applied to the eyelid up to the crease, and then blended in with a brush or fingertip. A wide selection of colors is available; the choice will depend on the model's coloration, clothing, and the mood or feeling the photographer wishes to convey. White shadow can be used just under the eyebrows to highlight the eyes themselves.

The model should practice these techniques at home to gain experience and judgment. (*See:* MAKEUP.)

Hints on Posing and Apparel

Not every model has a perfect face or figure. When photographing women, try to pose them in a way that brings out their best features and at the same time minimizes any slight problem areas. There are relatively easy ways of doing this. Some of the following suggestions may be helpful.

> For a slenderizing effect, use full-length stretched-out poses.
>
> A fuller, more rounded-out appearance can be given to a slender woman by having her pose seated or in a curled-up position.
>
> The female figure generally looks more shapely when turned at an angle of 45 degrees to the lens axis. The model's feet should be gracefully pointed and one leg slightly bent at the knee.
>
> Shoes or boots with fairly high heels bring out the curves and flatter the legs.
>
> Sheer seamless hose give legs a smooth, finished look, especially with short skirts or shorts.
>
> If the model commonly wears panty hose, specify that she use a sheer-to-the-waist type so that the unsightly, darker reinforced area found in other styles will not show below short clothing.
>
> Good-looking legs look even better when the model wears a swimsuit, leotard, or body shirt that is cut high at the thighs. The resulting "leggy" look is very flattering and lends itself to a wide range of poses. Any garment (especially a swimsuit) that is cut too squarely in the legs tends to make a model's legs look shorter and heavier.
>
> Use the "stomach in, chest out" pose. Have the model draw in her stomach just before you are ready to take a picture. This is especially important when she is wearing a snug-fitting garment, bare-midriff clothing, or a bikini—also when she's in a sitting or reclining pose. Her waist will look slimmer, her stomach flatter, and her general appearance will be immensely improved.
>
> To help minimize a prominent nose, use a telephoto lens from a frontal position; avoid profile views.
>
> Corrective hair styling can solve the problem of a girl with a high or prominent forehead, particularly in close-up pictures. Bangs, or a style that brings the hair forward, can make a definite improvement. Sometimes a properly styled wig can be helpful.
>
> Keep a supply of straight pins, safety pins, and clothespins handy. They can be used to great advantage to remove gathers and wrinkles in loose-fitting clothing. Naturally, these accessories should be strategically placed so that they do not show in the pictures.
>
> Body makeup can be very helpful for touching up untanned areas of the body that show when various articles of clothing are worn by a model. It takes considerable skill and practice to be able to blend in the makeup so that it is not noticeable, especially when the area to be covered is extensive.

• *See also:* ADVERTISING PHOTOGRAPHY; BOUNCE LIGHT; FLASH PHOTOGRAPHY; MAKEUP; MODELS AND MODELING; PORTRAITURE; SOFT-FOCUS EFFECTS; THEATRICAL PHOTOGRAPHY; UMBRELLA LIGHTING.

Further Reading: Eisenstaedt, Alfred. *People.* New York, NY: Viking Press, 1973; Farber, Robert. *Images of Woman.* Garden City, NY: Amphoto, 1976; Ockenga, Starr. *Mirror After Mirror: Reflections on Woman.* Garden City, NY: Amphoto, 1975; Smith, J. Frederick. *Photographing Sensuality.* New York, NY: T.Y. Crowell, Inc., 1975; Yeager, Bunny. *Art of Glamour Photography.* Garden City, NY: Amphoto, 1962.

When the background is glass or a mirror, the most common means of eliminating reflections or glare is to change the camera angle, the subject position, or both. (Top) Flash aimed directly at the subject is reflected in the glass door behind her. (Bottom) Changing the subject position, the camera angle, and the flash angle to the side and above the subject eliminates unwanted reflections. Photos by John Menihan.

Glare and Reflection Control

Reflections are images seen or photographed in smooth, shiny surfaces. Unwanted reflections are images of things that are outside the camera field of view, but that show up in the scene because of a smooth, shiny surface in it.

Glare is also a visual and photographic effect. It is the spreading of light around a bright light source, or around the reflection of a light source. Glare interferes with vision because of bright light bouncing around in the eye. It can also interfere with the photographed image because of light bouncing around in the camera, and irradiation and halation in the film. Control of both effects is often necessary. Following are some of the methods used to control glare and unwanted reflections.

1. Change the camera angle so that the reflection of the unwanted glare does not enter the lens. This is the primary method of eliminating the image of the camera and photographer when the background is glass or a mirror. It also avoids the problem of on-camera flash causing a hot spot in a polished background.
2. Place black masking material so that the unwanted element is not "seen" by the reflective surface in the picture. Black cloth pinned to a crossbar on a light stand makes an easily positioned baffle.
3. Hide the camera behind black masking material so that it can be directed head-on to a reflective surface without being seen. The lens can poke through a slit in the material. This is a convenient way of photographing objects displayed in glass or plastic cases when the camera must be at a distance from the case wall.
4. Place the lens directly against a glass or plastic surface in order to photograph something on the other side.
5. Spray the reflective surface of the object with a dulling spray. Such sprays, available in art and theatrical-supply stores,

deposit a thin coat of wax on a shiny surface which eliminates specular (mirror-like) reflections by diffusing the light. The spray may easily be wiped from most surfaces when no longer required.

6. Diffuse the light by reflecting it from a white, dull surface, rather than aiming the light source directly at the subject.

7. Place the reflective object inside a "tent" of diffusing material, with the light sources outside; extend the camera lens through a small hole in one side. (*See:* TENT LIGHTING.)

8. Use a polarizer. Rotate the polarizer until the glare or reflection is minimized or eliminated. Place the polarizer in front of the lens with the same orientation. Reflections from polished metal surfaces cannot be eliminated in this way. Be sure to increase exposure to compensate for the eliminated light. (*See:* FILTERS.)

9. Use polarized light in combination with a polarizer. Two light sources, one at either side of the subject, equipped with polarizing screens are required. (A) Turn on one light and set its screen so the polarization is horizontal; a reference mark on most screens makes this easy to do. (B) Rotate the polarizer in front of the lens until the glare or reflection at the subject is eliminated or minimized. (C) Turn out the first light. Without changing the position of the lens polarizer, turn on the second light and rotate its screen until glare or reflection from the subject is eliminated. (D) Turn on both lights and make the exposure, with appropriate compensation. Reflections from polished metal surfaces can be controlled in this way.

• *See also:* COPYING; FILTERS; FLARE; POLARIZED-LIGHT PHOTOGRAPHY; TENT LIGHTING.

(Left) Glare and reflections on glass and other shiny surfaces can ruin a potentially good photograph. (Right) A polarizer in front of the camera lens will eliminate reflections from glass; while the polarizer will not affect glare from shiny metal, such as the chrome trim around the windshield, it will considerably improve the quality of the image.

Glare and Reflection Control

Because it has form without apparent substance, glass is generally represented photographically by its outline. Only through complete control of lighting is clear glass made visible to the camera's eye. Photo by Stephen Stuart.

Glass, Photographing

Glass, Photographing

Taking pictures of a glass object is like photographing an illusion. Glassware presents a challenge because it has form almost without photographic substance. Because it is transparent, glass itself is seldom seen. Instead, reflections, color, surface etching, or designs are seen. Shape, refracted light, the contents of a container also may be noticed, but you literally look and photograph through the glass itself. The visual aspects that can be seen provide the key to successfully photographing glass. The secret of making these aspects visible is the complete control of light. Drinking vessels, for example, perhaps the most common of transparent materials, can be portrayed clearly by lighting them in such a manner that they stand out as a dark-outlined shape against a light background, or as a light-outlined shape against a medium or dark background. These techniques of photographing glass are not fundamentally different, but rather variations of a basic silhouette method. They produce a finished illustration that matches closely the mental picture most people have when they think of clear glass objects.

There are two approaches to making pictures of glass containers and objects. One is to photograph the object itself as the main subject, using techniques that reveal its shape and transparency. The other is to use glass as an element in a decorative picture in which the modulation of light and color for visual effect is the main intention. This article describes some techniques for both approaches.

Photographing Glass Objects

Basic Requirements. The following are basic requirements for photographing glass objects:

1. A studio or shooting location that can be darkened completely.
2. View camera and lens equipped with a deep lens shade. (To minimize distortion, focal length should be longer than the diagonal measurement of the film size.) A 35 mm single-lens reflex camera can be used for making color slides, one of the most popular formats for decorative photographs. Whatever the camera, through-the-lens viewing and focusing is essential to observe the effects being created and to adjust composition.
3. Sturdy camera stand or studio tripod.
4. White and medium-gray seamless background paper.
5. Clear (water-white) sheet of plate-glass and assorted glass shelving.
6. Textured sheets of glass or plastic, clear and colored, for decorative pictures.
7. Strong colored filters or pieces of theatrical gelatin or plastic film to color the light thrown on the subject.
8. Sawhorses and wood blocks to support glass working surfaces.
9. Studio lights, including spots and mini-spots, *all* with barn doors.
10. Moderate-speed film.

Basic Setup. Hang white, seamless background paper from a high (10- or 12-foot) horizontal support and curve it forward on the floor so that it is underneath the entire area containing the setup. Place two sawhorses on the forward part of the background paper, spaced to support the edges of a large sheet of plate glass. This provides a transparent worktable through which bounce light from the background paper behind and below the subject will pass. Strips of paper, other than white, can be attached to the background (out of camera range) to produce edge effects in the glass.

The camera angle, or height of the camera, will vary with the subject. Since glassware is essentially three-dimensional, showing the ellipse, or oval, of the rim will add depth and roundness to the finished photograph.

Most camera exposures will be rather long because reflected light from the background is normally the sole source of illumination. Because of the length of the exposure, proper camera equipment and a *sturdy* camera stand are a necessity to prevent movement.

It is also advisable to have a working area that can be darkened *completely*. A ceiling light fixture, an exit sign, or even a crack around a doorway have all been known to cause annoying reflections. Not eliminating these sources of unwanted reflections can result in a great deal of wasted time and effort.

(Left) Because glass is seen mainly as an outline, it is generally portrayed either as a dark-outlined shape against a light background, or as a light-outlined shape against a dark background. Use of carefully controlled lighting combines the two means of portrayal in this sophisticated image. (Above) In a different approach, the shape of the glass is defined by its contents. Photos by Viles Studio Inc. for Editorial Photocolor Archives.

Specular highlights which add depth and form, as well as sparkle, to clear glass, are obtained through use of front lighting. The technique required for this effect must be handled with great care and control. Photo by Stephen Stuart.

Glass, Photographing

A basic setup for photographing glass consists of white, seamless paper curved from wall to floor as a background, and a large sheet of plate glass mounted on sawhorses as a working surface. Strips of paper in colors other than white may be attached to the background for producing edge effects in the glass.

Lighting is largely a matter of personal taste; it can be described best by referring to photographs. The accompanying illustrations show variations of the basic silhouette treatment of lighting. They were executed for a color assignment. The vessels were filled with colored water, but the lighting technique would be similar if the vessels were empty. By studying these photographs and the lighting diagrams with them, it is easy to see the infinite variety of effects that can be obtained by simply changing or redirecting the bounce light from the background.

Controlling Flare. There are no hard-and-fast rules for the placement of lights in this type of photography. The lights should be handled, as the subject matter: *with care.* Changing the angle of a beam of light by a fraction of an inch can change the lighting effect drastically and, at the same time, can create some serious flare problems. In the case of the accompanying illustrations, a great deal of reflection from the background is present. Uncontrolled, this reflection causes lens flare and in turn flat negatives.

An easy way to control lens flare is to construct a black hood to extend from the lens board to the subject, just outside the angle of view. Focusing cloths or black felt draped over wood dowels do a good job in controlling flare.

Lens flare may be easily controlled by building a framework extending from the lens board to the subject, and draping it with black material.

Glass, Photographing

With the main light aimed low against a white backdrop and a secondary light aimed directly at a gray backdrop, a shaded white-to-gray background effect is produced. Bounced light from the white backdrop is transmitted through the liquid in the glass.

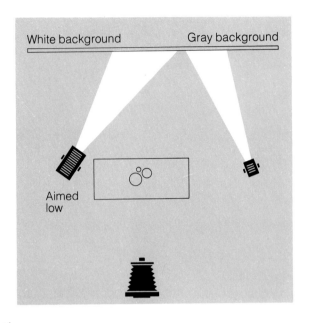

A gray card hung at approximately subject level provides darker gray for the liquid color; a black card hung directly above the subject adds an edge effect to outline the glass.

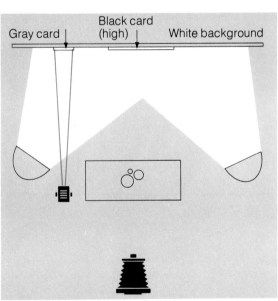

Glass, Photographing

A black background effect is produced by using a dark gray backdrop. A white card lighted from below and above adds the white edge effect. The square shape of the gray card hung at left, when transmitted through glass, adds volume to the rounded objects.

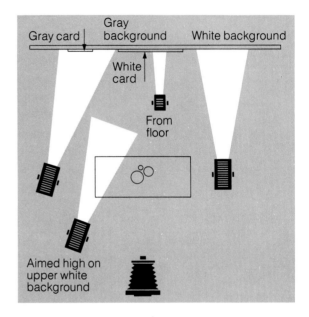

When a particular lighting technique does not create excessive bounce from the background, a normal lens hood may be sufficient to control flare.

Adding Sparkle. If a true silhouette is desired, all light must be shielded from the front and sides of the subject, as was done by lamp position in the setup shown in the accompanying photograph. Should some highlights be desired to create more sparkle in plain or thin glassware, front bounce light from a narrow, diffuse source is advisable. A simple way to improvise such a source is to clip a sheet of mounting board to one barn door of a flood lamp and control the width of the slit of light emitted by the opposite barn door. This light can be placed on either side of the camera, about lens height or higher, with the bounce light from the cardboard striking the subject. When the subject is a cylindrical object, two specular highlights will result from this technique, one from the front surface and the second from the rear. The spacing between the highlights is easily controlled by moving the light either closer to or farther from the lens axis.

Placing the lights behind the subject and letting no light strike it directly, will produce a true glass silhouette. Only reflected light from behind hits the subject.

Glass, Photographing

Adding frontlight to glass should be done with caution. Front or side specular highlights can add depth and form, as well as sparkle, but if the subject is etched glass, be sure such highlights do not obliterate the etched design. Each piece of glass should be examined carefully to determine if any frontlight is desirable.

Exposure and Contrast Control. Most photographers find the "highlight method" of making an exposure-meter reading the most successful. Many meters have a "highlight with detail" setting. If not, simply take a normal reading from the background and expose for four times the indicated amount.

A shorter-than-average developing time is normal for black-and-white glass photography because the lighting ratio is often rather great; burned-out

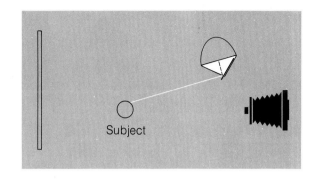

To obtain highlights for greater sparkle, a sheet of mounting board is clipped to one barn door of a floodlamp, creating a very narrow light source. The small beam of light striking the front of the subject is diffused by bouncing it from the mounting board.

Three silhouetted brandy snifters make an interesting repetition of the same shape in three different sizes. As the diagram illustrates, a clear spotlight and a red-filtered spotlight behind two sheets of fluted glass and a sheet of opal glass created the textured peppermint-stripe background. There was no direct light on the glassware. Photo by Frank Pallo.

Glass, Photographing

highlights (with the exception of an occasional specular highlight) should be avoided. The density range of the negatives should, of course, be adjusted to the enlarging equipment.

Decorative Photographs of Glass

A dealer in glass, plastics, or building materials can supply a wide variety of textured surfaces to be used as backgrounds for decorative glass pictures. Of these, the fluted, ribbed, hammered, pebbled, and dimpled surfaces offer the most variety for unusual glassware pictures. The accompanying diagram shows a basic way to use them.

There are a number of ways to add color to the lighting setup. For example, use glassware that is color-tinted, insert colored cards in the background, place colored cellophane or plastic filters in front of the light, or use colored filters over the camera lens. Of these methods, using colored filters over the light source will probably be most versatile.

Decorative Lighting. Because the pieces of glassware reflect as well as transmit light, it is essential to first turn off all the room lights. In order to avoid merging the objects with the background, arrange them and/or the lights so that a definite outline is created. This is usually accomplished by aiming the main spotlight at the background from a high or low angle. It is necessary to experiment until the right effect is obtained.

The worst mistake, with any kind of glassware, is to aim the light directly at the glass objects. Generally speaking, no direct light should be used at all.

To create a definite outline of the pieces of glassware, the main spotlight should be aimed at the background from a high or low angle. (Above, left and right) A spotlight provides an eye-catching circle of light behind the subject. (Below) This watery effect was created by taping small patches of colored cellophane to the back of a sheet of translucent glass. Only the champagne glass itself was in front of the background. Illumination was from a single clear spotlight directed at the background. Photos by Frank Pallo.

1232

A wooden box can be made to store sheets of background glass. It also holds them in place for shooting pictures. A slide projector and a 150-watt floodlight supply the illumination.

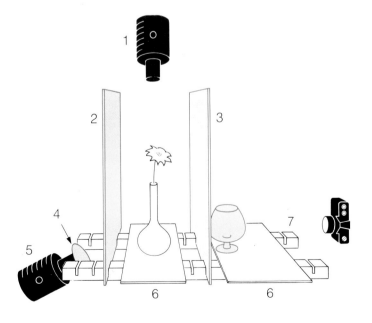

Rather, the background should be lighted, and the glass arranged in front of it.

If a spotlight has a variable-beam adjustment, try increasing and reducing the size of the beam. Also, raise and lower the light. These same suggestions apply whether the arrangement is placed in front of a wall, a piece of cardboard, a seamless paper background, or a textured-glass background. The only difference is in the placement of the main light. In the first three instances, it is aimed at the background from in front of the subject. In the last instance, the textured glass is illuminated from the rear.

To use textured-glass backgrounds, get various pieces cut to the same size in order to fit them into a wooden rack, like the one shown in the accompanying illustration. This rack serves as both a background holder and a storage box. A convenient size for use with small glass pieces is .19 square metre (2 square feet) and 20 centimetres (8 inches) deep.

The exposure can be determined by taking a reading from a reflected-light meter at the camera position. However, because the color-saturation effect can vary with different exposures, it is always a good idea to make several exposures at different lens openings or shutter speeds.

A Tabletop Setup. Using a tabletop setup similar to the one shown in the accompanying illustration is a very versatile way to achieve a variety of lighting and subject arrangements. The opal glass is necessary for all of the pictures made with this setup; the use of textured glass is optional, depending on the effect you desire.

Tabletop Setup for Photographing Glassware.
(1) Spotlight with snoot; (2) 2'×2' opal glass;
(3) 2'×2' textured glass; (4) Color filter; (5)
Spotlight with snoot; (6) Plastic or opal-glass
shelves; (7) 2"×2" hardwood, grooves cut 1¼"
deep for holding glass. Grooves are spaced 1"
apart and are alternately ⅛" and ¼" wide to
accommodate different thicknesses of glass.

(Above and right) The sparkle and light-refracting qualities of glass are shown to best advantage by these interesting photographs made with a combination of overhead light and movement. Photos by Viles Studio Inc. for Editorial Photocolor Archives. (Left) Lighting alone delineates the forms of these small crystal statuettes in this classically high-key photograph. Photo by Stephen Stuart, Ad Team, Inc.

Glass, Photographing

Glass, Photographing

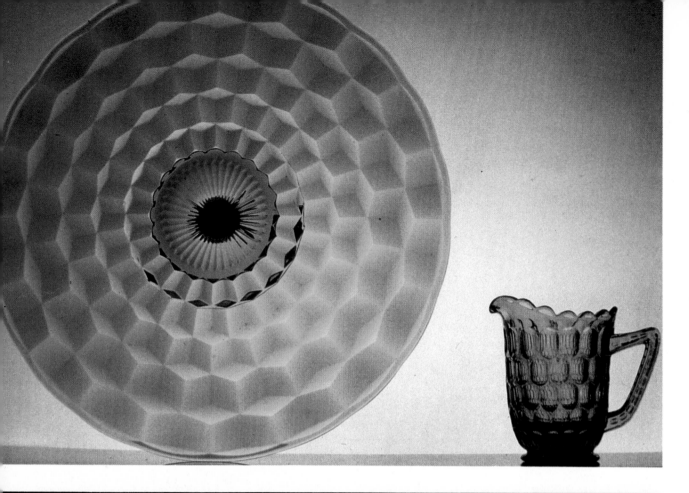

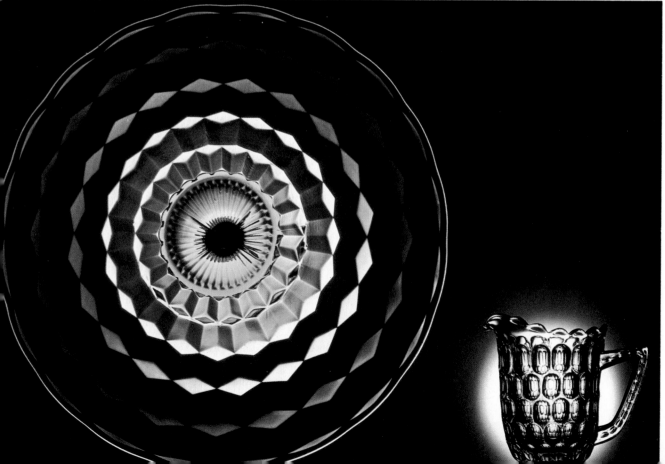

◄ *The same subject illuminated (left) with photolamp and (below left) with two spotlights illustrates the considerably different effects achieved with the two different types of lighting. Photos by Frank Pallo.*

For lighting, spotlights are better than floodlights. The concentration of light from a spotlight is essential for creating good highlight and shadow effects, and for producing halo effects with all types of glassware. The accompanying photographs show the dramatic difference between floodlight and spotlight illumination. When arranging lights, as well as when taking the picture, turn off all the other lights in the room.

Arrange the setup so that the front side is near the edge of a table. This will permit placing the camera in the best position for attaining good composition and lighting effects. For most glassware pictures, use a low camera angle, with the lens almost level with the opal-glass shelf. The low angle de-emphasizes the separation between the shelf and the background, and helps emphasize the size and shape of the objects being photographed.

A big advantage of this setup is that it offers the opportunity of lighting solid objects that are placed behind the textured glass. Although the tabletop diagram shows a spotlight above the subject being photographed (as well as another spotlight behind the opal glass), it is often necessary to aim the light from the side of the setup rather than from above it. For example, in the accompanying photograph of the lily in the vase, because the stem of the day lily in a dark vase was curved, the flower was lighted from the side. With subjects like this, make sure that the beam of light does not spill onto the textured or opal glass. If it does, there will be a flare effect similar to that produced by aiming the camera into the sun.

Backgrounds. Textured glass is available in many designs and can be cut to practically any size. A sheet of glass .19 square metre (2 square feet) is ideal for many objects. The square format is especially desirable with fluted or ribbed glass, because the pattern can be oriented vertically or horizontally for different effects and still cover the same area.

Some of the textures are quite coarse, and therefore more suitable for backgrounds. Others are fine

Because the stem of the lily was curved, sidelighting was necessary to bring out the form of the flower. With such lighting, care must be taken not to allow the light to "spill" onto the textured or opal glass; if it does, flare will ruin the image. Photo by Frank Pallo.

enough to place in front of objects for an etched effect. The first picture in the accompanying series shows the result of placing wine glasses and a wine bottle in front of the opal-glass background. The remaining pictures in the series were made by positioning glass of various textures between the wine glasses and the wine bottle.

For the first photo in this series (above), the wine glasses and carafe were positioned in front of the opal-glass background. All the other photos were made with various types of textured glass placed between the glasses and the carafe. Photos by Frank Pallo.

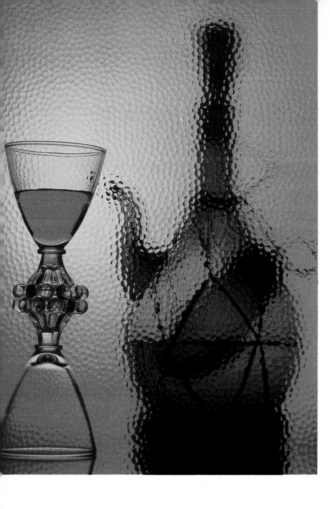

(Left) A decorative grid has various colored filters taped to the openings. (Below) A gradual blending of the colors in the grid is obtained by moving the grid closer to the light source. (Right and below right) Two versions of the same arrangement: the photo at right was made with the multicolored grid in back of the opal glass. Photos by Frank Pallo.

Many photographs will show objects in their natural color against a plain or textured background. This is especially true if the glassware or liquid in the glassware provides the color. To get more color, place colored plastic or glass filters over the light source. For a multicolored background, purchase a decorative grid from a local building supplier, hardware store, or upholstery shop. Then tape various colored filters over the openings. These grids are usually made of plywood 3 millimetres (⅛ inch) thick and are used to decorate room dividers, hi-fi speaker cabinets, and so forth.

Tape the filters to the grid at random, or select a combination of colors that would be particularly effective for a specific subject. In either case, position the grid between the background light and the opal glass. For a brilliantly colorful abstract effect, place the grid close to the opal glass. For a more gradual blending of colors, move the grid closer to the light source.

• *See also:* BLACK-LIGHT PHOTOGRAPHY; LIGHTING; PRODUCT PHOTOGRAPHY.

Glass, Photographing

Glycerin

Glycerol; glycyl alcohol; 1, 2, 3-propanetriol; propenyl alcohol

Glycerin is very hygroscopic; it absorbs atmospheric moisture readily. At one time this quality led to its being used as an ingredient of emulsions that kept them flexible, and permeable by processing solutions. Today it is the primary ingredient of print-flattening solutions because it keeps the moisture content of an emulsion relatively constant—the emulsion does not expand and contract with changes in humidity.

Glycerin is used to prepare collotype plates prior to inking. It may be used for controlled or selective development of platinum prints (see the article PLATINUM PRINT PROCESS). "Liquid gate," or glycerin-sandwich negative carriers are used to suppress or eliminate scratches in optical printing and enlarging. The negative is sandwiched between pieces of glass coated with glycerin; the glycerin fills in surface scratches to equalize their refractive index with the undamaged portions of the film.

Formula: $CH_2OH \cdot CHOH \cdot CH_2OH$
Molecular Weight: 92.09

Clear, syrupy, colorless liquid; mixes freely with water and alcohol.

• *See also:* COLLOTYPE; PLATINUM PRINT PROCESS.

Glycin

Parahydroxyphenyl aminoacetic acid, parahydroxyphenyl glycine, Athenon (a discontinued trademark of Eastman Kodak Company)

A developer that produces brown tones on papers. It was formerly believed to produce fine-grain images on films, but actually had little advantage in this direction; it was, however, used in fine-grain formulas in combination with paraphenylene diamine.

Formula: $(C_6H_4OH)(NH \cdot CH_2COOH)$
Molecular Weight: 167.16

Whitish gray powder, slightly soluble in water, very soluble in sodium sulfite solutions or alkaline solutions.

CAUTION: Photographic glycin must not be confused with medicinal glycine; the former is a parahydroxyphenyl derivative of the latter, and is highly poisonous.

Godowsky, Leopold

(Born 1902)
American musician; co-inventor of Kodachrome film

Leopold Godowsky's interest in color photography began during his high-school years. With fellow musician Leopold Mannes, he invented a method of color photography using a three-lens camera equipped with red, green, and blue filters that made black-and-white color separation records. These images were projected through filters of the same colors to create an additive color image.

While studying physics and chemistry at the University of California—and while simultaneously holding positions in the violin sections of the Los Angeles and the San Francisco symphony orchestras—he collaborated with Mannes (who was studying physics and musicology at Harvard University) to produce an additive color motion-picture process. A public demonstration of the process in 1921 did not lead to commercial success.

During the 1920s, Godowsky and Mannes worked in New York City to perfect a color photographic system, supporting their research with employment as classical musicians. In 1922, their work attracted the attention of Dr. C. E. K. Mees, director of Kodak Research Laboratories, who arranged for them to obtain supplies and special materials at cost. At the same time they secured some financial support from private investors. Their work concentrated on subtractive color processes, using plates with two (rather than three) emulsion layers to limit the complexity of experimentation. They obtained a number of patents for key developments in their work.

In 1930, Godowsky and Mannes joined the staff of Kodak Research Laboratories in Rochester, N.Y. Leading a team of Kodak research scientists, they produced an improved two-layer color film for which marketing plans were made. But their rapid progress beyond that point produced a far superior three-layer reversal color film. It was introduced as Kodachrome 16 mm motion-picture film in April 1935, and as 35 mm and size 828 (8 exposures, 28 × 40 mm) still films in August 1936.

The three emulsion layers individually produced blue, green, and red negative silver-image records that were reversal-processed into corresponding yellow, magenta, and cyan positive dye images. Development in the original Mannes and Godowsky process was accomplished by controlled diffusion of dye-forming developers to the individual layers. The film characteristics and processing procedures have been refined and improved several times by Kodak scientists in the subsequent decades.

Because of the quality of the dyes as well as the thinness of the emulsion—the three layers have a total thickness that is little more than that of a conventional black-and-white single-layer film—Kodachrome film images are characterized by color brilliance coupled with sharpness and fine grain. As a result, Kodachrome film has remained the most widely used color transparency film for more than 40 years.

Godowsky and Mannes carried out further research at the Kodak Research Laboratories during the latter 1930s. Mannes later became head of the music school founded by his family in New York City. Godowsky continued independent research in color photography in New York and Connecticut on a contractual basis with Eastman Kodak Company.
• *See also:* ADDITIVE COLOR SYNTHESIS; COLOR FILMS; COLOR THEORY; *KODACHROME* FILM; MANNES, LEOPOLD; SUBTRACTIVE COLOR SYNTHESIS.

Goerz, Carl Paul

(1854–1923)
German optician and manufacturer

Goerz founded C. P. Goerz AG in Berlin in 1886. There he manufactured an extensive line of cameras and lenses, including such noted items as the Goerz Double Anastigmat (later named Dagor), which was designed by Emil von Hoegh, and the

Wide-Angle Hypergon. The company was eventually merged into the Zeiss-Ikon cartel. A semi-autonomous branch factory existed in New York for many years, and its products are marked "C. P. Goerz—New York."

Gold Chloride

Gold trichloride, chlorauric acid

A metallic salt, used in toning baths to produce, in various formulations, brown, red, or blue tones on photographic papers.
Formula: $AuCl_3 \cdot HCl \cdot 3H_2O$
Molecular Weight: 394.09

Golden yellow crystalline powder. It is very hygroscopic and can dissolve in its own absorbed water; hence it is usually sold in sealed glass tubes. To prepare the solution, the tube is broken under water, and agitated to transfer all the chemical to the liquid. Since the chemical is approximately 50 percent gold by weight, it is quite expensive.

GOST Speeds

GOST Speeds refer to the film-speed system used in Eastern Europe and the Soviet Union; it gets its name from Gosudarstvenny J. Standart, which is the national standards organization of the USSR. The system is basically similar to the ASA/BSI system, although it is based on a different exposure/density point and a different multiplier. The final scale of numbers is close to those of the ASA/BSI arithmetic systems and usually may be used interchangeably with the latter.
• *See also:* ANSI; ASA, ASAP SPEEDS; BSI SPEEDS; DIN SPEEDS; SENSITOMETRY; SPEED SYSTEMS.

Gradation

In a picture area, the gradual, continuous change in value or density, or in color is referred to as gradation. There is no gradation in an even-tone area.

Gradation is related to contrast; when it is steep (a rapid change in a short distance), the visual contrast is high. When it is less steep, the visual contrast is low or soft. Printing a negative on a high-contrast paper increases the gradation in the print, while printing on a low-contrast paper lowers it.
• *See also:* CONTRAST; GAMMA.

Graininess and Granularity

The terms "graininess" and "granularity" are used throughout photographic literature. One of these characteristics can determine the success or failure of a photographic product in a particular application, while the other can affect the perception of the quality of the results.

Graininess is the subjective sensation of a random pattern apparent to a viewer seeing small local density variations in an overall uniform density area when the image is enlarged.

Granularity is the mathematical expression of an objective measurement, made with a densitometer having a small aperture, of the local density variations that give rise to the sensation of graininess.

The most widely used photographic processes depend upon the light sensitivity of the silver halide crystal. Usually, only a few silver ions in each exposed crystal are altered by light during exposure. By means of development, however, the photographic process achieves an enormous amplification of the effects of light. As a consequence of this image-forming process, a photographic image is made up of discrete particles of silver. Even in color processes (where the silver is removed after it has served its light-capturing function), the dyes form "dye clouds" centered on the sites of developed silver grains.

The granular structure of the image is of no concern when the eyes do not resolve the pattern. It is when the structure is enlarged, projected, or otherwise viewed with sufficient magnification that the visual sensation called graininess is experienced.

Randomness of Silver Halide Crystals

Most photographic materials consist of silver halide crystals dispersed in gelatin and coated in

A segment of photographic emulsion is represented here by a model with spheres (grains) of various sizes filling the volume. This model has been used by scientists investigating graininess and its measurement.

thin layers on a support. The crystals vary in size, shape, and sensitivity, and generally they are randomly distributed (see the accompanying illustration). Not all of the crystals in an area that receives uniform exposure *are* made developable. The locations of those crystals that are developable are also random. In the photographic process, those crystals that are sufficiently exposed by light are reduced to metallic silver by development. Development usually does not change the position of the grain, so the image in a uniformly exposed area is a random distribution of opaque silver particles, separated by the transmitting gelatin matrix (see the accompanying illustration).

The fact that a granular pattern is seen does not mean that the eye can resolve the individual silver particles. Such particles range from about 2 micrometres ($\frac{2}{1000}$ of a millimetre) down to about one-tenth that size. At normal viewing distance (25 to 35 centimetres), the eye can just distinguish a particle in the order of a 0.05-millimetre diameter.

When a photographic image is viewed at moderate magnification—say 2.5 times enlargement from the original—there usually is no appearance of grain structure because the eye does not see the pattern at such low magnification. At 20 times enlargement, however, the granular structure becomes apparent, even in materials with relatively fine grain. Enlarge-

Graininess and Granularity

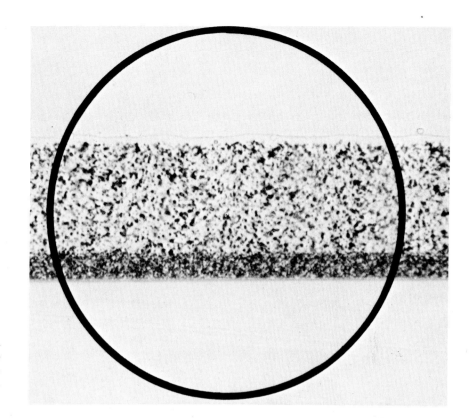

Grains of silver halide are randomly distributed in the emulsion when it is made. This cross-section of a raw emulsion shows silver-halide crystals in two layers.

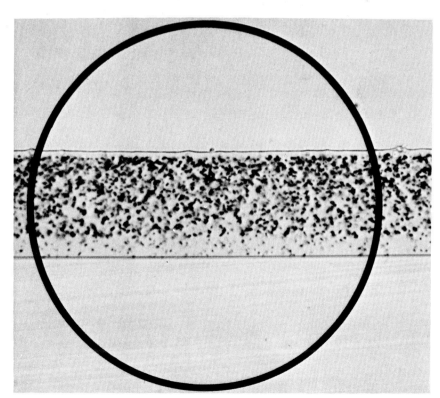

Silver is developed or clouds of dye formed at the sites occupied by the exposed silver halide. Contrary to widely held opinion, there is little migration or physical joining of individual grains. Compare the distribution of silver particles in this cross section with the undeveloped silver halide above.

Graininess and Granularity

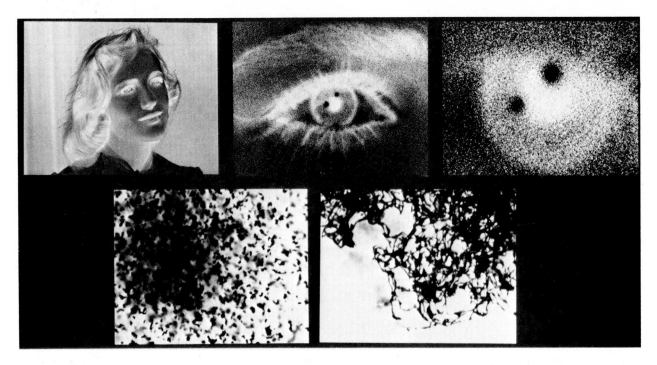

Top row: (Left) a 2.5X enlargement of a negative shows no apparent graininess. (Center) At 20X, some graininess shows. (Right) When a segment of the negative is inspected at 60X, the individual silver grains start to become distinguishable. Bottom row: (Left) With 400X magnification, the discrete grains are easily seen. Note that surface grains are in focus while grains deeper in the emulsion are out of focus. The apparent "clumping" of silver grains is actually caused by the overlap of grains at different depths when viewed in two-dimensional projection. (Right) The makeup of individual grains takes different forms. This filamentary silver, enlarged by an electron microscope, appears as a single opaque grain at lower magnification.

ment to 200 times or greater is really required before the individual grains of silver that usually blend to produce the sensation of graininess can be seen. This relationship of magnification to the appearance of graininess is shown graphically in the accompanying illustration.

The Necessity for Randomness. Without randomness, the sensation of graininess does not occur. For example, if many small particles are arranged in a regular pattern, such as that of the halftone dot pattern used in graphic arts, an observer does not have a sensation of graininess. If the observer views a halftone at a magnification sufficient to resolve the dots, the regular pattern will be seen and recognized as such. This is shown in the accompanying figure. With lower magnification—at which the observer can no longer resolve the individual dots—the dot pattern ceases, and the observer sees only a uniform area.

On the other hand, the observer viewing a random pattern of small spots with a magnification such that he or she resolves the ultimate small spots cannot recognize any orderly or intelligible image. As the magnification is decreased, the tiny spots do not disappear. Instead, because they are randomly located, the observer associates them in random groups. The groups, which are often called clumps, become the new units of graininess, as shown in the accompanying illustration. Because of their random character, a few spots located by chance relatively close to each other appear as a dense unit. Close by, another area that, again by chance, has fewer than the average number of opaque spots will be seen as a less dense unit.

This process of association of random groupings continues as magnification decreases. The observer progressively associates groups of spots as new units of graininess. The size of these groups gets larger and larger as the magnification decreases, but the difference in density between the darker and the lighter areas becomes less and less. Finally, the difference becomes so small that the observer is not sensitive to it, and he or she says that the area is uniform.

The clumps, or groups, of silver particles are not formed by movement of the silver in the gelatin. When the emulsion is made, the silver halide crystals are scattered throughout the emulsion, and the developed grains are located where the crystals were. The randomness is not an even distribution, but can be shown statistically. For this reason, it can be said that graininess is caused by statistical clumping of the silver grains.

Measurement of Granularity

The attributes of the photographic image that cause the human visual system to perceive graininess can be measured and interpreted by an electro-optical system, and this is the basis of the granularity measurement used for many products. To provide a numerical value that correlates with the visual impression of graininess, scientists analyze the image structure with a *microdensitometer* and some statistical tools.

The Microdensitometer. Ordinary densitometers measure density over an area that is very large compared with the size of individual silver particles. If the densitometer is used to read several positions on a uniformly exposed and developed photographic material, the density value will be essentially constant. Small variations in the number of particles measured will not affect the reading, since there are so many particles in the aperture. When the aperture of the densitometer is reduced in size, however, fewer particles are measured and a small change in the number of particles therefore causes the densitometer to show varying values of density. Analysis of the magnitude of these variations of density recorded with the small aperture of a microdensitometer can give a statistical measure of the granularity of a sample.

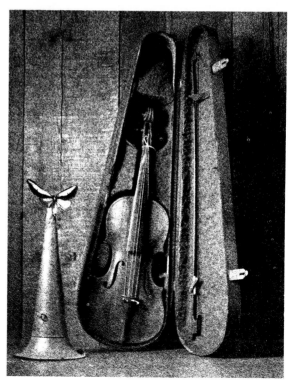

(Above right) If the uniform dot pattern of a conventional halftone is used to reproduce a scene, the eye accepts the image as a smooth, continuous-tone rendition. This is because the dots are regularly spaced. (Right) When the halftone dots are distributed randomly in an area to reproduce a scene, the image looks grainy.

Graininess and Granularity

The aperture of the microdensitometer is selected to give meaningful readings, or values, with the widest range of film samples. The measurement actually derived from the microdensitometer sampling is dependent, of course, on the size of the aperture.

With granularity measurements of uniformly exposed and processed coatings of silver particles, there is a correlation between the aperture size of the recording microdensitometer and the graininess apparent when the sample is viewed at certain magnifications. Higher magnification makes the sample look more grainy. Correspondingly, a higher value for granularity is recorded when the sample is measured with a small aperture.

In practice, the instrument is not used to sample discrete areas, nor does the operator take individual readings for calculation. Instead, an area of apparently uniform density is continuously scanned by the aperture. The transmitted light is imaged on a photosensitive pickup, and the current produced is then fed (through suitable electronic circuitry) to a meter that is calibrated to read the standard deviation of the random density fluctuations (see the accompanying illustration.)

The signal from a continuous density-scan of a grainy emulsion appears the same as random electrical noise when displayed on an oscilloscope. The rms voltmeter gives a direct readout of "noise level."

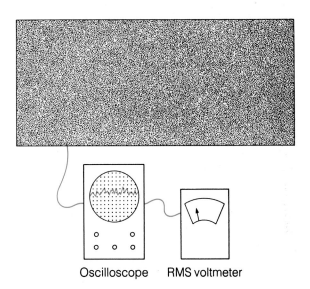

Oscilloscope   RMS voltmeter

Standard Deviation. Standard deviation is a statistician's term used to describe the variations of a group of samples about their average. In this case, it is used to describe the variations in density found when the grainy material is scanned with a small aperture. A term now generally used to designate the quantity is "root-mean-square (rms) granularity." The standard deviation and root-mean-square of the variations are actually different terms for the same quantity. The quantity derived from this analysis usually correlates well with the subjective observation, graininess.

When the standard deviation of density, or rms granularity, is recorded, it is a small decimal number. For ease in comparing numbers, the standard deviation is multiplied by a factor of 1000. This yields a small whole number, typically between 5 and 50.

Diffuse rms Granularity

Because a microdensitometer measures only a very small spot on a photographic material, and the mechanism of projecting and collecting a light beam in the instrument produces semi-specular, rather than diffuse, light, the microdensity reading is different from that recorded with a standard diffuse densitometer. Therefore, a correction must be introduced in the granularity measurement so that it will correlate with diffuse density readings.

Some film information includes only a descriptive phrase for graininess. These graininess descriptors are assigned according to classifications based on measured granularity values. The graininess classifications are:

Diffuse rms Granularity Value	Graininess Classification
45, 50, 55	Very Coarse
33, 36, 39, 42	Coarse
26, 28, 30	Moderately Coarse
21, 22, 24	Medium
16, 17, 18, 19, 20	Fine
11, 12, 13, 14, 15	Very Fine
6, 7, 8, 9, 10	Extremely Fine
less than 5, 5	Micro Fine

1248

No attempt is made to have separate classifications for different areas of application for films such as amateur, professional, aerial, or microfilming. Thus, films within such a category usually do not have a range of graininess classifications from coarse to fine. The differences of films within one category, for instance, might be covered completely by the terms fine, very fine, and extremely fine. Another category might include only films classified as medium, moderately coarse, and coarse.

Color Graininess and Granularity

It is generally recognized that most color materials do, indeed, exhibit a grain structure. This is due to the formation of the dye image from the original silver halide grains. Even though a complicated sequence of chemical reactions is initiated by the reduction of these silver halide crystals to produce dye images, the necessary conditions for graininess are usually not disturbed. That is, the fundamental small units of the colored dye image are still numerous and randomly distributed. So graininess persists.

After the color-forming process is complete, the silver is removed. The dye usually forms semitransparent clouds with centers at the silver sites. The clouds become less dense, and then disappear, a short distance from the central sites. In practice, these dye clouds vary in size, uniformity, transparency, and density distribution. They do, however, give rise to a sensation of graininess similar to that perceived in black-and-white materials. So it is possible to measure the granularity of color materials and assign a granularity value. However, the microdensitometer must see the color films as the eye sees them.

It might be expected that a photographic image made up of cyan, magenta, and yellow dye particles would appear more grainy than the corresponding silver image because of color contrast. In fact, the eye does not distinguish color in very small detail close to the resolution limit of the eye. It sees only brightness differences. Graininess of color materials, at least at the threshold limit, depends primarily upon the luminosity contribution of the separate dye layers. The magenta dye layer contributes most to the appearance of graininess. This occurs because the magenta dye absorbs the green light to which the eye is most sensitive. The yellow dye layer, on the

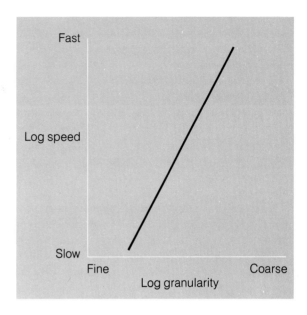

As the speed of a photographic material increases, so generally does the granularity.

other hand, contributes very little to the perception of graininess in a color material. For these reasons, measurements of granularity in color materials must be made with a carefully controlled and filtered light source in order to record values that correlate with the visual perception of graininess in the samples.

Some Practical Effects of Graininess

With the trend to smaller and smaller film formats has come the need for greater and greater enlargement. This is true both for prints from negatives and for projected movies or transparencies. With this requirement for great enlargement has come a renewed awareness of the granular structure of films.

The photographer wants a fine-grain film, but not at the expense of sensitivity or film speed. Unfortunately, faster films usually have larger grains. In a fast film with large silver halide crystals, these crystals have a greater probability of being made developable. The larger silver halide crystals normally develop to larger particles of metallic silver. The selection of a film is usually a compromise between available speed and tolerable grain (see the illustration on the preceding page).

The pursuit of more favorable speed-grain ratios is a constant concern of photographic researchers. The relationship of emulsion speed to the grain structure is of practical concern to the photographer. It is of vital importance to the scientist who uses photography. The speed-grain relationship indicates whether or not the photographic material will detect radiation, and if it is detected, whether or not it will form an image that can be recognized.

Graininess and granularity depend primarily upon the grain size, or the range of grain sizes, built into the film by the manufacturer. However, the effective graininess of most negative films is significantly increased by overexposure (and subsequent normal development), by extended development, or by the use of highly active, high-contrast developers. So to get a fine-grain negative, you must start with a film having inherently fine grain. Normal development of a fine-grain film will yield a more satisfactory negative than the attempt to modify the grain structure of a comparatively coarse-grain film with a special-purpose solvent developer. While the graininess of the coarse-grain film may be reduced with the solvent developer, this is usually at the expense of film speed and image sharpness.

Developers formulated to yield moderate contrast with normal development times and having low-to-medium activity will preserve the inherent grain characteristics of a film without suppressing film speed. High-energy developers that produce high contrast can significantly increase the granularity of a film. So also will the granularity increase with overdevelopment, which usually increases contrast.

Printing a grainy negative can further increase the appearance of graininess in the image, although the fine grain of the positive material does not usually contribute to the effect. The change in graininess is caused by the contrast index of the print material. In the print, the coarser grains of the negative ap-

The differences of grain in segments of three prints made from a fine, a medium, and a coarse-grain negative are evident in these enlargements.

pear as associated groups of the finer grains in the print material. Graininess increases whenever the contrast index of the print material is greater than unity; the more it exceeds unity, the greater the increase.

When a motion-picture film is seen at great magnification (as from a front-row theater seat), the viewer may be aware of graininess in the form of "boiling" in the image. The sensation that is caused by the frame-to-frame change of grain position is one of grains "crawling" or "boiling" all over the uniform areas of the image. Graininess is most noticeable in projected motion pictures, or projected transparencies, at a critical density level. The critical diffuse density is about 0.9 for color and 0.6 for black-and-white.

• *See also:* CONTRAST; CONTRAST INDEX; DENSITOMETRY; DEVELOPERS AND DEVELOPING; DEVELOPMENT; IMAGE EFFECTS.

Further Reading: Baines, H. *The Science of Photography,* 3rd ed. London, England: Fountain Press, 1969; Fritsche, Kurt. *Faults in Photography: Causes and Correctives.* Garden City, NY: Amphoto, 1968; Horenstein, Henry. *Beyond Basic Photography.* New York, NY: Little, Brown and Co., 1977; Katz, Jerome and Sidney J. Fogel. *Photographic Analysis: A Textbook of Photographic Science.* Hastings-on-the-Hudson, NY: Morgan and Morgan, Inc., 1971; Neblette, C.B. *Fundamentals of Photography.* New York, NY: Van Nostrand Reinhold Co., 1970.

Graphic Arts Photography

Photomechanical processes used in the graphic arts trades include letterpress, lithography, gravure, flexography and serigraphy, or silk-screen process. All the photomechanical processes except gravure have one thing in common—they are "go or no-go" processes. That is, a printing plate either deposits ink on paper or it does not. There is no way to make it print partial amounts of ink. Thus, a basic printing plate (except for gravure), like a stick of type, prints either black (or full color) or white (no ink). The gravure process is an intaglio process. That is, the ink is held in small depressions in the printing plate before its transfer to the paper. The depths of the depressions vary—deep depressions hold more ink than shallow ones. In the gravure process, light and midtones are achieved with partial amounts of ink.

The original processes were direct processes. That is, the paper was pressed directly against the printing plate to receive the ink. Both letterpress and lithography are also used today as offset processes. In an offset process, the ink is transferred to a smooth flexible surface, called the blanket, which is mounted on a cylinder. The paper is pressed against the blanket to transfer the ink. Most lithography used today is offset lithography.

The first step in making any kind of printing plate is to make a high-contrast photographic negative from the original copy. (Exceptions are the electronic-mechanical direct engraving of plates for letterpress printing, and films for making gravure plates.) If the original subject is linework, such as ink drawings, diagrams, or black lettering on white paper, the negative is made by copying the line copy in a camera. If the original copy is a photograph or other continuous-tone image, such as a painting, then the exposure of the negative is made through a patterned screen that breaks up the various tones of the original into tiny dots of different sizes. Light tones form tiny clear dots in a black surround, middle tones form a square checkerboard pattern, while dark tones form tiny black dots in a clear surround in *the negative image.* They are just reversed when the negative is used to make the printing plate. The dot image, whether on the negative, on the printing plate, or printed onto paper, is called a *halftone* image.

The spacing of the dots is controlled by the halftone screen. Screens are classified in terms of lines per inch—meaning rows of dot-forming screen images. Screens are available in a variety of spacings, from 50 lines per inch to 150 lines per inch or greater. The factors that lead to the choice of halftone spacing are paper type, method of printing, and the ability of the particular printing press to print a fine dot. Newspapers, for example, are printed on comparatively low-cost newsprint, which is not as smooth as some papers, and which is highly absorbent. This requires widely spaced dots. Halftones for newspaper printing are generally made with screens of from 50 to 100 lines per inch, depending primarily on the type of paper used.

Because the paper used for them is smoother and often coated with a smoothing clay material, the halftones used to make the illustrations for books and magazines are made with 100- to 133-line

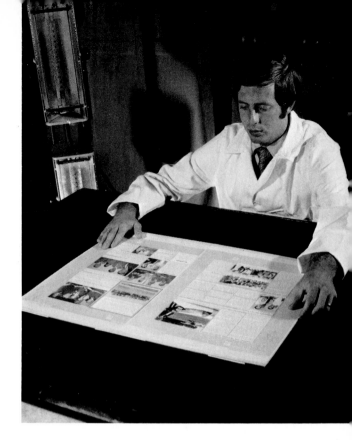

(Above left) To prepare a page spread for printing, paper prints made from halftone negatives are stripped into position on the mechanical, along with appropriate line (type) copy. (Above right) A line negative is made from the mechanical. (Below left) After processing, the finished line negative is ready for platemaking. (Below right) Following a series of trial runs on the press, the plate is washed of all residual ink. It is then re-inked and set up for final printing.

THE

Lorem ipsum dolor
eiusmod tempor
Ut enim ad minim
laboris nisi ut aliquip
irure dolor in
illum dolore eu fugiat

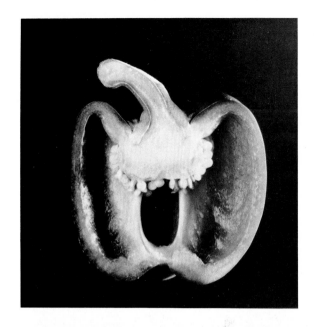

To make any printing plate, a high-contrast photographic negative is first made
from the original copy. (Above) If the
original is linework, such as this ink drawing, it is copied in a camera to make a
negative. If the original is a continuous
tone image like a photograph (above
right) it is exposed through a patterned
screen (right) that breaks up different
tones into dots of different sizes. The result is a halftone image.

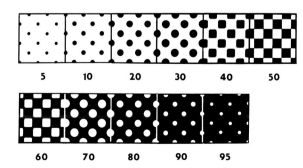

| 5 | 10 | 20 | 30 | 40 | 50 |

| 60 | 70 | 80 | 90 | 95 |

(Left) Different tones of a continuous-tone original are broken
down into variously sized dots. In the negative image, light
tones appear as tiny clear dots on a black ground; middle
tones as a checkerboard pattern; dark tones as tiny black
dots on a clear ground. When printed, as illustrated here, the
clear (white) and black images are reversed. Numbers under
each square indicate the percentage of black.

Graphic Arts Photography

Halftone screens are classified in terms of lines, or dot-forming screen images, per inch, and vary according to a variety of factors. Results of four different screens are shown here: (Top left) 50 lines per inch; (top right) 100 lines per inch; (bottom left) 133 lines per inch; (bottom right) 150 lines per inch.

screens, occasionally 150-line screens if very high-quality paper is to be used. Screens finer than 150 lines per inch are available, but are mostly used for specialty work where the highest quality paper is to be used, and the printing presses are in the best possible condition. If not, plates made with such fine-screen halftones tend to clog with ink when being printed.

Photomechanical Films

To make negatives that contain only lines and spaces (line negatives) or dots and spaces (halftone negatives), an extremely high-contrast film must be used. In the trade, such films are often called *lith* films, and the term lith often becomes part of the film name. There are a number of Kodalith films, for example. In addition, special extremely high-contrast developers are used, both to obtain the contrast needed in the negatives and to achieve high maximum density in the blacks. Such developers usually

contain paraformaldehyde and hydroquinone along with other ingredients. A typical formula is:

Kodak developer D-85

Water 32 C (90 F)	500.0 ml
Sodium sulfite, dessicated . . .	30.0 g
Paraformaldehyde	7.5 g
Sodium bisulfite	2.2 g
Boric acid (crystalline)	7.5 g
Hydroquinone	22.5 g
Potassium bromide	1.6 g
Add cold water to make . . .	1.0 litre

Most graphic arts people use packaged developers rather than mixing their own. Such developers are usually packaged as concentrates in bottles. Often two concentrates are required for one developer because the solutions keep better separated. The two solutions are mixed and diluted with water

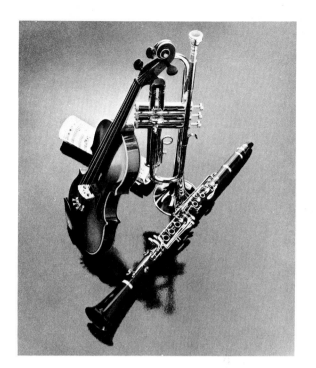

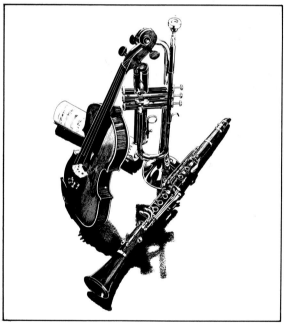

to make a working solution. Much processing of lith films is done in roller-transport processing equipment. Special mechanical processing (MP) lith films with prehardened emulsions are used so that higher than normal temperatures can be used in the processors to reduce processing time. Both tray processing and roller-transport processors utilize the normal fix, wash, and dry procedures after development. Because the lith emulsions are relatively thin, processing, wash, and dry times are relatively short.

Halftones from black-and-white copy are made on orthochromatic (sensitive to blue and green) lith film. This permits the use of red safelights, while retaining some expanded color sensitivity for use in contrast control. When indirect methods of color separation of color originals is used, resulting in continuous-tone separation negatives and masks, orthochromatic lith film is generally used to make halftone positives from the separation negatives. Halftone negatives are then made by contact print-

Color transparencies (top left) may be made into continuous-tone black-and-white halftones (top right) by making separation halftone negatives, which are then photographed on panchromatic lith film; panchromatic film is capable of translating all the original colors into tones of black, gray, and white. Line copies (bottom) are made on extremely high-contrast orthochromatic lith film from black-and-white originals.

ing the halftone positives on a blue-sensitive contact lith film. When color transparencies are separated directly into halftone negatives, panchromatic (sensitive to all colors) lith film is used.

Process Cameras

Cameras for making line or halftone negatives are called process cameras; they are made in a variety of sizes and styles. For relatively small-scale work, vertical process cameras are often used. Such cameras contain all the essential features for graphic arts work: copyboard, lights, and camera with a vacuum back and process lens.

For larger work, horizontal cameras are used. Lighting equipment and copyboard may be part of the camera, or separate. Many horizontal cameras are built into the building. The "light" end of the camera is in one room, while the camera back is in a darkroom. The camera is literally built into a wall. The copyboard and focusing controls are at the back of the camera so that the process camera operator can size and focus the image on the ground glass from the darkroom. These cameras have a vacuum back if they are used with contact halftone screens so that the screen and film emulsion are in tight contact when the exposure is made.

Some process cameras have tapes or scales calibrated for both sizing and focusing. Sizing is done by linear percentage. 100 percent means the negative is the same size as the original. Percentages less than 100 percent indicate reduction, while percentages larger than 100 percent indicate magnification. In the absence of tapes or scales for focusing, a parallax method of viewing the ground glass, along with a 6- to 10-power magnifier, provides sharp focus.

Lenses for process work are usually relatively long focus, small aperture (f/10) with apochromatic correction. They must cover relatively large fields, and they must be corrected to have a flat image field at the usual magnifications near 1:1. Because process lenses are not used for distant objects, f-numbers have little value. Process lens diaphragms are calibrated in a series of aperture ratios, which serve instead of f-numbers for the various percentage sizes.

Copyboards and Lamps

The copy from which the line or halftone negative is to be made is placed on a copyboard and

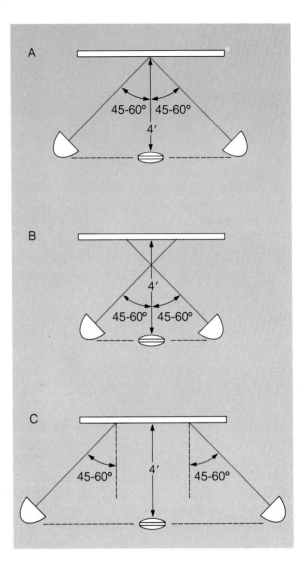

Lamp arrangements A, B, and C all have equal angles and distance. With A, however, the lamps illuminate the center at the expense of the edges. The resulting negatives are warm in the center (too much exposure) and cold at the edges and corners (too little density). Note that B and C over-illuminate the edges relative to the center. The effect of this imbalance at the copyboard is uniform illumination across the film plane.

lighted evenly. Most copyboards have a sheet of glass to hold the copy flat. The glass must be kept scratch-free and scrupulously clean. The copyboard background is black to minimize lens flare. The copyboard, when in place, is held rigidly in a position centered with and exactly perpendicular to the

Graphic Arts Photography

lens axis. Many horizontal camera copyboards have a tilt feature that lets them lie flat for placing the copy and cover glass.

The lamps used for lighting the copy must provide very even illumination. They are usually from 2 to 4 feet from the copy (even farther for large copy) and arranged as shown in the accompanying illustration. Arrangements B and C permit even illumination without direct reflections from the cover glass and glossy originals.

Printing Methods

The type of photography required for graphic arts reproduction varies with the method of printing. The requirements for some types of printing are simple, but for others, quite different.

Letterpress Printing. Historically, the first type of printing was with sticks of type with raised letters. A greasy ink was applied to the surface of the letters and paper was pressed against this surface. The ink transferred to the paper, resulting in a printed image of the letters on the type. This method of printing is letterpress, which is called a relief process. It is still used. Flexography is a type of letterpress that uses rubber plates.

While type was made from cast metal, illustrations were printed from wooden blocks on which pictures were engraved by hand. This method was used from about 1450 until 1850, when Henry Fox Talbot, the inventor of the negative-positive form of photography, invented a method of etching metal printing plates of line drawings.

In this process a flat metal plate, usually zinc or copper, is coated with a layer of fish glue (a colloid) sensitized with bichromate. The plate is exposed by contact to a negative image of a line drawing. The glue partially hardens in the exposed areas and is further hardened by heating the plate. It is then washed with water, which washes away the unhardened (unexposed) glue but leaves the hardened glue. The plate is etched with an etching solution, which eats away the unprotected metal. The hardened glue acts as a resist, which protects the metal from the etch. This forms a relief image on the surface of the metal plate, which can be put in a printing press and printed.

Henry Fox Talbot, as early as 1852, conceived the idea of breaking up the continuous tone of a photograph into dots so that it could be printed—like his plate of line drawings. He used various cloth materials and plates with ruled lines to break up the image, but was not very successful.

In 1893, Max Ernst invented a successful method of making halftone plates. He used a screen made of two pieces of glass on which he had placed black ruled lines. The lines were at right angles to each other, creating a pattern of clear squares on a black background. He focused the image of the photograph on the film, as in copying, but placed his screen a few millimetres in front of the film. This cast an unsharp image of the screen on the film that varied in brightness both because of the variations in tone of the picture being copied, and because of the shadow effect of the screen. By using a high-contrast film, this created a halftone image (where the film was developed) in which the dot size varied with the tone being reproduced. This halftone negative was contacted on the sensitized glue plate, and a halftone printing plate resulted. This method was the only method used up until 1939, but is little used today.

In 1939, a new type of screen was invented for making halftone negatives—the contact screen. This was invented by Alexander Murray of Eastman Kodak Company. Instead of containing sharp-edged squares like the original glass screens, contact halftone screens are dye images on film, containing variable density dye dots in rows. Magenta dye screens are made in various screen sizes (lines per inch), and in positive and negative forms to make halftone negatives or halftone positives. Gray screens are also made for direct color separation work and for some black-and-white work, as well.

In use, a contact screen is placed in close, direct contact (as the name implies) against the film, and the image of the continuous tone being reproduced is photographed through the screen.

The metal printing plates must have small black dots in the lightest areas and small clear dots in the blackest areas in order to print well. A single exposure of a black-and-white original on a lith film through a contact screen may not contain these dots. In order to get the little dots in the clear areas of the negative (dark areas in the plate), a second *flash* or fogging exposure through the screen is needed. This is usually accomplished by using a yellow safelight. Just enough exposure is given, overall, to create a minimum dot exposure in the original dark areas.

Graphic Arts Photography

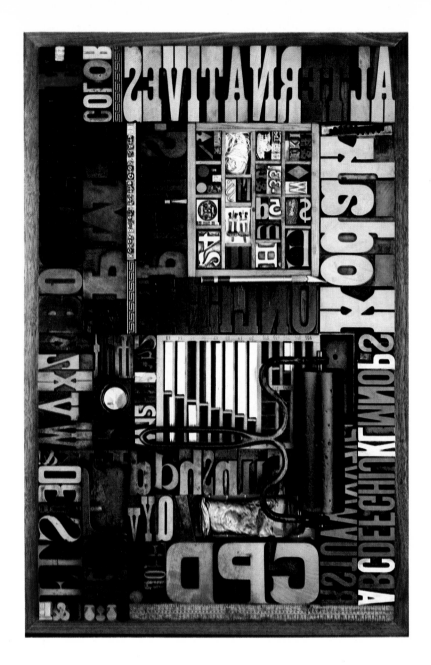

As this artistic rendition illustrates, letterpress printing is done by applying ink to raised type, then transferring the inked surface of the letters to paper. In order for the image to read from left to right, the type itself must, of course, read from right to left.

Often the highlights will not be well separated in the halftone negative—the highlight dots in the plate are too large. In order to improve the dot sizes in the light areas, a third exposure, called a *bump* exposure, is given. For this exposure the halftone screen is removed from in front of the film, and the film is exposed directly to the unscreened image.

Just enough exposure is given to give the highlight areas a small additional exposure so that in the lightest tones the dot size is reduced.

By controlling these three exposures—the main, or detail exposure, the flash exposure, and the bump exposure—the process camera person can produce halftone negatives that will make high-quality printing plates.

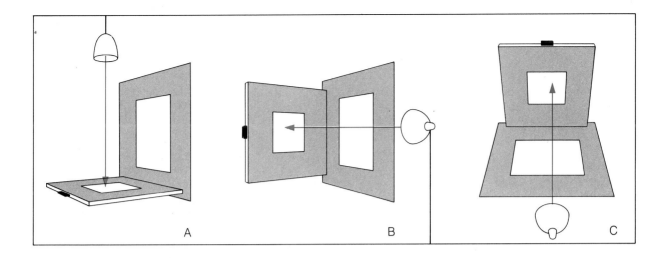

For regular use, locate the flashing lamp in the most convenient position. Setup A can be used for cameras that have backs that open to a horizontal position. For cameras that are hinged vertically, setup B can be used. The flashing lamp mounted as shown in C can be used for most vertical cameras.

Lithographic Printing

Letterpress printing was described earlier as a relief printing process—the printing surfaces of a plate are physically higher than nonprinting areas. Lithography is a planographic process—the printing and nonprinting areas are essentially in the same plane. However, they differ chemically so that printing areas accept ink and nonprinting areas do not.

A grained plate (stone, metal, or even paper) is coated with a light-sensitive colloid-type material and is exposed to a halftone negative of a picture and/or a line negative of text material. The exposed material is developed and washed. This leaves the colloid on the plate in areas not to be printed (the whites) and bare plate surface in areas to be printed.

The plate is printed in a wet condition. The colloid accepts water; the base plate does not. The wet colloid repels the greasy printing ink, but the base metal accepts it. If paper is pressed against the plate, the ink transfers to the paper, creating the printed images.

Nearly all lithography in current practice is offset lithography. Rubber blankets pick up the ink from the plate and transfer it to the paper.

Offset litho presses vary from small duplicating machines that run typing-size paper and use inexpensive paper litho plates, to very large web presses that run rolls of paper up to 76 inches wide—with 5 or 6 printing sections to print four or more colors,

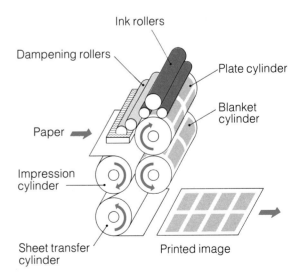

Basic setup of offset-lithography press.

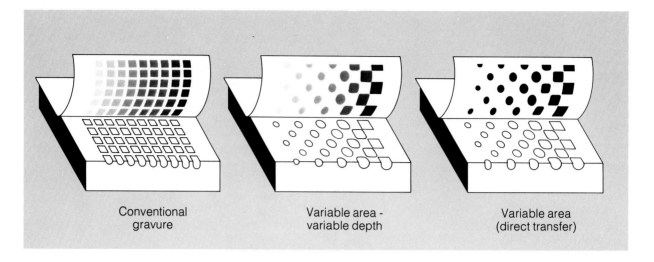

Conventional gravure | Variable area - variable depth | Variable area (direct transfer)

The three types of gravure are: (left) conventional gravure, (center) variable area-variable depth, and (right) variable area (direct transfer).

as well as to apply fast-drying varnishes in a single pass through the press. They run at speeds up to nearly 2000 feet per minute and print from aluminum litho plates.

The halftone photography used to make plates for litho printing is nearly identical to that for letterpress printing in both color and black-and-white. One slight difference is that the highlight dots in planographic printing can be smaller—or even nonexistent—in small-area whites, while letterpress plates must have a dot everywhere. For this reason, the bumping exposures are more common in making black-and-white halftone negatives for lithographic plates.

Gravure Printing

Gravure printing is direct, intaglio printing. The printing plate contains the image of both line copy and halftone copy in the form of rectangular depressions in the surface of the plate. In both web and sheet-fed presses, the copper plate is wrapped around a cylinder. The ink is applied to the cylinder by roller or by spray, and the surface of the plate is cleaned by a scraper called a doctor blade. The paper is pressed against the surface of the plate by an impression roller made of rubber.

While letterpress and offset lithography are widespread, with thousands of printers using the same basic techniques, gravure printing is limited to a relatively few large practitioners, and the processes are largely proprietary. It is known that there are basically three types of dots used:

1. Constant rectangular dot size, variable depth.
2. Variable dot size, constant depth.
3. Variable dot size, variable depth.

For the constant-dot-size, variable-depth plate, a positive transparency is made on black-and-white continuous-tone film. This film is contact-printed onto a photosensitive material called carbon tissue, which is a bichromate sensitized gelatin with carbon particles in it coated onto a tissue paper. A second exposure to a positive-line contact screen (black rectangles in a clear surround) form the lines around the dots.

Exposure hardens the sensitized gelatin in proportion to the amount of exposure. The exposed tissue is positioned on the copper plate or cylinder, and the tissue backing is removed. The gelatin is "developed" in hot water, which leaves gelatin of

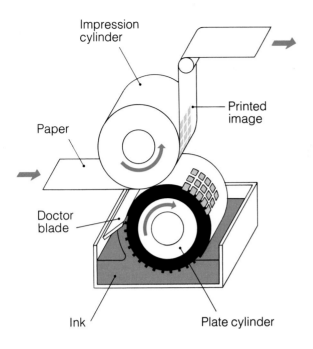

Basic setup of gravure press.

various thicknesses in the dot areas between the hardened screen lines. The copper surface is then etched with ferric chloride solution, leaving the dots with varying depths. This method produces high-quality reproduction, but the plates deteriorate so that it will print only relatively short runs.

The variable-dot-size, constant-depth plate is printed from a halftone positive, similar to one made for lithography. It uses the dot pattern like a checkerboard in the dark tones so does not require the line screen exposure. The scale of tones is therefore limited; it is primarily used in the printing of packaging materials.

The variable-dot-size, variable-depth plate has dots that are a combination of the other two. It produces high-quality reproductions, while the plates hold up for relatively long runs. It is the process used to print catalogs, newspaper supplements, and magazines. It is primarily the process used for four-color reproduction.

Screen Process (Silk Screen, Serigraphy)

In the basic silk-screen process, a stencil is applied to silk or other open-weave fabric stretched on a frame. The frame is placed on paper or other surface to be printed, and silk-screen paint is squeezed through the openings in the stencil, thus printing the paper.

In photographic silk screen, the silk is coated with a photosensitive gelatin layer. This may either be in the form of a liquid emulsion that is painted on the cloth screen, or a layer of emulsion coated on a stripping paper. It is exposed to a line or very coarse halftone positive and developed; this hardens the gelatin in the exposed areas. The screen is washed in hot water, which removes the soft, unexposed gelatin, but leaves the hardened gelatin attached to the silk, thus creating the stencil.

A line original (drawing, typeproof) is copied onto a lith film in a process camera, creating a line negative. This is contact-printed onto lith film, making the line positive. If the screen size is large, the line negative can be made the largest size for which an enlarger is available, and can be enlarged onto lith film to make the positive.

Very coarse halftones are sometimes printed by screen processes—equivalent to a 5-line screen or coarser. A 50-line screen can be used to make a halftone negative, which is then enlarged $10\times$ to make the coarse halftone positive. Four-color halftones are sometimes printed this way for large posters or for billboard signs.

Manufacturers have adapted screening techniques to apply labels to plastic and glass product containers, or to apply decorations on glassware. A third manufacturing use of a screen printing process is in the production of some types of electronic circuit boards.

Color Reproduction

The same principles of color reproduction used in color films are used to reproduce color by graphic arts methods. A halftone color reproduction is printed with three subtractive-primary-colored process inks—cyan, magenta, and yellow. They are often called blue, red, and yellow inks in the trade. In addition, because of deficiencies in the process color inks, a black printer is required to add depth and neutrality to the dark tones. Hence the term four-color reproduction. A full amount of each of the colored inks produces a brown, not a black—primarily because of a lack in density of the cyan (process-blue) printing ink.

Before the final printing in the offset process is begun, press proofs are checked to make sure the halftones are of the desired quality. (Left) In black-and-white printing, the metal printing plates must have small black dots in the lightest areas and small clear dots in the blackest areas in order to print well. If they do not, further exposures of the negative may be necessary. (Right) Color press proofs must have the color key (printed along the edge of the paper) checked for accuracy in order to maintain proper color balance in the pictures. Additionally, the color separation negatives must be in exact register so pictures will not appear out of focus.

Another intrinsic characteristic of the process inks makes special photographic procedures necessary. Ideal subtractive primary colors transmit all of two primary colors of light and absorb all of the third. For example, the magenta (process-red) ink should transmit all of the red and blue light and absorb all of the green. No perfect primary pigments

have yet been found, so corrections for the imperfect nature of the printing ink pigments are made photographically by masking.

The Indirect Method. The first step in making halftone plates for printing full color is to make a set of masks. The masks are low-contrast, positive, continuous-tone film images that are made from the original through filters that provide the necessary correction for the printing inks, and that help control contrast. For indirect color reproduction, the masks are black-and-white. If the original is reflection copy, they are made in the process camera, and are usually exposed behind a diffusing material to make "soft" definition masks, which makes the final reproduction appear sharper. With transparencies, the masks can be made in the camera or by contact.

When the masks are made, continuous-tone color-separation negatives are made through tri-color separation filters. When the process camera is used, these filters are special photomechanical (PM), thin, gelatin, sharp-cutting red, green, and blue filters. For contact work, regular gelatin filters can be used. A greenish-colored filter is used for the negative for the black printer. Special negative separation film is used, and the film is exposed to the image of the copy through the appropriate mask, in register.

Halftone positives are made from the separation negatives through a special magenta positive contact screen. A simple exposure is used—the flash and bump exposures are not required because of the control of contrast provided by masking and by adjusting the developing time of the separation negatives. A fine-tooth adjustment of contrast can be attained by using yellow or magenta color compensating filters over the exposing light.

To avoid a moiré pattern caused by overlapping of the halftone dots, the screens used to make the positives have the rows of dots at different angles.

The halftone positives are contact-printed onto a slow-speed lith film to make halftone negatives. Four plates are made as described earlier and are printed in the four colors in register.

Basically the same indirect method is used to reproduce color transparencies and color prints (paintings), except that a lower contrast separation film is used for transparencies because they have a much greater density range.

The Direct Method. An alternative photographic method of producing color printing plates is

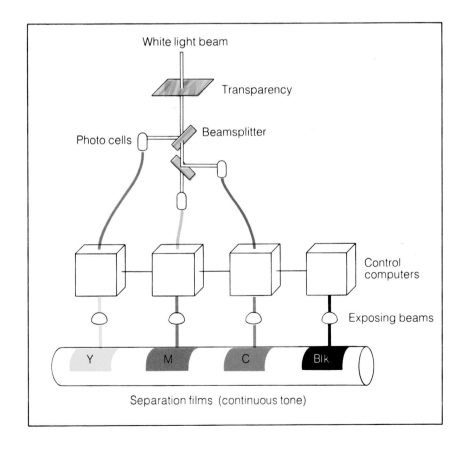

Soft-dot electronic scanner. This type of indirect, continuous-tone scanner uses light and exposes through a halftone screen.

White light beam

Transparency

Photo cells

Beamsplitter

Control computers

Exposing beams

Y   M   C   Blk.

Separation films (continuous tone)

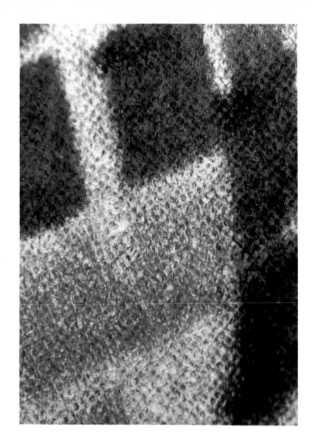

Shown under great magnification, color halftone dot patterns appear to break down into three colors—cyan (blue), magenta, and yellow—plus black, which is required to add depth and neutrality to the dark tones. Especially apparent in photo at right are the different angles at which the dots on the four screens are positioned to avoid a moiré pattern that might be caused by overlapping dots.

Graphic Arts Photography

the direct or direct-screening method. This can be done with a photographic enlarger, with a process camera, or by contact methods. The enlarger method is typical. A transparency is put in the enlarger and focused on the easel.

Four direct halftone separation negatives are made on panchromatic lith film by projecting the transparency through the masks and through gray negative halftone angled screens that are held in close contact with the pan lith film by vacuum.

The four printing plates are made from these halftone negatives as described above.

Optical Scanning

In the 1930s, Alexander Murray and R. S. Morse of Kodak invented an optical scanning device to make the separation negatives from transparencies by electronic-optical means. Such a scanner is controlled by electronics, and it optically scans the transparency and exposes panchromatic film bit by bit, automatically masked and separated for color. From the separation negatives, halftone positives are made. These are used to make halftone negatives, which are used to make the printing plates.

The latest scanners are called direct-screen scanners. There are two types. The laser scanners scan either color prints or transparencies, and use a laser beam to expose the dots directly onto a lith film, producing the four halftones (either negative or positive) directly. This eliminates the need for the continuous-tone separation negatives. The other type uses light and exposes through a halftone screen. Both indirect and direct scanners are in current use.

• *See also:* COLOR SEPARATION PHOTOGRAPHY; HALFTONE; NEWSPAPER TECHNIQUES; PHOTO-MECHANICAL REPRODUCTION, PREPARING PHOTOGRAPHS FOR; SCREENED NEGATIVES AND PRINTS.

Further Reading: Ballinger, Raymond A. *Art and Reproduction: Graphic Reproduction Techniques.* Florence, KY: Van Nostrand Reinhold Co., Div. of Litton Education Publishers, Inc., 1965; Brunner, Felix. *Handbook of Graphic Reproduction Processes* (Visual Communications Books). New York, NY: Hastings House Publishers, 1962; Cogoli, John. *Photo Offset Fundamentals.* Bloomington, IL: McKnight, 1973; Eastman Kodak Co. *Basic Photography for the Graphic Arts,* pub. No. Q-1. Rochester, NY: Eastman Kodak Co., 1978; Jussim, Estelle. *Visual Communications and the Graphic Arts: Photographic Technologies in the Nineteenth Century.* Ann Arbor, MI: R.R. Bowker Co., 1974; Shapiro, Charles, ed. *The Lithographer's Manual.* Pittsburgh, PA: Graphic Arts Technical Foundation, 1966.

Gray Card

On occasion, when taking reflection exposure-meter readings of certain subjects, it is desirable to use a substitute for the subject itself. This may be necessary (1) because the subject is inaccessible, (2) because it reflects too much or too little light for a proper reading, or (3) because it is too small to give a proper reading. The best substitute for the subject in such cases is a piece of gray cardboard of about 18 percent reflectance. (The Kodak 18 percent gray card is called the Kodak neutral test card.) Statistical studies have shown that the average scene — whether a portrait, a room interior, or a landscape* —if averaged overall, reflects just about 18 percent of the light falling upon it. Therefore, the usual reflected-light meter is calibrated for a subject of 18 percent reflectance, and will give correct readings on most ordinary subject matter.

Now and then you will find a scene that is either much lighter than normal (as, for instance, a sunny beach) or much darker than normal (as a scene in a dense forest, with almost no true highlights present). In such a case, a reflected-light meter, used in the normal way, will produce an erroneous exposure reading. However, if the reading is taken not from the scene itself but from a gray card of 18 percent reflectance, and it is made certain that the card is receiving the same illumination as the subject itself, then the reading obtained from the card will produce a correctly exposed negative or transparency.*

Such a substitution method is also useful in copying materials such as written matter—a sheet of white paper with a few lines of type on it or a black card with a few lines of white lettering. In both these cases it is difficult to determine the correct exposure; the use of a gray card will simplify the matter greatly.

The principle here is merely to substitute a gray card for the subject, and to obtain a reading that is the same as the reading that would be obtained from

*For some reason, there is a slight difference between the average subject reflectance of studio subjects and outdoor subjects. Readings made in the studio are used directly. However, outdoor subjects nearly always will be slightly underexposed if the gray-card reading is used directly. Increasing the exposure by ½ to ⅔ stops is recommended.

OUTDOOR EXPOSURE METERING WITH *KODAK* NEUTRAL TEST CARD

Meter Type	Light Condition	Light Direction	Subject Type	Meter Location	Meter Aim	Special Meter Handling	Correction for Subject Brightness in Stops*				
							Very Light	Light	Normal	Dark	Very Dark
Reflection averaging and spot meters with *Kodak* neutral test card	Sun	Front	All	Near subject or camera	Aim meter at neutral card. Hold averaging meter about 6″ from card. Do not cast shadow on card.	Hold card vertically with gray side angled to face halfway between camera and sun. Aim meter squarely at card face.	−½	Ind	+½	+1	+1½
	Sun	Side	All	Near subject or camera			+½	+1	+1½	+2	+2½
	Sun	Back	Scenes	At camera		Hold card vertically with gray side facing toward camera. Shade meter if sunlight falls on it. You are measuring shadow brightness.	−2½	−2	−1½	−1	−½
	Sun	Back	Close-ups	Near subject			−1½	−1	−½	Ind	+½
	Overcast and Shade		All	Near subject or camera	At card	Hold card vertically, gray side facing directly toward camera.	−1	−½	Ind	+½	+1

*Ind = indicated exposure. This means to give the exposure found by using the meter without correction. The − and + figures mean to give less or more exposure than the dial indicates. If the correction is −½, give ½ stop less than the indicated exposure; if the correction is +½, give ½ stop more than the indicated exposure.

an average subject of 18 percent reflectance. Almost anything can therefore be used as a substitute, provided its reflectance is known and the meter calibration is corrected accordingly.

Thus, when lacking a gray card, photographers often take an exposure reading from the palm of their hands. But the reflectance of the palm is about 35 percent, even with very dark or very light persons, or twice the average reflectance of the ordinary scene. This does not prevent the use of such a substitution provided the difference in reflectance is taken into account. Since the palm of the hand reflects 35 percent of the incident light, or twice as much as the average scene, the meter will read double the amount of light, and if this reading is used directly, the picture will be underexposed by one full stop.

There are several ways to compensate for the difference in reflectance in such a case. One way is to use the meter normally, taking the reading from the palm of the hand and then, when setting the camera, simply to use one stop larger than the meter calls for. Or, you could use the lens aperture indicated by the meter, but halve the exposure time—for example, 1/50 sec. instead of 1/100 sec. To avoid

any arithmetic, and to prevent accidentally underexposing by forgetting to make the compensation, you could simply set the meter to half the film speed (for example, use ASA 200 for an ASA 400 film) and use the reading directly from the palm of the hand.

Once this principle is understood, any convenient object of a known percent reflection can be used for a substitution exposure reading. There are times when the light is so dim that you cannot get a readable indication either directly or with a gray card. In this case, you can use a white card (the Kodak neutral test card is white on the back) and take the reading from it. This will usually put the reading well up on the meter scale where it is easy to read. But it must be remembered that the white card reflects about 90 percent of the light falling onto it; this is 5 times as much as the gray card or an average scene reflects, and if the reading is used directly, an underexposure of 5 times will result.

Again, any convenient method can be used to compensate for this difference. For instance, a 1/20 sec. exposure could be used instead of a 1/100 sec. exposure. Trying to compensate by varying the lens diaphragm is difficult for a factor of 5, but the compensation would be about 2¼ stops, and the lens could be opened by that much. Probably the easiest way is simply to divide the film speed by 5.

For example, if you are using a film rated at ASA 400, set the meter at ASA 80 and use the resulting reading directly. This system avoids errors; in addition, most film-speed ratings are easily divisible by 5.

Exactly the same thing is done when an incident-light reading is taken. Most incident-light meters are calibrated for an 18 percent reflectance, just as reflected-light meters are. Incident-light attachments for ordinary meters consist of diffusing disks or hemispheres, made of a white plastic material. When the incident meter is used correctly, it will give the same shutter-speed and *f*-number readings as the reflection meter used with a gray card. In outdoor scenes, it is important to hold the gray card at the correct angle to the sun and camera. The accompanying table indicates correct usage.

• *See also:* EXPOSURE; EXPOSURE METERS AND CALCULATORS; EXPOSURE TECHNIQUES; GRAY SCALES.

Gray Scales

A gray scale is a photographic film or paper with a series of steps of different densities, usually covering the entire range from minimum to maximum density. In some gray scales, the density change from step to step is uniform, and is most often either 0.15 or 0.30, which correspond to equivalent exposure differences of one-half and one stop, respectively. Some paper gray scales may also be made with approximately equal visual differences between steps. In such a scale, the density does not change uniformly because less difference is required between light tones than between dark tones for equivalent visual separation. The accompanying illustration compares some types of scales.

The term *gray scale* is more often used for a paper print scale that is to be viewed or photographed by reflected light; its steps are measured in terms of their reflection densities. A gray scale on film or other transparent base material is called a *step scale* or a *step tablet;* it is used with transmitted light, and is measured in terms of transmission densities. A scale with continuous, rather than stepped, density changes is called an *optical wedge,* or a *density wedge,* or a *continuous-density scale.* Paper gray scales are, of course, calibrated in reflection density units, while film step scales are calibrated in transmission density units. A special gray scale used for copying or photographing line originals for reproduction is called an opposed gray scale guide; it is made by cutting a gray scale in half, lengthwise, and then rejoining the sections again in opposing directions.

Uses of Gray Scales

Reflection gray scales are frequently photographed alongside a subject to help in balancing a set of color separation negatives or positives. They are also used in black-and-white work to compare the tone values or densities of a reproduction with the original, and to find correct exposures and development times for negatives made through filters. A calibrated scale can be used in place of a densitometer to make close approximations of print densities by visual comparison.

Transmission step tablets are generally used to make contact exposures on films or print materials to determine exposure and development, and to make comparisons of contrast. They may also be used in an enlarger, in place of a negative, for controlled tests, or they may be photographed by transmitted light, for example, alongside a transparency being copied.

Continuous-density wedges have less direct use for the working photographer than do stepped scales. Wedges are used primarily to control the intensity of the reference light in visual densitometers, and in making wedge spectrograms to evaluate the spectral sensitivity of emulsions.

Obtaining Gray Scales

Although it is possible for an individual to make rudimentary gray scales and step tablets, it is very difficult to insure uniform density changes between steps and to measure the densities precisely without a sensitometer and a densitometer. It is far better to use scales that have been manufactured with precise sensitometric control. There are several gray scales and step tablets that are inexpensive and that can be obtained through photo or graphic arts dealers.

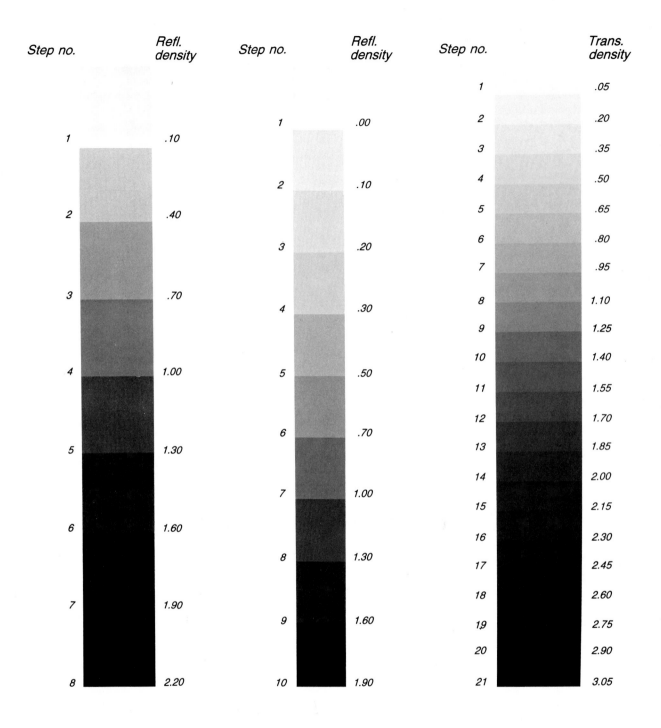

Step no.	Refl. density	Step no.	Refl. density	Step no.	Trans. density
				1	.05
		1	.00	2	.20
1	.10			3	.35
		2	.10	4	.50
				5	.65
2	.40	3	.20	6	.80
				7	.95
3	.70	4	.30	8	1.10
				9	1.25
		5	.50	10	1.40
4	1.00			11	1.55
		6	.70	12	1.70
5	1.30			13	1.85
		7	1.00	14	2.00
				15	2.15
6	1.60	8	1.30	16	2.30
				17	2.45
		9	1.60	18	2.60
7	1.90			19	2.75
				20	2.90
8	2.20	10	1.90	21	3.05

Gray scales and step tablet equivalent tones. Although these illustrations are based on actual photographic materials, the limitations of halftone reproduction make them only diagrams, not true facsimiles. The densities given relate to the original materials, not to these reproductions. (Left) An 8-step scale of equal density differences. (Center) A 10-step scale of equal visual differences. (Right) A 21-step scale of the type found in a step tablet on a film base. Ink reproduction cannot clearly distinguish the equal density differences between all steps.

The *KODAK Professional PHOTOGUIDE,* publication No. R-28, contains an 8-step reflection scale with a difference of 0.3 density (one stop) between steps. The *KODAK Color DATAGUIDE,* publication No. R-19, has a similar 8-step gray scale. A 10-step scale with approximately equal visual differences between the steps and mounted on card stock is included as a component of the *KODAK Color Separation Guides* packet; publication No. Q-13 has a 7-inch gray scale; publication No. Q-14 has a 14-inch gray scale. Other Kodak paper gray scales, consisting of 10 steps (density range 0–1.80) on double-weight print paper either 2″ × 10″ or 8″ × 10″, are available from photo and graphic arts dealers.

Kodak photographic step tablets on film are supplied in three sizes, each covering a density range of approximately 0.5 to 3.05:

No. 1A—¾″ × 3³⁄₁₆″; 11 steps; step increment, 0.30.
No. 2—1″ × 5½″; 21 steps; step increment, 0.15.
No. 3—35 mm × 9⅞″; 21 steps; step increment, 0.15.

Kodak paper gray scales and photographic step tablets are available in either calibrated or uncalibrated form. A calibrated scale or tablet is supplied with a record of the exact density of each step, as it is individually measured after the scale has been manufactured. An uncalibrated scale has a nominally uniform density change from step to step. It is less expensive than a calibrated scale, and is satisfactory for all but the most precise technical or scientific use. Calibrated step scales are usually furnished by the manufacturers of transmission densitometers to be used in setting the adjustments.

Specialized Scales. The Kodak calibration gray scale, supplied as a component of the *KODAK Graphic Arts Exposure Computer,* publication No. Q-12, is a 12-step reflection scale with holes punched through the edges of adjacent steps. Densities in original reflection copy can be determined by holding the scale against the copy and moving it until the tone seen through a hole matches one of the adjoining scale steps. (See the accompanying illustration.)

The *KODAK Reflection Density Guide,* publication No. Q-16, is a 24-step gray scale with densities up to 2.00. It has holes punched in the center of each step for use similar to that of the calibration gray scale.

The *KODAK Projection Print Scale,* publication No. R-26, is a circular transmission scale divided into 10 wedge-shaped steps. (See the accompanying

The Kodak Calibration Gray Scale is used to determine densities in original reflection copy.

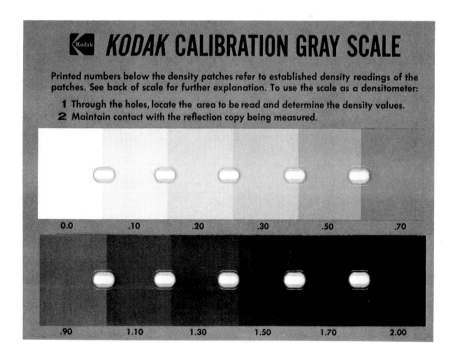

illustration.) It is useful in determining the correct printing time for contact prints and enlargements made on photographic film or paper. The scale is placed in contact with the print material and an exposure is made for a stipulated time through the scale. This produces a test strip with a single exposure because the ten sectors of the scale indicate different printing times corresponding to their different densities. After development, the exposure time can be read from the best-appearing sector in the test print.

A number of small-size and special-purpose gray scales and step tablets are available for use in graphic arts applications. Consult a dealer in graphic arts products.

Using a Gray Scale

The accompanying table relates typical full-scale subject values to an 8-step gray scale such as that in the KODAK Professional PHOTOGUIDE. The table is based upon a typical illumination of 7200 footcandles and vertical gray-scale position. (For a method of determining footcandles from exposure meter readings, see the article LIGHT UNITS.) Equivalent reflectances of other gray scales may be approximately related to subject values by reference to this table as well.

A gray scale may be used to determine exposure, development, or exposure compensation for filtration. The general method is to photograph the gray scale under the same conditions as will be used with actual subjects, and to evaluate the results either by taking densitometer readings from the film, or by making comparison prints. The scale must be evenly illuminated; mounting it on a medium-gray or dark card will make it easy to handle and will minimize the effects of flare or reflections from surrounding objects that otherwise would be within the lens field. If it is being photographed with a subject, it must receive the same light as the subject.

When a gray scale is mounted on a dark background and photographed under low-flare condi-

GRAY-SCALE AND PERCENT-REFLECTION TABLE

Gray-Scale Step	Step Refl. Dens.	Step % Refl.	Step % Refl. Range	Cdls/Ft² In Sun	Step Range Cdls/Ft²	Subject Step Range Definition	Commonly Photographed Subjects in the Sun
—	—	—	90	—	>2100	Specular highlights	Light sources, specular reflections from shiny surfaces
1	.10	80	60–90	2000	1400–2100	Diffuse highlights	Whitest clouds, whitest snow, Bright white paint
2	.40	40	30–60	1000	700–1400	Light tones	Light Caucasian skin, dry white sand, new unfinished wood, light blue sky, dusty dirt, lemons, white paint
3	.70	20	15–30	500	350–700	Medium-light tones	Caucasian skin, wet white sand, medium dry earth, red brick, weathered wood, deep blue sky, light grass and foliage, oranges
—	.74	18	—	400	—	Middle gray	Kodak Neutral Test Card (gray side)
4	1.00	10	8–15	250	175–350	Medium-dark tones	Black skin, medium to dark grass and foliage, dry dark earth, dark tree trunks
5	1.30	5	4–8	125	87–175	Dark tones	Black fresh-turned earth, very black skin, dark clothes
6	1.60	2.5	2–4	64	44–87	Very dark tones	Most black objects, very dark clothes
7	1.90	1.3	1–2	32	22–44	Black	Blackest objects
8	2.20	0.6	.5–1	16	11–22	Deep black	Black velvet
—	—	—	.5	—	11	Deepest black	Blackest objects in shadow

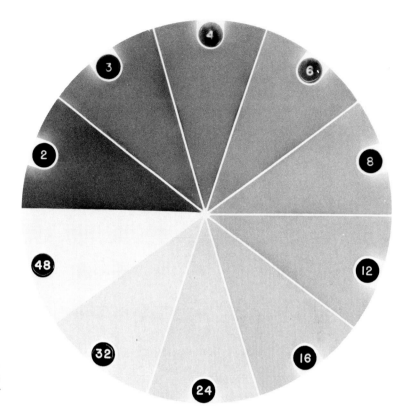

The Kodak Projection Print Scale is used in determining correct printing type for prints made on photographic paper or film. Instructions for its use are explained in the text.

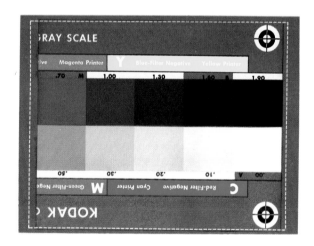

A 14-inch Kodak gray scale would produce step images only ⅛" wide in the length of a 35 mm frame. By cutting the scale in half and arranging it as shown, closer framing (broken line) will produce step images more than ¼" wide in 35 mm format. A neutral gray or dark backing card will eliminate flare. This illustration has been drawn to scale using a 14-inch gray scale; size of the gray or dark card may vary.

tions such as frontlighting in the studio, densitometer readings from the resulting negative can be used to plot a characteristic curve of the film's response. The higher levels of flare encountered in exterior situations will affect low-value (shadow-area) densities enough to make characteristic curves plotted from the results show the results of both film and flare characteristics, so that they do not show the characteristics of the film alone.

If densitometer readings are to be made, the image of each step of the scale must be large enough to fill the area covered by the densitometer probe. With small-format negatives such as 35 mm, the size of a Kodak 14-inch gray scale is too small when its length fills the frame. It is possible to get a larger image by cutting the scale in half as shown in the accompanying diagram. The 8-step gray scale in the KODAK Professional PHOTOGUIDE is arranged in two rows so that each step can be up to ⅜-inch wide in a 35 mm format image.

Exposure and Photographic Quality. The purpose of achieving correct exposure is to obtain maxi-

mum photographic quality. With transparency films, this means getting a tonal reproduction in which the specular highlights are clear film; diffuse highlights (step 1 in the gray scale table) have a slight tone, while step 7 or 8 black subjects which are sunlit are reproduced as just lighter than black. Shadowed objects of step 4 or 5 reflectance will reproduce as black, while shadowed step 1 to 3 reflectance subjects will reproduce in the same tonal range as sunlit 4 to 7 reflectance subjects.

With negative films, correct exposure means the achievement of negatives with the minimum exposure that will produce prints with the same type of quality reproduction described earlier. While giving somewhat more exposure than the minimum will nearly always give the quality tonal reproduction

described, it results in increased negative densities, which mean longer printing times, increased graininess, and decreased sharpness. Further, more exposure requires longer shutter speeds or larger lens openings, often limiting the ability to stop motion or to obtain the desired depth of field.

Exposure Determination

To determine exposure, a series of test exposures should be made based on an incident-light reading, or a reflected-light reading from an 18 percent neutral test card held in the gray-scale position; the meter should be set to the manufacturer's ASA rating for the film being tested. The exposure series should bracket a total of two stops more and less than the meter-indicated exposure, using third-stop

Where correct tonal rendition is critical, as in art reproductions, a gray scale is photographed with the art itself to give correct exposure. (Left) Vincent Van Gogh, "Van Gogh's Room at Arles" photo by Scala New York/Florence. (Below) Joan Miró, "Girl in Front of Sun," photo by Joseph Martin/Scala. Both photos for Editorial Photocolor Archives.

Gray Scales

intervals for a transparency or slide film, and full-stop intervals for a negative film. The series for a black-and-white film should include an additional exposure with the lens capped to produce a blank frame or sheet. If a color film is being tested, a color scale or various colored objects should be included with the gray scale.

Color transparency films are evaluated visually to determine the best exposure, either by projection or examination over an illuminator, while negative color films are evaluated by making the best possible print from each usable exposure. The frame that produces the best results is the "speed frame."

Black-and-white films may be evaluated by density readings, or visually. To use a densitometer for evaluation, read the blank exposure (made with the lens cap on) to determine the filmbase-plus-fog density. Then read the test exposures to find the one in which the black step of the gray scale—which will be the most transparent step in each negative—has a density approximately 0.10 above filmbase-plus-fog density. A density increase in the range of 0.08 to 0.15 is acceptable. This frame is the speed frame. Less than this causes a noticeable loss in shadow detail. More than this makes the negatives unnecessarily dense, which increases print exposure time, increases graininess, and decreases definition.

To evaluate the negatives visually, first establish a standard printing time from the blank exposure. Using one of the test exposures, raise the enlarger and focus it for the usual print size; then shift the film to the blank frame. For contact printing, simply place the blank frame on the print material. Use the normal grade of paper to make a test strip of exposures through the blank frame by shifting a card to cover or uncover the exposure area in a series of equal time steps. Process the strip and examine it to find the *shortest* exposure that produces a maximum black through the blank frame; this is the standard printing time.

Without changing the enlarger settings, make a print from each of the bracketed test exposures on the film; use the standard printing time for each print. Examine the processed prints to find the one in which the black gray-scale step (clearest step in the negative) prints a very dark gray just distinguishable from the maximum possible black. (It helps to trim the end from each test print so the black scale step can be compared directly with a piece of paper

exposed and processed to maximum black.) The negative from which this print was made is the speed frame.

However it has been identified, the exposure that produced the speed frame can be used to find the film speed, or exposure index, for the conditions, as follows:

EXPOSURE INDEX	
Exposure for Speed Frame	Multiply ASA Speed By
+2 stops	0.25×
+1⅔ stops	0.32×
+1⅓ stops	0.40×
+1 stop	0.50×
+⅔ stop	0.64×
+⅓ stop	0.80×
Meter indication	1.00× (no change)
−⅓ stop	1.25×
−⅔ stop	1.60×
−1 stop	2.00×
−1⅓ stops	2.50×
−1⅔ stops	3.20×
−2 stops	4.00×

For example, with an ASA 400 film, if the speed frame resulted from an exposure one stop more than the meter-indicated exposure, the true film speed, or exposure index, is:

$$400 \times 0.50 = \text{EI } 200.$$

Development Testing

To use a gray scale for development tests with black-and-white films, first determine the density range of a negative that prints with the kind of contrast you like on a normal contrast grade of paper. Read the thinnest part of the negative image that will produce a print density just lighter than black, and the most dense diffuse highlight area. Subtract the smaller reading from the larger; the resulting negative density range will usually be about 0.80 for negatives to be printed on a condenser enlarger and 1.05 for diffusion enlarger negatives.

Photograph an evenly illuminated 8-step gray scale, using the exposure given by an incident-light or neutral test card reflected-light reading with the meter set to the true exposure index of the film, as determined by the procedures in the preceding section. In order to give different developments, expose several sheets of film or give each frame of a roll of 35 mm film the same exposure; the length can be cut into shorter pieces in the dark before processing.

Develop the film with planned developing time variations (keep the temperature and agitation constant). Take density readings of steps 1 and 8 in each processed variation. Proper development is indicated by the negative in which the step 8 density is about 0.10 above filmbase-plus-fog, and step 1 has a density about 0.80 or 1.05 (or your negative density range) above that of step 8. If the step 8 density is much above or below 0.10 above filmbase-plus-fog density, the exposure needs correction. If the density difference between steps 1 and 8 is low, increase the development; if it is high, reduce development.

This same method can be used to find proper development using a different developer with a known film, or a new film with a known developer.

Plotting Characteristic Curves. As noted previously, when a gray scale is photographed under low-flare conditions, the resulting negative densities can be used to plot a characteristic curve of the film response. The method of plotting curves is discussed in the articles CHARACTERISTIC CURVE and DENSITOMETRY. Since the various reflection densities of the gray-scale steps create the exposure differences in the negative, the steps must be properly spaced along the horizontal or Log E axis of the curve graph. In the Kodak 8-step gray scale previously mentioned, the density difference between all steps is 0.3, so they can be uniformly spaced along the graph axis. But the steps of the Kodak 10-step gray scale do not have equal density differences, and

Comparative spacing of gray-scale steps on the Log E axis of characteristic curve graphs. (A) Kodak 8-step gray scale; (B) Kodak 10-step gray scale; (C) Kodak step tablet. Spacing is based on a value of 0.1 for each graph division. The step numbers and densities correspond to those given on the gray scales and the nominal step-tablet values, as shown on page 1268. The step numbers run backward from left to right because the maximum density in a gray scale or step tablet produces minimum density in the exposed material.

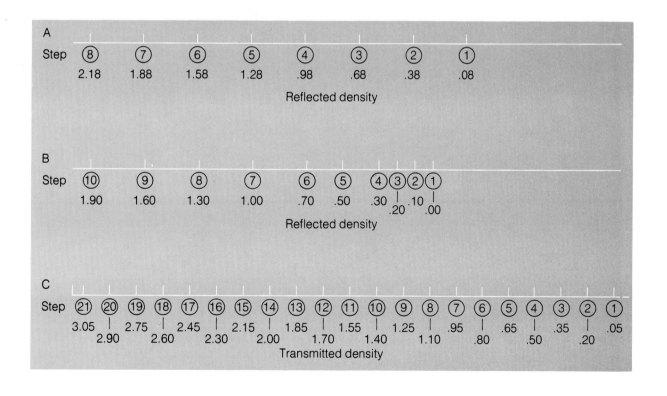

therefore cannot be equally spaced on the graph. The accompanying diagram compares the spacing required for the steps of these two scales, and for those of a 21-step negative step tablet.

Determining Filter Compensation

Photograph a gray scale without the filter. Then make a series of exposures through the filter, each one stop more than the other. Usually five stops over normal will be enough to find the factor, but if the filter is dense go to six or seven stops over normal. When the negatives are processed, read the density of a mid-scale step in all the negatives. Plot the densities of the negatives taken through the filter on a graph as shown in the illustration. Draw a horizontal line at the density of the step in the unfiltered negative. Where the two lines intersect shows how many stops increase are necessary to duplicate the density with the filter on the lens. Using the accompanying table, calibrate the filter factor.

FILTER FACTOR CALIBRATION	
+ Stops	**Filter Factor**
+1	2.0×
+1⅓	2.5×
+1½	2.8×
+1⅔	3.2×
+2	4.0×
+2⅓	5.0×
+2½	5.7×
+2⅔	6.3×
+3	8.0×
+3⅓	10.0×
+3½	11.0×
+3⅔	13.0×
+4	16.0×
+4⅓	20.0×
+4½	23.0×
+4⅔	25.0×
+5	32.0×
+5⅓	40.0×
+5½	45.0×
+5⅔	50.0×
+6	64.0×

Violet Filter No. 34A Daylight Tungsten

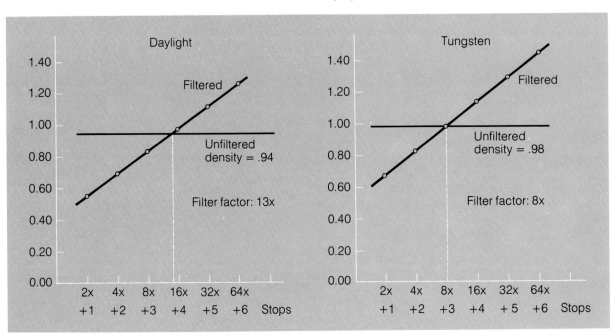

Determining filter compensation. After the filter factor has been determined, read the density of a mid-scale step in all the processed negatives, filtered and unfiltered. Plot the densities of the filtered negatives on the graph (oblique lines). Draw a horizontal line at the density of the step in the unfiltered negative. The point (indicated by the dotted lines) where the two lines intersect shows how many stops increase is required to duplicate the density of the unfiltered negative in the filtered negative.

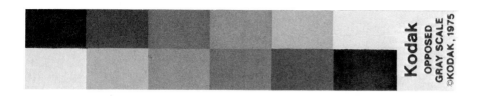

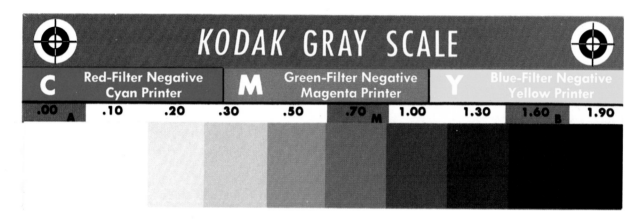

An opposed gray scale (top) Kodak 7-inch gray scale (bottom).

Gray-Scale Use in Line Copying

Whenever charts, drawings, engravings, or other line originals are being copied or photographed for reproduction, the need for a quick visual reference for checking exposure/development changes (whether intentional or unintentional) can be met by using an opposed gray-scale guide. This guide is made by cutting a gray scale in half, lengthwise; then the sections are joined again, but in opposing directions.

The opposed gray-scale guide can be made from the Kodak gray scale, a component of the *KODAK Color Separation Guides* (7-inch), Kodak publication No. Q-13. The guide is made from a section of the gray scale itself. Although a part of the gray scale is removed in making the guide, there will be enough of the gray scale remaining to preserve its use as a color separation guide. To make the opposed gray-scale guide, cut about ⅝ inch from the edge of the separation-guide gray scale. Next, cut the ⅝-inch piece into two ³⁄₁₆-inch strips. Join the two strips together in the opposed position so that

the 0.30 step is opposite the 0.50 step. Place transparent tape on the back of the strips to hold them together. To square the guide, trim away the high densities on the ends. If convenient, the steps can be numbered or otherwise identified for easier reference.

A small (⅝″ × 3″) 6-step opposed gray scale, Kodak publication No. Q-18, is also available.

By including the guide with all camera line copy, you should be better able to match line-width rendition from similar copy, confirm normal exposure and development for certain copy, monitor processor activity, and control development compensation when processing in a tray.

Using an Opposed Gray Scale. Position the guide next to some good line copy and make some test exposures to determine the best exposure and development time. These test exposures are also used to establish the density value at which certain exposure and development conditions will produce the most significant density change (or break) in the scales. The term "break" is commonly used to describe the point at which a print of a gray scale appears to have lost most, if not all, of the tonal separation between the steps and shows a major shift in density. This is especially true with materials of very high contrast, such as Kodalith films, in which density values in the copy are essentially reproduced as either black or white. Consequently, the guide will look different at the break as exposure is adjusted to suit the different types of copy. If the copy has colors, a colored filter is sometimes used to get good black-and-white separation. The use of a colored filter may cause slight changes in the break point that has been established as being ideal for good line copy without such a filter.

The test exposure that gave the best negative from good line copy, and established a visual reference (break point) in the guide, will be the proper aim point for a fairly wide range of copy conditions. This is especially true when using Kodalith ortho films, type 3, because these films have a wide copying latitude. When properly photographed, difficult types of copy will indicate a shift in the break on the guide. This shift will be about one step less for weak copy (or very fine lines) and about one or two steps more (overlap or break) for bold copy with an off-white or dirty background.

Because of the differences in working conditions and operations, experience in using the guide will soon establish the visual reference that is most suited to your needs. Once you have established the best reference points on the guide for different types of copy or conditions, you will be able to interpret the results very quickly, and you will get more repeatable results from day to day. You can also run a

Interpreting Results from an Opposed Gray Scale In Line-Copy Work

Indicates normal exposure and development, and is the correct reference point for average copy.

Indicates underexposure or weak developer, or is correct reference point for weak copy or very fine lines.

Indicates overexposure, or is correct reference point for bold copy with off-white or dirty background.

routine check on conditions of exposure and development whenever it seems necessary to keep a system from "drifting." If you are using a mechanical processor, looking at the guide will give you a double-check on the processor conditions as well.

The opposed gray-scale guide is also useful with tray development of films that can be handled under safelight conditions. By checking the guide against moderately overexposed or underexposed films during development, you can make corrections in development time more reliable. When development progresses to the point where the guide shows the proper break, the film should then have a good image, because you will have adjusted the development time to compensate for the exposure error. Of course, extreme overexposure or underexposure of the film will not respond well to development compensation, so the exposure will need to be adjusted.

Using Step Tablets

Because they are on transparent base materials, step tablets may be used for contact or projection exposures, or may be photographed by transmitted light. Whenever a film emulsion is being exposed by contact or projection through a step tablet, it should be backed with black material to prevent unwanted exposure from light reflected back through the base. The step tablet must be masked in all situations so that light passes only through it; light passing around the tablet can cause flare, which will degrade results. The following are some practical uses of step tablets.

Characteristic Curves. A tablet is an ideal way to give precise step exposures to a film in order to obtain data for plotting a characteristic curve. A contact exposure avoids flare effects; a projection exposure is useful for investigating exposure/development factors when enlarged negatives of film positives are to be made. Camera exposures of a transilluminated tablet provide data for duplicating transparencies. However, none of these methods provide results that take into account the combined lens-camera factors encountered in conventional photography of subjects by reflected light; for that, a reflection gray scale rather than a step tablet must be used.

Contrast Evaluation. The printing scale of various contrast grades of paper can be determined by contact or projection exposures with a step tablet;

the method used should correspond to the method normally used for printing. Identify the tablet step that has a density that matches the filmbase-plus-fog density of the film used for your negatives. If a densitometer is not available, expose through a piece of blank processed film and the step tablet, side-by-side, and make a visual tone match. Place a small corner of opaque tape on the base side of this step to serve as a reference mark.

Expose samples of various contrast grades of paper through the step tablet. Adjust exposure each time to the minimum required to produce a maximum black at the marked step; the required exposure will increase as the contrast grades increase. Compare the processed results when dry. Count the number of distinct steps between maximum black and pure white (do not count these extremes). Note whether the increase/decrease in the number of steps is the same from grade to grade. It may well be that a No. 2 paper produces three more steps than a No. 3, but that the No. 3 grade produces only two more steps than a No. 4. If a Kodak 21-step tablet is used, each step corresponds to a half-stop difference in subject brightness or contrast; with an 11-step tablet, each step is a full-stop difference.

Negative Density Range. To determine the approximate negative density range that each paper grade can accommodate, multiply the number of visible steps by the step increment. (Do not include the maximum black or pure white at the ends of the scale in the step count, because these correspond to densities outside the meaningful negative density range.) For example, if the density increment is 0.15 from step to step, and seven steps can be distinguished, the paper requires a negative with a density range of $0.15 \times 7 = 1.05$. Standard step scales may be made of a material that has a different Callier factor from the negative film to be enlarged, so their use may give misleading results. It is better to make up a step scale using the film that is to be enlarged to get meaningful results in this test.

Paper Comparisons. The step-tablet method of contrast evaluation can be used with selective- or variable-contrast papers as well as with graded papers. It also is an excellent way to find equivalent contrasts among different papers from the same manufacturer, or among papers of different manufacture. For example, if a European No. 3 paper and a U.S. No. 2 paper reproduce the same number of steps from a tablet exposure, they have the same overall contrast and require negatives of the same density range, no matter what differences there may be in the numbers or words used to designate their contrast characteristics.

Exposure Control. Some special processes, such as the platinotype and palladiotype (platinum and palladium prints), the cyanotype, and the gumbichromate processes, require long printing exposures that cannot be determined conveniently or accurately by the usual method of making test strips beforehand. However, test samples of the print material can be exposed under a step tablet at the same time as the image negative is being printed. From time to time, a test strip can be removed from under the tablet and processed to evaluate progress without interrupting the main exposure.

An alternate method is to use a more responsive material such as Kodak studio proof paper as a kind of printing timer. Tests must be made to determine how many tablet steps will print in the time required for normal exposure of the special print material. Once this is established, proof paper is exposed under a step tablet alongside the image being printed. The proof exposure can be examined at intervals as the main exposure progresses. Because the proof paper is a printing-out material, it does not have to be processed in order to evaluate the printing exposure.

• *See also:* CHARACTERISTIC CURVE; CONTRAST; CONTRAST INDEX; DENSITOMETRY; NEUTRAL DENSITY; TONE REPRODUCTION.

Greeting Cards

Photographic greetings can be as simple as a snapshot enclosed with a card or note, or as complex as multiple images and overlays on a cleverly folded card. Whatever the occasion or the technique, photo-greeting cards can be attractive and personal.

Pictures for Greeting Cards

A card can be made from any well-exposed negative, slide, or print. The first thing to do is to select an appropriate picture. If one is not already at hand,

it should be taken as far ahead of time as possible. There are many opportunities for taking greeting-card pictures well in advance of most occasions. If the card is to be a Christmas greeting, for example, pictures showing people dressed in winter clothing and enjoying winter activities can be just as seasonal with or without snow. Props such as a carefully placed bough of greens decorated with an ornament or two, some candles, a wreath, or a few pine cones will provide the needed seasonal touch.

On the other hand, it is not essential for a Christmas-greeting picture to have a Christmas or winter theme. A picture taken on a summer vacation can be a welcome sight in the middle of winter. Or a picture of the family with a background of fall foliage can make a colorful card. Setting aside suitable pictures all year long provides a stock of material to choose from as an occasion approaches.

When it is not possible to get a picture before a special event—a picture for a birth announcement, for example—the card can still be planned in advance. Then, when the day arrives, the picture can be taken and quickly processed, and the vital statistics added to produce the card without delay.

Ideas for Taking Pictures

Greeting within the Picture. One of the easiest ways to make a greeting card is to include the greeting in the picture itself. A simple "Happy New Year" attractively written on a piece of colored poster board held by someone in the picture makes an excellent greeting. A simple idea for a picture is more effective than a complicated one.

Another method of including a greeting in a picture involves combining the picture negative with another negative containing a suitable message. Photograph the message in white letters against a black background such as black felt; for best results, use a high-contrast film, or a high-contrast developer with a normal-contrast film. Of course, the best results are obtained with an extremely high-contrast film, such as Kodalith ortho film, type 3, developed in a high-contrast developer, such as Kodalith developer. Position the message in the frame so that it corresponds with a dark, uncluttered area in the picture—such an area will appear as a clear or light area in the picture negative. Sandwich the two negatives together in the enlarger and print them as one.

Merry Christmas
and
A Joyous New Year

(Above) A personalized greeting card, generally made up by a photofinishing lab, uses the customer's photograph; a stock greeting or a personalized message can be printed below or alongside the picture. (Right) This photograph of a watercolor painting was used with a commercial lab's stock message to make an appropriate and attractive card.

Season's Greetings

Greeting Cards

(Above) Combination of the picture negative with a message negative works particularly well if the picture has a light area into which the lettering, which prints up black, can be positioned. (Below) A family photograph and paper cutouts are combined in a collage.

7515 Old Oak Way
Carmine, Ohio 12572

This photograph was made up into an announcement of a new address. It is not always necessary for the photograph to illustrate the theme too closely. A picture like this says considerably more than would a photo of a new house.

Greeting on a Mirror. Another way to include a message in the picture is to print or tape it directly on the face of a large mirror. Position the subject so it is reflected in the mirror, and take the picture of the combined reflection and message. To avoid their being included, place the camera and any lighting equipment at an angle to the surface of the mirror. Frame the picture inside the edges of the mirror.

If flash is used with a nonadjustable camera, the combined camera-to-mirror-to-subject distance must not exceed the recommended flash-to-subject distance. This is usually from 4 to 9 feet, so if the subject is 3 feet from the mirror, the camera and

flash cannot be more than 6 feet from the mirror. Aiming the flash into the mirror from the camera position will make certain that the message is lighted and that light is reflected onto the subject. With an adjustable camera, the total flash-mirror-subject distance should be used to determine the proper camera exposure settings. Because the mirror is closer than the subject, any message on the mirror is likely to be overexposed; therefore, it is best to use dark lettering. With adjustable cameras, use the depth-of-field indicator in the lens to make sure the greeting and the subject are both in focus. (*See:* FLASH PHOTOGRAPHY; GUIDE NUMBERS.)

Family Activities. A photo-greeting card intended for a particular occasion need not have that occasion as its theme. A picture used in a Christmas card, for instance, can show all or part of the family at some other time of the year. If the family took a special vacation, a good travel picture showing family members in some foreign locale or in a national park can be of interest to those receiving the cards. The rest of the card can convey the message.

A picture of some special activity or sport clearly showing family members participating can be suitable, and welcome to the recipients of the card. Dad and mom preparing a gourmet dish with family members tasting, or the family with a special pet are types of activity especially appropriate for Christmas cards.

If some member of the family is a pictorial photographer, an attractive picture with or without a Christmas theme can be admired by those who know it represents the photographic skill of the sender.

Tabletop Pictures. Tabletop pictures usually include several small subjects arranged in a pleasing composition on a tabletop. Such pictures are easy to create and can be appropriate for photo-greeting cards. Any season of the year can be represented in the table setup, regardless of the weather outside. For example, to create a snow scene in the middle of the summer, use detergent for snow.

Come To My Birthday Party

A birthday-party invitation may have only the guest of honor's photo pasted on the front of a heavy, unfolded card. Pertinent information (date, time, address) might be handwritten on the back.

Greeting Cards

Robert Z. Philbin
University of Rochester
June, 1978

This photograph was an obvious choice for a graduation announcement. The black gown makes a perfect background for type printed on a combination negative.

A charming child photograph combined with a Mother's Day message can be made by sandwiching the photo negative and the message negative and printing together, then pasting the print onto heavy, single-folded paper. The rest of the message may be handwritten on the inside. This type of card is best done only in small quantities.

For Grandma

Happy Mother's Day

A tabletop picture of a jack-o'-lantern can become a photo-greeting invitation to a Halloween party. For an invitation to a birthday party or a confirmation, make an arrangement of pictures of the child that were taken at various ages, from birth to his or her present age, and add some appropriate props to complete the composition.

Silhouettes. Silhouettes are dramatic; they can make unusual pictures for greeting cards. To make a silhouette, pose the subject in profile several feet in front of a plain, light-colored wall. Place a light source behind the subject, aimed at the wall. Make an exposure based on a major reading of the wall, but give it about two stops more exposure than the meter indicates.

For a colorful silhouette picture, pose the subject in front of a colored-glass window with the light coming through it. Expose for the window brightness, and the subject will be recorded as a silhouette. To create "colored-glass" windows at home, tape pieces of different-colored cellophane or plastic to the back of a window, using clear tape. Pose the subject several feet in front of the window. By focusing on the subject, the window will be slightly out of focus and there will be no chance of the tape being visible.

If silhouette pictures are to be printed commercially, be sure to specify that they are to be silhouettes. Automatic printing equipment can mistake silhouette images for underexposures, and will try to compensate in order to show detail in the subject. That ruins the silhouette effect and washes out the backgrounds of color pictures.

Kinds of Cards

Collage Cards. A collage is a picture made up of several sections of various pictures. To make the master card, combine whole photographs or cutouts from photographs with cutouts from other sources. A razor-edged knife makes it easy to do a neat, accurate cutting job. Assemble the pictures on a plain background; use glue or double-faced tape to hold the cutouts in position. Artwork can be added to establish a theme, along with the message, and a signature if desired. When the paste-up is complete, light it evenly and copy it onto film to produce a single negative from which any number of cards can be reproduced. (*See:* COLLAGE; COPYING.)

Photograms. A photogram is an illustration made on a sheet of photographic paper without using a negative. It consists of white or gray letters and designs on a black background. The high-contrast appearance of a photogram is dramatic, and photograms are easy to make. Only a few small props and some photographic paper are required. Under suitable safelight conditions, arrange opaque or semiopaque objects suggesting the greeting-card theme on a sheet of photographic paper. The emulsion side of the paper must face up. Pine boughs, pine cones, block letters, and paper cutouts are objects appropriate for Christmas-card photograms.

When the arrangement is suitable, turn on the exposing light. Use the light from an enlarger or a 15-watt bulb in a desk-lamp reflector, and experiment a bit with the exposure time. Process the paper in the usual way. After the paper is processed and dried, sign it or add a message with white ink on the dark background. If only a few cards are needed, just regroup the props on unexposed photographic paper for each exposure. To produce cards in quantity, make a copy negative of the best photogram and use it for printing additional cards.

Color photograms can be made on color enlarging paper. Filters are placed over the enlarger lens provide the background color. If transparent objects are being used in the photogram, pieces of color filters or lighting gels can be placed in the objects to produce different colors. The list below indicates what filters to use on a negative color paper, such as one of the Kodak Ektacolor papers, to get the background color you want.

Kodak Wratten filters	*Print color*
Yellow: No. 8, No. 15	Blue
Yellow-green: No. 11, No. 13	Violet
Green: No. 58, No. 61	Magenta (fuchsia)
Bluish-green: No. 44, No. 65	Red
Blue: No. 47, No. 47B	Yellow
Violet: No. 34A	Yellow-green
Magenta: No. 33	Green
Red: No. 25, No. 29	Cyan (blue-green)

Cards from Greeting-Card Masks. Anyone with darkroom facilities can turn a black-and-white negative into a photo-greeting card by combining the negative with a greeting-card mask. A greeting-

A black-and-white photogram is easy to make by arranging opaque or semi-opaque objects suggesting the desired theme on a sheet of photographic paper, and exposing and processing the paper normally.

Color photograms are not difficult to make on color enlarging paper. Translucent objects, such as flowers, must be used so that light from the enlarger can pass through them onto the paper below. To add lettering, cut letters from colored cellophane and arrange on the paper.

Greeting Cards

An invitation to a Halloween party can be easily made by cutting out paper figures and contact printing them on photographic paper.

Holidays such as Valentine's Day, with readily recognizable symbols, are good occasions for making photogram greeting cards. The designs used on this card were cut out from commercially available border stencils.

Greeting Cards

With a little imagination, almost any photograph can be converted to greeting-card use. While the photographer probably did not have a "Bon Voyage" message in mind when he photographed this sailing vessel, he later turned the photo to an attractive and amusing purpose.

card mask is a high-contrast negative with a design and a greeting such as "Merry Christmas" on it. The mask comes with an opening in a standard negative size. Many photo dealers stock such masks.

To use, put a negative over the opening in the mask and hold it in place with small pieces of tape from behind. The tape will not show on the card. Print the mask-and-negative sandwich on a contact printing paper such as Kodak Azo paper (double weight), and process the paper normally. The result will be an original photo-greeting card.

To make a high-contrast greeting-card mask, use a camera that accepts 4″ × 5″ sheet film. Arrange the message for the card on a plain white background, allowing space for the picture. Use black paint, india ink, dark press-on letters, or cut-out letters from magazines or printed materials. Old greeting cards can be a source of message ideas and letters. Photograph the message on high-contrast sheet film. After the negative is processed and dried, cut an opening just a little smaller than the picture negative to be used. When printed, the picture will appear in a black area with the message in white letters alongside.

French-Fold Cards. To make a French-fold greeting card, take a sheet of paper and fold it in half twice, once lengthwise and once widthwise. The result is a card similar to a great many commercial greeting cards. An important point in making folded cards is that most photographic papers crack when folded. However, Kodak Ad-Type papers are lightweight, black-and-white printing papers especially designed to fold without cracking. The 8½″ × 11″ size French-folds to 4¼″ × 5½″ to fit a standard-size card envelope.

Most French-fold cards have a picture on the outside fold and a printed greeting inside. This re-quires two negatives—one for the front picture, and another for the message. If the negatives are 2¼ inches square or larger, use an 8½″ × 11″ sheet of opaque black paper to make a mask with cutout areas slightly smaller than the negatives. Place the two openings for the negatives in opposite corners (upper left and lower right). For the card to fold and read correctly, the picture and greeting negatives should be oriented in opposite directions, as shown in the accompanying illustration. Tape the negatives in position on the mask and contact-print the combination onto a suitable paper.

For small negatives (110, 35 mm, 126, or 127), use a 4″ × 5″ piece of black paper to make the mask. Be sure the greeting negative is compatible in size

A French-fold card has the picture printed on the outside fold and the greeting printed inside. Since the paper is folded twice, picture and greeting negatives must be oriented in opposite directions.

Season's
Greetings

Holiday Joy from Coral Gables

Nancy and George Smithers

A Christmas card need not show snow; some people live in climates where it is warm all year round. A photograph such as this, showing personal warmth and friendship, would make an eminently suitable seasonable greeting card.

with the photo negative. Insert the negative in the mask, following the same procedure as for the large-size mask, place the negative/mask combination in the negative carrier of an enlarger that will accept 4″ × 5″ negatives, and make enlargements on 8½″×11″ paper such as Kodabromide A or Polycontrast A paper (either will fold like Ad-Type paper).

Process and dry the photographic paper for French-fold greeting cards by following the directions included with the paper. When the paper is dry, fold it and add a signature.

Photo Cards for Purchase

A number of greeting-card folders and special greeting-card printing services are available through photo dealers.

The most versatile item is a basic folder into which a suitable print can be mounted, either on a self-contained strip of pressure-sensitive tape or with dabs of adhesive at the corners. The folder may be of the two-fold variety, made of lightweight cardboard, or of the French-fold type, made of card stock paper. Some folders have slits in the inside leaf

for inserting the corners of a standard-size print. This is quicker than mounting a print with adhesive, but it limits the size of the print that can be used.

Stock folders of this sort are usually available throughout the year in plain ivory, off-white, or color tints, and at holiday seasons with preprinted messages or decorative details. They can also be ordered with special printing.

Some photofinishing labs print greeting cards from a customer's color negative or slide, along with a stock greeting or a personalized message of one or two lines printed below the picture. A handwritten signature or message can even be printed. Kodak Slim-Line and Trim-Line photo-greeting cards are of this type; they are furnished with envelopes as well. It is also possible to have cards printed with the message in reverse—that is, in white letters—within the picture area. Most photo dealers can assist in ordering these special printing services.

• *See also:* COMBINATION PRINTING; MULTIPLE PRINTING; TABLETOP PHOTOGRAPHY; WRITING ON FILMS AND PAPERS.

Ground Glass

Ground glass is made by abrading one side of a glass sheet to form a translucent screen. The usual methods are sand-blasting, grinding with an abrasive, or etching with acid. Similar sheets of embossed or molded plastic are sometimes generically referred to as ground glass when they are used in cameras.

The most common use of ground glass is as a viewing and focusing screen in reflex and view cameras. The screen is placed with the textured (ground) side toward the lens to show the image being made by the camera lens. It must be located exactly the same distance from the lens that the film will be.

Otherwise, an image sharply focused on the ground glass will not be focused on the film with the same precision. In a view camera, the screen is usually mounted in a panel that lifts out or moves away on spring or lever arms to permit insertion of a film holder in its place. In a reflex camera, the screen remains fixed in its position above the mirror that reflects the image from the lens. The screen is often ruled with a grid of horizontal and vertical lines to aid in aligning the subject with the frame edges.

Ground-glass screens form images that are bright in the portion directly in line between the lens and the position of the viewing eye, but that fall off considerably all around, forming a hot spot. A coarse-texture screen diffuses the image light more and thus has less of a hot spot than a fine-texture

Whether held in horizontal (left) or vertical position (right), the ground-glass screen of a camera provides critical control over image sharpness and alignment within the limits of the frame. Note the "hot spot" effect inherent in this focusing aid. Photos by Norm Kerr.

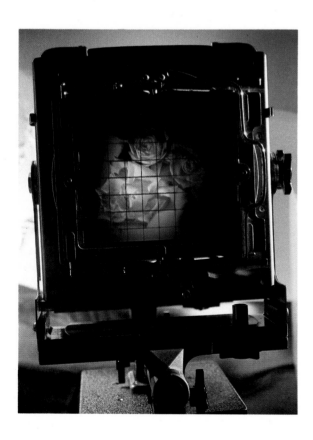
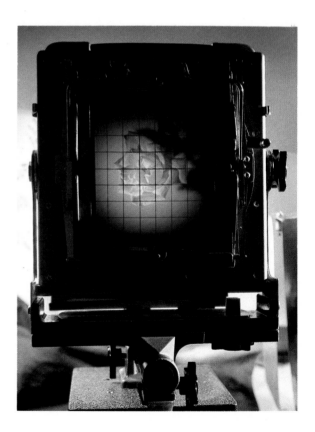

In a view camera, the ground-glass screen is mounted on a panel that lifts out or moves away to permit replacement with a film holder.

screen. However, the coarse screen does not resolve fine detail in the image, which makes critical focusing difficult. The best solution is to use a fine-texture ground glass with a field lens placed against the textured side. The field lens may be a very thin, plastic Fresnel lens that produces an image with much more uniform brightness, or it may be an actual plano-convex lens that serves the same field-lens function.

The corners of the ground glass in a view camera are often cut away, creating triangular openings to the camera interior. These permit air to escape as the bellows are compressed whenever the lens board and camera back are moved closer together. The purpose is to avoid damaging the bellows with air pressure when quick-focusing or when closing the camera for dismounting and packing. The corner openings also permit looking in to see if extreme lens or back movements will cause any degree of vignetting. If the entire circle of light at the lens cannot be seen from a corner, the extreme angle of adjustment will cause part of the outer edge of the image to be cut off.

In reflex cameras, the ground glass is usually made of molded plastic with special focusing aids molded in the central portion. A pair of opposing prisms may be incorporated that act as a range finder, or the central area may be molded into a microprism surface that breaks up out-of-focus images, but that appears clear when the image is focused sharply. Molded ground glasses may have an anular ring of fine ground glass around the central area, and be clear in the outer area. Fine focus can be achieved in the anular ring, while clear viewing with no focusing capability exists in the clear, outer area.

A ground-glass panel is often used to form the working surface in a retouching stand. Small illuminators and transparency viewers may use ground glass to diffuse the light. When even illumination is required over a large surface, white, translucent glass or plastic gives better results than ground glass. Kodak flashed opal glass, for example, is coated on one side with a milky diffusing layer that produces very even light distribution.

To improvise a ground glass, tape a sheet of frosted or matte acetate, or a sheet of tracing paper, to a piece of plain glass of proper size. A small magnifier will make it easier to focus the image sharply.

• *See also:* FRESNEL LENSES; RETOUCHING; VIEWING AND FOCUSING.

Guide Numbers

The five factors affecting flash exposure are:

1. Light output of flash (includes reflector characteristics).
2. Film speed.
3. Shutter speed (including sync).
4. *f*-number.
5. Distance.

The first three factors are usually constants in a given situation, and are combined into a number called the *guide number*. The last two factors are interrelated variables by which the flash exposure is controlled.

The reason for this is that light from a source has lessening intensity falling on objects the farther they are from the flash, and increasing intensity the closer they are to the flash. Some modern electronic flash units automatically control the light they emit for flash by measuring light being reflected by the subject. However, with most flashbulbs, flashcubes, flipflash, non-automatic or manual electronic flash units, and automatic units set in a manual mode, flash guide numbers provide the most convenient means for determining flash exposure for a given subject.

Since the guide number includes the factors of light output, film speed, and shutter speed (including synchronization), there is a change in guide number for each different value of each of the above factors.

Light from a source has lessening intensity falling on objects the farther they are from the camera. Therefore it cannot be expected that an entire photograph will be evenly illuminated by the light from a single flash, if the subjects are at varying distances from the light source. Photo by John Menihan.

Using Guide Numbers

Divide the proper guide number by the flash-to-subject distance in feet to find the *f*-number for average subjects. For example, if the guide number is 80 and the subject is 10 feet away from the flash, divide 80 by 10. The answer, 8, means that the lens should be set to *f*/8. If the answer is between two *f*-numbers marked on the camera lens, set the lens opening at the nearest *f*-number or halfway between the two, whichever is closer to the answer.

Guide numbers given in American film sheets, and in this encyclopedia, are for distances measured in feet. If distances are measured in metres, different guide numbers must be used. See the guide-number calculations section in this article.

Guide numbers are just *guides;* they are for average subjects in average-size rooms. They do not take into account subjects that are lighter or darker than average, or small rooms with light-colored walls that reflect a lot of light. In small rooms with light-colored walls, use one stop less exposure than the guide number indicates. Outdoors at night, or in very large rooms, give one stop more exposure.

If necessary, you can change the guide numbers to improve results. If your pictures are consistently

Guide-Number Calculations

The following formulas can be used to adjust the guide number for a normal situation to arrive at correct exposure for different conditions. A small calculator with a square-root function will help provide quick answers to any problem.

1. Guide-Number Test.

Set up the flash unit at a convenient distance from the subject; 10 feet makes calculation easy. Make a series of exposures at half-stop intervals; keep a record of the *f*-number used for each exposure. Examine the processed results and select the best exposure (using color reversal film with laboratory processing will minimize processing variations and will make exposure differences quite apparent). The guide number (GN) for the flash unit can then be derived from the *f*-number used for that exposure:

$$GN = \textit{f}\text{-number} \times \text{flash-to-subject distance}$$

2. Guide-Number Conversions.

To change for distances measured in metres or feet:

$$GN \text{ for feet} \times 0.3 = GN \text{ for metres}$$
$$GN \text{ for metres} \times 3.3 = GN \text{ for feet}$$

3. Required *f*-Stop Setting.

For the required *f*-Stop setting use the following formula:

$$\textit{f}\text{-number} = GN \div \text{flash-to-subject distance}$$

4. Required Flash Distance.

To determine where to place the flash in order to use a desired *f*-stop:

$$\text{Flash-to-subject distance} = GN \div \textit{f}\text{-number}$$

5. Electronic Flash Guide Numbers.

The guide number is related to the beam or effective candlepower-seconds (BCPS, ECPS) output of the unit and the arithmetic ASA speed of the film:

$$\text{Electronic flash GN} = \sqrt{A \times ECPS \times \text{Daylight ASA of film}}$$
$$\text{OR}$$
$$\text{Electronic flash GN} = \sqrt{ECPS \times (\text{Daylight ASA of film} \div B)}$$

NOTE: For GN for feet, $A = 0.05$; $B = 20$
For GN for metres, $A = 0.0045$; $B = 222$.

6. Electronic Flash Output.

The ECPS rating of a unit can be determined from its guide number for a given speed film:

$$ECPS = GN^2 \div (\text{Daylight ASA} \times A)$$
$$\text{OR}$$
$$ECPS = GN^2 \div (\text{Daylight ASA} \div B)$$

See note with formula under electronic flash guide numbers above for values of *A* and *B*.

7. Guide Number for Different Film.

The guide number to use with a new film can be determined for a given flash unit when an accurate guide number for another (old) film is known:

$$\text{New GN} = \text{Old GN} \times \sqrt{\text{New ASA} \div \text{Old ASA}}$$

8. Bounce Flash Exposure.

When flash is bounced from an average-height white ceiling with no direct light from flash falling on subject:

$$f\text{-number} = 0.7 \times (\text{GN} \div \text{flash-to-ceiling-to-subject distance})$$

9. Guide Number for Multiple Frontal Flash.

When light of the *same intensity* from *independently powered* units overlaps on the camera side of the subject:

$$\text{Combined GN} = \text{GN for one unit} \times \sqrt{\text{Number of units}}$$

10. Guide Number for Multiple Electronic Flash.

When two or more electronic flash heads are connected to the *same power supply,* multiply the guide number for each head by the square root of 2 (1.4), add the results, and divide by the total number of units (n). That is:

$$\text{Combined GN} =$$

$$\frac{(\text{GN No. 1} \times 1.4) + (\text{GN No. 2} \times 1.4) + \ldots (\text{GN No. n} \times 1.4)}{n}$$

11. Guide Numbers for Bracketing Exposures.

The following guide-number calculations can be used to bracket exposures.

GN × 0.5 = GN for exposure change of: +2 stops

0.7	+1
0.84	+½
1.2	−½
1.4	−1
2.0	−2

underexposed, that is, if your negatives are too light or your slides are too dark, use a lower guide number. If your pictures are consistently overexposed— if your negatives are too dark or your slides are too light—use a higher guide number.

The guide-number calculations in this article include several methods for adjusting guide numbers for various subjects and conditions.

• *See also:* ELECTRONIC FLASH; FLASH PHOTOGRAPHY.

Gum Arabic

Vegetable gum; chief component of mucilage and similar adhesives

Used mainly in photography in the rather obsolete gum-bichromate printing process. Currently used in lithographic printing-plate desensitizer.

Formula and Molecular Weight: Indeterminate

Yellowish-to-white or amber lumps, freely soluble in water, insoluble in alcohol and ether.

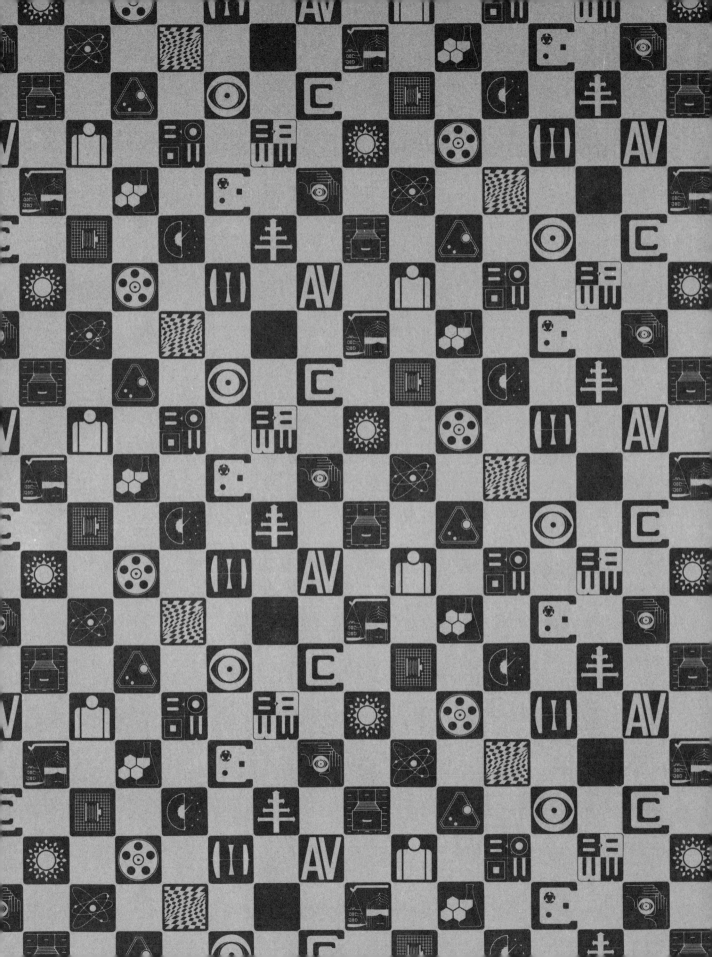